The Church at the Centre of the City

The Church at the Centre of the City

Edited by
Paul Ballard

✜ EPWORTH

British Library Cataloguing in Publication data

A catalogue record for this book is available
from the British Library

978 0 7162 0639 2

First published in 2008
by Epworth
4 John Wesley Road
Werrington
Peterborough PE4 6ZP

Typeset by Regent Typesetting, London
Printed and bound in the UK by
MPG Books Ltd, Bodmin, Cornwall

Contents

Acknowledgements

As the Introduction indicates, this volume comes out of a long process. Thanks are, therefore, due to a considerable number of people who have been involved along the way. It would be impossible to enumerate them all. They have included many who have given time and expertise, not least those who attended the conference in Cardiff in 2005 where they shared their experiences and encouraged the production of this book. Some, however, deserve special mention.

Noel Davies, himself, has been at the heart of the project from the beginning. He brought with him his experience in the world Church as a former General Secretary of Cytun (Churches Together in Wales), as well as his academic standing as the historian of ecumenism in Wales. Without his dedication and support nothing would have happened.

Then there are the other members of the Cardiff Steering Group who set up and followed up the Cardiff conference and who gave unceasing encouragement: Tom Arthur, Minister of the United Reformed City Church; Peter Collins, Dean of the Catholic Metropolitan Cathedral; Keith Kimber, Rector of the parish of St John the Baptist, Church in Wales; Monica Mills, Chaplain at the Lightship to Cardiff Bay.

In the editing of this volume it was also a privilege to have the expertise and advice of Angela Graham, a writer and broadcaster, and Norman Shanks, formerly Leader of the Iona Community and minister in Glasgow, who, together with Chris Baker and Noel Davies, read and commented on the draft text.

Moreover, neither the conference, nor any follow-up, nor the volume would have been possible without the generous support of the Conference for World Mission, the Jerusalem Trust and the Gibbs Trust.

Editors and authors always depend on the quiet and patient work behind the scenes. This has been afforded in abundance by Natalie Watson and her team at Epworth Press who, thereby, enabled the finished product to emerge.

So far as is known, the requirements of copyright have been observed.

Any short quotations from other works have been illustrative of or part of a discussion and have been acknowledged in the referencing and the bibliographies. Where explicit permission has been granted, that has been acknowledged *in situ*. If, however, copyright has been infringed, apologies are hereby expressed and assurance given that the matter will be appropriately rectified on request.

Paul Ballard

Contributors

Cate Adams is City Centre Chaplain, Aberdeen.

Chris Baker is Director of Research at the William Temple Foundation, Manchester.

Paul Ballard is Emeritus Professor in the School of Religious and Theological Studies, Cardiff University, where he taught practical theology.

John Bradbury is Director of Studies in Church History and Theology at Westminster College, Cambridge.

Geoff Cornell is Superintendent Minister of the West London Mission of the Methodist Church.

Mary Cotes is Ecumenical Moderator of the Mission Partnership in Milton Keynes.

Andrew Davey is National Advisor on Community and Urban Affairs of the Church of England.

Noel A. Davies is Director of the Centre for Ecumenical Studies at Trinity College, Carmarthen and Tutor in Ministerial Studies for the Union of Welsh Independents.

Ben Edson is Anglican City Centre Missioner in Manchester Diocese.

Barbara Glasson is Superintendent Minister of the Methodist City Centre Circuit, Liverpool.

Leslie Griffiths is Superintendent Minister of Wesley's Chapel, City of London, and a Life Peer.

John Inge, formerly Bishop of Huntingdon, is Anglican Bishop of Worcester.

Peter Macdonald is Minister of St George's West, Church of Scotland, Edinburgh.

Jonathan Meyrick is Dean of Exeter.

Len Simmonds is an independent business consultant.

Huw Thomas is Senior Lecturer in the School of City and Regional Planning, Cardiff University.

Peter Willis is Superintendent Minister of Life at the Centre Methodist Mission, Nottingham.

Introduction

The Setting and Purpose of the Study

NOEL A. DAVIES AND PAUL BALLARD

The focus of this volume is the city centre, that is, the commercial, administrative and retail area that is to be found at the centre of our large industrial cities and towns, indeed in any town of some size. This, usually the historic heart of the city, is what the Americans call 'down town' and the urban geographers call the Central Business District (CBD). The claim is that, while each city or town has its unique features, the CBD is sufficiently recognizable, with its own typical characteristics, to constitute a particular context for the Church's ministry and mission that needs to be taken seriously on its own terms. It is hoped, therefore, that together the contributions that follow, with the commentary, will raise the consciousness of the wider Church and challenge it to see the importance of this much-neglected field. If the city is the creative heart of the modern world then the city centre is at its heart, where all the lines of communication and power come together. To neglect it is to abandon the city itself.

The idea for this book was born in a research project undertaken by Noel Davies during 1999. The Cardiff Churches' Centre, an ecumenical body based in City United Reformed Church in Cardiff's city centre, commissioned the research. The project was located within the School of Religious and Theological Studies of the then University of Wales, Cardiff (now Cardiff University), and funded by a generous grant from the Council for World Mission. The primary aim of the research was to develop a new vision for the Churches' Centre and to recommend ways in which this vision could be implemented in a changing and developing city.

It soon became clear, however, that this could not simply be a project that made practical recommendations about the way forward. Any pro-posals for a renewed city centre strategy would need to be grounded in theological and missiological reflection drawn from a range of disci-plines and contexts. The result was the report *God at the Centre:*

Exploring Theology and Mission in the City Centre (1999), which sought to set out preliminary pointers to an analysis of the contemporary city centre (focused in this case on Cardiff), and began to explore possible ingredients of such a perspective for the city centre as a basis for detailed recommendations for ways forward in the city for the Cardiff churches.

A number of insights emerged from this process that have shaped the present book. The most significant of these was that considerable attention had been given over a long period to Urban Priority Areas (UPAs), normally found in the old industrial areas of the inner city or some post-war council estates: that is, those often vast areas of contemporary cities that are, more often than not, characterized by multiple deprivation, but also by vigorous engagement in social regeneration by civil society and religious communities, including churches. Indeed, urban ministry and mission had become virtually identified with these concerns. This is true not only in Britain but across the world, especially in the southern hemisphere where rapid urbanization results in vast slums and massive urban poverty. At the same time, in the UK, attention had also been given to rural ministry and the changing countryside. Concern has been shown for the collapse of traditional communities and the spread of a dispersed suburbia in many areas. But two areas in the modern city have been strangely neglected: the suburbs and the city centre. For the first, it might suggest that suburbanization has become the norm both socially and for the Church. What is normal is unremarkable. There are signs, however, that in the face of contemporary pressures this assumption is being challenged (Brown, 2005). The city centre, too, is undergoing a remarkable make-over. Every town or city of any size has its inner core which buzzes with activity every day but which is virtually empty in the evenings and weekends. But more and more this is changing as a second, mobile population flows in to take advantage of the newly awakened entertainment bonanza in the city centre. To this aspect of urban life, until recently, little if any attention has been given within the churches. Yet increasingly we are aware of this dimension to our lives. It became clear, therefore, that the kind of reflective exploration that had been undertaken in Cardiff should be offered to a wider constituency as a service to the life of the Church in Britain.

The second, though not of course original, insight was a recognition that each city centre has its own particular characteristics that give it an identity that is distinctive and unique. These differences include the variables of history and size. All cities show, in their physical and cultural environment, the influences that have shaped them down the years. We can think of places dominated by their cathedral or castle, or which boast of their industrial or commercial power of yesteryear. Some have lost out while others flourish. For some the city centre is hardly differentiated from the rest of the city. Others have clear quarters for different functions where similar enterprises gather in solidarity. Nevertheless it is possible to recognize certain common characteristics. The city centre is about power and decision-making structures, economic and commercial driving forces; a very mobile – and until recently a diminishing – population; communities (often small communities) of marginalized people, often those who are the poorest, the homeless and addicted, who crave anonymity but who also need support and assistance; a vigorous and attractive leisure and entertainment culture; a rapidly changing infrastructure which has often meant shifts in the focus of the city centre; and churches with generally declining membership usually drawn not from the centre but from other areas of the city.

The third insight, which was given particular attention in the initial project, was that any theological and missiological reflection on the city centre would, almost by definition, need to be contextual. Theology had to emerge from a vigorous engagement with the forces at work in the city centre (such as those outlined above) and could not be a philosophical or systematic exposition that was not rooted in the contemporary cultural, social, economic and political realities. It has to be a theology of God's Kingdom (or realm) shaped by the lives of persons in communities. The first consequence of such a recognition was that the theological task had to be undertaken in partnership, not only between different areas of theology but also between theology and other academic disciplines, not least sociological analysis, cultural studies and urban planning. Second, while we were aware that responses to the analysis and reflections of Latin American liberation theology had been, to say the least, varied and often rigorously critical over recent decades, we believed that its basic methodology and insights were still valid. The pastoral cycle of analysis, reflection, action and evaluation, as a methodology of approaching mission in the centre, was thought to be helpful, and the many attempts – for example, through the longstanding study and research centre, the Urban Theology Unit in Sheffield – to apply the insights of liberation theology to Urban Priority Areas offered some helpful paradigms for our own efforts.

The report also recognized that for the churches in the city centre this has to be an essentially ecumenical commitment. This is not to say, of course, that only ecumenical church structures and partnerships (which can be weak in some city centre situations) can undertake effective city centre witness and service. It is to claim that denominational commitments and programmes in city centre mission and ministry need to have ecumenical identity, partnership and commitment at their heart. At a time that has been described as 'an ecumenical winter', when churches at all levels of their life together, whether international, national, regional or local, are withdrawing in varying degrees from previous ecumenical relationships, it became clear that a renewed ecumenical commitment and partnership is an essential foundation for Christian witness in the city centre. The ecumenical maxim of 'the unity of the church for the sake of the unity of the human community' continues to be a valid insight. The ecumenical dimension of the then weakened Cardiff Churches' Centre needed to be vigorously maintained and, indeed, developed, if it was to have a significant role in the future of Cardiff city centre. What is true of Cardiff, we believe, is also true in other contexts. The city centre challenges the churches' vision of and commitment to ecumenical renewal, not least through adequate resources, at a time when forces of decline in most aspects of the life of the traditional churches (at least in western Europe) are in danger of causing entrenchment and withdrawal rather than the risk of what can be costly ecumenical engagement and practice. A renewed ecumenical vision and praxis for the city centre was (and is) urgently called for.

With the support of the Jerusalem Trust and the Gibbs Trust, it was decided to initiate a threefold programme. The first move was to hold a conference in Cardiff (September 2005) that would bring together practitioners in city centre ministry and mission and academics in a range of disciplines. That the conference was over subscribed confirmed the conviction that there was a need that had hardly been met. Second, it was hoped that this would lead to a number of local initiatives where practitioners would explore how best to forward their concerns. As was to be expected among busy people, this was patchy; nor was it necessary for activities to be reported. Nevertheless there were a number of events and meetings, including seminars in Cardiff, Bristol and Birmingham. More important were the efforts to ensure that the city centre agenda is sustained. This was done in three ways. First, the city centre was put into the programme of the 'Jesus in the City' congress in Bristol, June 2007. A workshop of about twenty interestingly included a number of persons from overseas, especially the 'new Europe', where there are similar problems for the city centre. Second, the city centre has become a firm part of the agenda of the ecumenical co-ordinating project on urban mission, of which Erica Dunmow is the Urban Mission Development Advisor, based at the Wilson Carlile Church Army training centre in Sheffield. Third, the Methodist City Centre Network, which has been the only group to be constituted around these concerns, opened its biennial conference to ecumenical partners in May 2007 and a number took up the invitation. Subsequently it has been agreed that the group will be the national focus for city centre ministry.

But the third aspect of this continuing commitment grew out of the recognition that there had been very little, if any, serious writing on the theology of and mission in the city centre. The intentionally very slender report, *God at the Centre*, was one of a very few attempts at offering preliminary reflections in this particular field. Yet, as the proposal for this book put it, 'this is a crucial area of the missiological thinking of the churches if it is to meet the challenge of power and influence in modern society. There needs to be some assessment of what is happening and some reflection on the theological responsibilities and models of engagement appropriate to the social and economic climate of the early twenty-first century.'

The idea of preparing a publication in this area was, therefore, enthusiastically encouraged by academic theologians (and other scholars in related fields) and city centre practitioners. The structure of the book reflects some of the insights that have already been explored. Part I examines 'The City Centre Today', and seeks to bring into our reflection an examination of the demographic and socio-economic changes that have been occurring in city centres during recent decades. Part II offers some theological reflection on the Church in the city centre, firmly focused on the realities, which could provide a much-needed foundation for further theological and missiological work as well as for constructive engagement in the city centre. Finally, Part III offers a wide range of essays on reflective practice under the heading 'Witness and Service in and for the City'. What is offered here may be seen in terms of a series of reflective case studies on different aspects of life in the city centre and the churches' engagement in the city.

This collection, therefore, should be of interest to a wide readership:

- Those already engaged in city centre ministry of different kinds who can hereby enter into dialogue and reflection with their colleagues.
- Christians working in the city centre in whatsoever capacity wishing

to understand the Church's involvement and looking for opportunity for a more active role.

- Students and teachers on theological courses, whether in preparation for ministry or as part of the 'learning Church'.
- Church leaders making appointments to city centre jobs and planning urban mission strategies.
- Christian communities bewildered by the rapid change in the city centre and wondering how to react creatively.
- Those with responsibility for the life of the city, especially the city centre, such as the civic authorities, the police and the welfare services, not least in their dealings with the churches.
- Anyone concerned about the quality of life in the city, whether working there or living there and wondering what contribution the churches can make.

The focus of this book is the United Kingdom. All the authors' work, either as academic specialists or city centre practitioners, is in UK towns and cities. This limited context provides a clear focus for an exploration into the theology and practice of the contemporary city. But this is not a local or recent issue. A broader perspective is needed.

It was the rise of the modern industrial city, first in Britain, then in Europe and North America and now across the world, so that soon the majority of the world's population will be city dwelling, if it is not already, that posed questions about the nature and meaning of the modern society. The extremes of wealth and poverty, noted most radically by Marx and Engels, have produced a tradition of social critique and social action. In the churches also there were those who engaged theologically and practically with the issues of urbanization, from the slum parishes and settlements to various expressions of Christian socialism and political involvement.

After the Second World War we find a new phase, at least in the West. It was a time of hope and expectation. The imperial structures of the nineteenth century were breaking down into the new nations of Africa and Asia. The intention, through development and trade, was to break down the barriers of poverty. In Britain and elsewhere the welfare state was designed to overcome the demons of the past, providing health, education and security. What Harold Wilson called the 'white heat of technology' would be harnessed in the service of the common good. The city, as the locus of human creativity and endeavour, became the place of freedom and discovery. Harvey Cox, in *The Secular City* (1965), argued that the city was the birth place of the new society of opportunity, choice and equality, a pointer to the Kingdom.

This sense of euphoria, however, was not to last. From the 1970s and into the 1980s a new phase emerged. It was increasingly apparent, not least in a time of deindustrialization, unemployment and growing poverty, that the city was equally a place of despair. The inner city had become and remains problematic, the object of a string of political and economic initiatives. This was clearly brought out in Britain by the report *Faith in the City* (1985). Urban Priority Areas, or Community First Areas as they are now called, have more or less defined the urban context both politically and in terms of ministry and mission.

Perhaps, however, the mood has swung back somewhat. The negativity of deindustrialization has given way to a fresh technological optimism. The age of the microchip and exponential scientific advances spells out new possibilities and new utopias. Globalization seems to make everything possible. And the city has become the arena where those hopes are to be realized. The postmodern world is where the Christian faith and practice has to be worked out in fresh and, perhaps, startling ways. It is the city centre that has become the symbol of all this. This it is that lies behind all the contributions that follow. Here is another reason why such a volume is timely.

Yet there has to be an air of caution. The story outlined shows that not only are there fashions in our perception of the city but that there is also an inbuilt ambiguity. Positive and negative go together. In theological terms this is something to do with sinfulness. So, despite the excitement, there is also a dark cloud over the scene, not least in the face of the immense social, political, economic and environmental issues that confront our world. But the gospel is all about a cautious realism about human existence that takes seriously the forces of destruction that mingle with the aspirations and hopes. The city, and especially the city centre, is the stage where that human drama is enacted. There is both hope and frustration, possibility and danger, beauty and ugliness, truth and falsehood, virtue and vice. Thinking about the city theologically has to take into account the whole story and see it all in the perspective of the gospel.

It is, therefore, worth noting two contemporary attempts to reflect theologically on the city from beyond our shores, setting our endeavours in a wider context.

The World Council of Churches (WCC) launched its 'Peace to the City' programme in 1997. It is not confined to city centres as such, but it understands the city in ways that echo some of the insights of the project that is being developed in this present volume. The WCC Peace to the City webpage describes cities as 'centres of population, commerce, finance, political power and culture' which are 'a metaphor for the modern world'. Furthermore, they are seen as 'a microcosm of the most destructive forces of violence as well as of the most creative initiatives to overcome [them]'. But the WCC programme focuses on cities because it is believed that they also offer signs and possibilities of peace.

Some of the phraseology in what the WCC calls 'seven lessons from seven cities' (a deliberate echo of the seven letters to the churches in the Book of the Revelation to St John, in the New Testament) offers clues to the threats to the contemporary city and points to possible sources of renewal and transformation. Peace is 'nurtured by creativity and commitment' and demands a 'holistic' approach 'as all issues are connected'. It requires us to be willing 'to challenge our own self-perceptions and to make room for everyone's story'. Peace making challenges us to 'be bold and dare to cross "borders" by building bridges and strong partnerships'. Cities must create 'safe places . . . where all sides can be invited as equals'.

The Peace to the City Network was set up, through the WCC, 'to be a global grassroots network of churches, peace and justice organizations, faith communities and civil society movements in cities around the world, engaged in local initiatives to overcome urban, political, ethnic and religious violence.' The international context of the WCC project, then, offers a vision of the city not only as a metaphor for the modern world and a microcosm of the most destructive forces, but also as a safe place where peace becomes possible.

Another international perspective comes from Seppo Kjellberg (2000). He suggests that the city can be understood in the following terms:

(i) [the] meaning [of the city] lies in its plurality . . . (ii) [Human beings] are co-creators to the Creator and the Creation . . . (iii) The city society is the place where the necessary cultural diversity is possible . . . (iv) The city is a symbiotic form of life, planned and built by [human beings], but at the same time part of the evolutionary process . . . (v) [It] is a part of the common creation project of God, nature and [human beings] . . . (vi) [It] is a *developing* life form which enables real *emancipatory koinonia* (community).

On the basis of such an analysis he invites us to loosen theological reflection on the city from an anthropocentric perspective, where the primary focus is on individuals or even on communities of individuals, and to adopt what he calls 'an urban ecotheology', where the primary focus is rather on 'focusing ecotheology on the development of cities, and constructing a Christian alternative to the anthropocentric city' (p. 147) where 'the "community of all" as well as the "plurality of all"' (p. 153) find their place within a 'holistic, cosmocentric' understanding of the modern city (p. 155).

It is the basic affirmation of this present book that the perspectives offered here can help reinvigorate the churches' witness and service in the city centre in the context of the Christian reality. We believe that a renewed recognition of the importance of the city centre within the processes of urban transformation, of the powerful and changing forces that are at work there, and of the urgent need for contextual theological engagement with the range of individual and communal socio-economic influences that are brought to bear on and within the city, together with a renewed ecumenical vision of and commitment to Christian mission and ministry in the city centre, could offer channels and sources for much-needed renewal and transformation and bring to a new generation 'hope in the city'. This book is intended to be a beginning to such a process of study and reflection.

Bibliography

Archbishop of Canterbury's Commission on Urban Priority Areas, 1985, *Faith in the City*, London, Church House Publishing.
Brown, Malcolm, 2005, *Faith in Suburbia: Completing the Contextual Trilogy*, Edinburgh, Contact Pastoral Trust.
Cox, Harvey, 1965, *The Secular City*, London, SCM.
Davies, Noel, 1999, *God at the Centre: Exploring Theology and Mission in the Centre*, Cardiff, HOLI 9, Religious and Theological Studies, Cardiff University.
Kjellberg, Seppo, 2000, *Urban Ecotheology*, Utrecht, International Books.
World Council of Churches, www.wcc.coe.org/wcc/pcn/cities.htm.

PART I

The City Centre Today

Introduction: Pressure, Change and Speculation

The city centre, what urban geographers call the Central Business District (CBD) and Americans 'down town', has become again the focus of attention for the politician, planner and entrepreneur. Occupying, unless it is a modern planned city or new town, the site of the original settlement, the CBD reflects the story of the city itself. There will be found the historic buildings and monuments – castle, abbey or cathedral, guildhall – and the ancient walls, occasionally visible, marked by inner ring roads and railway stations. Everything happened in the city, living and working, the market and manufacture, civil and legal courts, worship and festival.

The industrialization and urbanization of society changed all that. Not only did the city spread out but different functions and classes tended to separate out. This was accelerated with the advent of modern mass transportation from the end of the nineteenth century, so it was no longer necessary to walk to work. This was the main factor in forging the urban landscape that we know today. From this, the city centre became indeed the CBD – banks, trading companies, offices, department stores and commercial hotels being the main components. The internal combustion engine and telephone further eroded the situation. Shopping malls and business parks are dispersed CBDs scattered around the periphery of the city, threatening to leave the original more or less empty.

The churches, too, migrated out or were largely abandoned for the suburban arcadia. Gibson Winter classically recorded this, in *The Suburban Captivity of the Church*, for the American scene in the 1960s. It was, perhaps, not so drastic in Britain and elsewhere in Europe, where historical factors such as the parochial structures and stricter planning regulations had a dampening effect. Nevertheless there was a sense, for those left behind, of being in a vacuum in which it was difficult to see the way forward.

Now it seems that, paradoxically, due to globalization, the process is rapidly being reversed. The city, in order to compete in the new markets, has to reposition itself. And it is the city centre that is at the heart of this transformation. The global parameters within which we are now compelled to live make it more important to establish an identity that has prestige and attracts the wealth from the activities that presently count – technology, learning, the new office culture, entertainment, leisure and tourism and modern living.

The chapters that make up this section open up something of what this means. It is impossible to avoid the impact of globalization, however that is understood and evaluated. Each city is part of the international network that is the global village. (Andrew Davey, chapter 1). That impact, however, means radical changes in the city centre as culture and the built environment are renewed. It also has implications for the rest of the city, those people and areas that do not immediately or obviously benefit from the new bonanza (Chris Baker, chapter 2). This process of change has also to be managed. It is a political as well as a socio-economic activity. There are competing interests, both within and beyond the city, some more powerful than others. It is easy for some voices, especially the poor and marginalized, to be drowned out. The churches are there too, concerned for their own presence in society but more importantly as advocates of those who seek support and justice. So it is important to recognize what it means to participate in the public arena (Huw Thomas, chapter 3).

Where is all this frenetic activity leading? It is impossible from the middle of historical change to predict what is going to happen. Yet it is necessary to be engaged. It is clear that there are real ambiguities in the whole process. Is this simply late capitalism run riot, widening the poverty gap exponentially? Or is it the possibility of greater human welfare than ever before? Does globalization herald growing international collaboration? Or is it another western hegemony? Do we control technology or does technology control us? What if, as seems from time to time a real possibility, the bubble bursts and it all collapses? Here is the classical Christian dilemma of living in the world with its hopes and destructiveness. Creative and prophetic living can only seize the times and seek to work both with them and against them to seek justice, peace and well-being. And this can only be done from the place where one is set. That is God's gift. 'Whatever your hand finds to do, do it with your might' (Eccles. 9.10). After that it is a matter of faith and the best use of skills and wisdom, trusting that

God will both honour the endeavour and work the mysteries of the Kingdom.

Bibliography

Winter, Gibson, 1961, *The Suburban Captivity of the Church*, Garden City, NY, Doubleday.

I

Cities and Globalization

ANDREW DAVEY

Cities have always been open to the world. Markets and forums have provided spatial settings for the exchange of goods and information, commodities that may have travelled far and will often flow on to other destinations. Urban populations grow through migration, with connections to many places of origin and many expectations about city life. Cities are about movement and exchange – apparent on the street through the goods displayed in the shops, advertising for communication and information services, the developers' hoardings, or the newspapers available in many languages.

This chapter explores how globalization has impacted on the social, economic and demographic realities of the city, particularly the core areas that have come to be associated with retail, commerce and leisure, but are being increasingly repopulated.

Location, location

The much-predicted death of the city as a business space with its close-knit working community has not happened. The internet has not killed off the forum and the market. While relational networks such as traditional chambers of commerce are declining, access to basic complementary commercial services remains important and new interdependencies emerge, particularly in those places where the global status is high. Businesses cluster for the convenience of customers, as well as access to the high-tech services on which they depend. Workspace is changing, with open-plan and hot-desk offices offering flexibility where floor space is at a premium. Retail spaces offer a combination of shelf-accessed goods and electronic catalogues. Commercial propinquity is vital, whether the location is city centre or out of town business park.

In the financial sector we see an increasing emphasis placed on cities, as nodal points enabling global networks and transactions. Cities become cluster points for corporations and those service businesses that support them.

> Trust, contact networks and social relations play pivotal roles in the smooth functioning of global business. Spatial propinquity allows these relations to be easily maintained, lubricated and sustained. Global cities are sites of dense networks of interpersonal contact and centers of the important business social capital trust vital to the successful operation of international finance. (Short, 2004, p. 14)

Position

It is the intensity of those transactions integrated with the global economy that defines the three cities which Saskia Sassen designates as truly global – London, New York and Tokyo. She identifies four new ways in which these cities (closely followed by Paris and Frankfurt) function:

> [1] highly concentrated command points . . . [2] key locations for finance and specialized service firms . . . [3] sites of production [and] the production of innovations . . . [4] markets for the products and innovations produced. (Sassen 2001, pp. 3–4)

Their significance, and ability to develop in parallel, is primarily explained by their regional position – each in a different time zone. But that position should not be assumed to be uncontested. While the big three complement each other they need a competitive edge in relation to the rising stars of their regions. How will Tokyo fare against the emerging hubs of the Chinese mainland; or will London lose out to the rise of Paris and Frankfurt, or the ability of Berlin to straddle East and West? Is New York unassailable against Chicago, Los Angeles or, eventually, the emergent cities of South America?

Sassen describes cities as being strategic sites in a new geography of centrality and marginality, which reproduces many of the old inequalities in new clusters, with little regard for national frontiers or regional geography. The intensity of the transactions binds cities into new hierarchies according to the traffic that passes between them. After the global financial and business centres another level is emerging, as the capacity and capability of cities in the global South is developed. This level includes cities such as São Paulo, Buenos Aires, Bombay, Bangkok, Taipei and Mexico City. The Globalization and World Cities Group,

Loughborough University, identifies ten alpha-level cities, graded for accountancy, advertising, banking/finance and law (Beaverstock, Smith and Taylor, 1999).

As she moves down the hierarchy Sassen comments, 'there has been a sharpening inequality in the concentration of strategic resources and activities between each of these cities and others in the same country' (2000, p. 51). These hierarchies are dominated by national or regional capitals whose connectivity and infrastructure are usually light years ahead of other cities in their territory.

The cities in these high levels take on new significance as they dominate their regions and often their nations. The decisions made in these cities impact on a global scale. Neil Smith notes the emergence of these cities as 'leading incubators in the global economy, progenitors of new urban form, process and identity' often eclipsing national government policy. This can be seen in the unrealized ambitions of Mayor Giuliani for 'a five borough foreign policy' in New York (Smith, 2002, p. 89) or Ken Livingstone's attempts to negotiate a discounted oil deal for London with the Venezuelan president Hugo Chavez.

Sassen also observes, 'Alongside these new global and regional hierarchies of cities is a vast territory that has become increasingly peripheral, increasingly excluded from the major economic processes that fuel economic growth in the new global economy' (Sassen 2000, p. 51). Castells describes the relationship between global cities and their regional contexts as being 'globally connected and locally disconnected' (Castells, 2000, p. 436).

Global or globalizing?

Alongside this we find the world is now predominantly an urban place. Globalization and urbanization are inextricably linked. All cities offer a level of connectivity which previous generations could not have imagined. Therefore it may be appropriate to speak of the 'global city' in the same way we once spoke of the global village. The urban experience is shared – over half the world lives in towns and cities. We depend on a handful of communication and media companies, on two personal computer systems, on a narrow range of transport and fuel options, on a global sourcing system for food.

Others would want to use 'global city' in terms of specific activities through which they dominate specific global networks: for example,

Los Angeles as a world city in terms of cinema or Milan in terms of fashion. 'Global city' may be a temporary categorization in terms of a particular event or meeting. So Athens becomes a global city for two weeks when it hosts the Olympic Games; other cities similarly when they host a political or economic summit (Short, 2004).

This may seem far away from the context of most British cities, but think for a moment: in what ways might sports make the locations of their teams global cities? The ownership and following of premier football clubs has significant global reach. What strategies or profiling give the illusion that a city is more prominent than it actually might be? Too often, Doreen Massey points out, the 'characterization of cities as "global" is a strategy whereby the part stands in for the whole, where the city is defined by its elite and the rest are confined to invisibility' (Massey, 2007, p. 216).

Globalization brings new dynamics to cities – we live in *globalizing* cities in a *globalizing* world. For John Rennie Short 'globalizing' describes well some of the dynamism and agony of cities at the beginning of the twenty-first century. 'Globalizing cities' captures 'that sense of becoming and longing. Globalizing cities are both global cities seeking to maintain their position and non-global cities seeking to become global cities. The terms are not permanent unchanging verities, but relational, spectral, temporal, shifting and unstable' (2004, p. 2). As globalization changes our urban context we find city government, hand in hand with economic interests, taking on new strategies. Maintaining or obtaining global position has led to a significant reshaping of our cities in terms of their demographics, their social profile and the levels of control experienced by their citizens. Previous caricatures of the local posed against the global need to be rethought: 'the local is not simply a product of the global but the global itself is produced in local places' (Massey, 2007, p. 167).

The centre and the margins

Taking this perspective means that just as cities are either centred and empowered, or marginalized and dominated – globally, regionally, nationally – those same divisions also emerge domestically in the interaction between neighbourhoods and communities within our globalized urban society. (You don't have to live at a geographical distance to be marginal in a global economy.) Cities (and churches) replicate the shaping of our global context. This is described as 'the dual city' or 'polarized city' – those who make up the different populations of a city do not meet or interact, yet they often occupy the same spaces, albeit in different roles and maybe at different times of day; the places they live, shop or have their children educated may be differentiated, 'worlds apart', even if they live in adjoining neighbourhoods.

In some places this seems unplanned. Elsewhere centrality and marginality are being planned and built into the city's structure. High-tech towers and executive residential buildings put core zones off limits to many citizens. Suburban gated communities similarly define social divisions in spatial terms. The increased use of CCTV, security guards and exclusion orders in what has habitually been considered 'public space' is marked in many of our cities. The social construction of differentiation is often found in other arenas: zoning and planning policy, immigration control and welfare contraction, pollution control and environmental measures, and, not least, where the garbage heaps, chemical factories, major roads and airports are situated in relation to housing.

In recent years city centres have been the focus of significant economic restructuring – what some urbanists would call the *revanchist* or *post-justice* city – as run-down neighbourhoods are forcibly persuaded into being repackaged for regeneration or gentrification. The state (local or national government often acting through new agencies or quangos) brings redundant or 'inactive' low-value real estate into circulation, creating a leaner city through a diminution of planning controls or civic obligation. Public land is sold, and school and welfare budgets are cut while city authorities hide behind the veneer of 'New Urbanism' with its new city living, and its cultural and architectural renewal.

The global market and the global mall

Globally cities are experiencing the same forces but each place's story will be different. Complexity and connectivity are significant aspects of our city centres – one cannot write of the spatial restructuring of the high street without reference to the interests of developers, global retailers or investors.

An encounter with the high street suggests many competing global claims. It might be the presence of significant global brands – 'high street names' such as Nike, Disney, Vodaphone or Gap. It may be a different type of store similarly dependent on free trade and low labour costs in another part of the world: Primark, Asda, Peacocks, Aldi, Lidl – often the preferred stores of migrants or the victims of global economic forces. Statistics from the Forbes List of the annual national sales of the world's leading companies show that, if Wal-Mart was a nation-state its sales would rank its gross domestic product twentieth in the world's economies – above Austria, Turkey and Saudi Arabia (Murray, 2006, p. 131).

Some global interests may be less apparent until one acquires a literacy in developers' hoardings. Bovis, Lend Lease, Persimmon are significant international players in the destiny of many high streets through new retail developments both in the city centre and out of town. Iconic buildings designed by global architectural gurus – 'starchitects' – are also seen as key to enhancing a city's profile and self-esteem. Behind these move concealed global players such as financial institutions, venture capitalists and hedge funds.

Cloning is rife. A 2005 New Economics Foundation survey designated Exeter as the leading example of 'clone town' Britain: 'In these towns, independent butchers, greengrocers, pet shops and dry cleaners had been driven out by national supermarket retailers, fast food chains, mobile phone shops and global fashion outlets.' The *Guardian* reported: 'Local people might be excited at first by the arrival of US retailers such as Gap and Starbucks. But they soon tired of "Latte-chino blandness".' The report added: 'Banality has taken root like a relative from abroad invited to stay because their foreignness seemed interesting, before realising they were tiresome and refused to leave' (Carvel, 2005). The combined forces of retailers and developers underpin this spatial as well as economic dimension to the city centre in the form of the shopping mall, a highly controlled space that reproduces and enforces a globalized consumer culture in highly controlled, air conditioned surroundings. Former high streets are remodelled to resemble or accommodate new mall developments – 'a destination, not a thoroughfare' (Chung, 2001, p. 654). Other forms of space, airports, museums and churches, follow suit.

> Shopping itself is homogenizing the environment in a way in which it needs to survive: by monotonizing physical variety to a type which services only the attraction of shoppers and assists only the activity of shopping. The dominance of the market economy has been so pervasive that despite resistance, all environments have been compelled to behave like shops. (Chung, 2001, p. 658)

Sze Tsung Leong suggests:

> Shopping is the medium by which the [global] market has solidified its grip on our spaces, our buildings, cities, activities, and lives. It is the material outcome of the degree to which the market economy has shaped our surroundings and ultimately ourselves. (Leong, 2001a, p. 129)

Employment and migration

With the emphasis on financial and service sectors, as well as retail and consumption, we increasingly witness the *devalorization* of (that is, the failure to give status or due reward to) people, places and activities that are not part of the control sectors of the economy, including many of those employed in the low-paid manual jobs (catering, security or cleaning) or supplying the street-corner services on which the daily life of the global city depends.

As the significance of certain cities and the activities they are based upon increases, a dysfunctionality enters the urban scene as the public and social infrastructure of the city is no longer sustainable. In London there have been a number of 'living wage campaigns', supported by churches, mosques and community groups. These campaigns urge an adequate wage for daily living, rather than merely a minimum wage, for the workers on whom such businesses depend – cleaners, security personnel, transport workers (often working in the premises of major trans-national corporations (TNCs) who are often themselves global migrants).

What are considered economically non-productive activities, including the care and education of children, and health care in the state sector, are similarly devalued. Teachers and some health professionals can no longer afford property prices and either endure long journeys to work or leave the major cities to work in the provinces. The direct recruitment of temporary foreign workers for these sectors from the Philippines, Eastern Europe or Australia is increasingly common.

On whom do our globalizing cities depend? Just as money and information streams across national boundaries so, too, do people: not just those who drive global business but also reserves of labour willing to work in these new globalized environments:

The top end of the corporate economy – the highly paid professionals and corporate towers that project engineering expertise and precision – is far easier to recognise as necessary for an advanced economic system than are truckers and other industrial service workers, or maids or nannies, even though all of them are a necessary ingredient. (Sassen, 2003a, p. 117)

Gender is a key factor in the contemporary working life of the city. Saskia Sassen has noted the patterns of female migration often absent in the plots of the dominant globalization narratives describing the new urban economy. As increasing numbers of professional women are employed in the higher levels of the global economy an often covert economy emerges, drawing other (usually migrant) women into work in their homes. The routes and networks of movement are often closely shadowed by those involved in the trafficking of women in the sex industry as well as drugs.

A growing share of . . . domestic tasks are relocated to the market: they are bought directly as goods or services or indirectly through hired labour. As a consequence we see the return of the so-called serving classes in all of the world's global cities, and these classes are made up of immigrant and migrant women. (Sassen, 2003b, p. 117)

Mobility becomes an asset in the global labour market: skilled professionals and workers, in health, education, planning and architecture, move, leaving countries skill-impoverished – and not necessarily to work in the professions for which they have trained.

In London researchers note the twin phenomena of the exclusion of the traditional working class and their heirs from the labour market, and the obstacles faced by many minority ethnic people from progressing in their careers. Michael Edwards describes the notion of 'bumping out':

Economic geographer Ian Gordon, has drawn attention to what he describes as a 'bumping out' of working class people from jobs through the availability and recruitment of more highly-qualified (often 'over-qualified') migrants, students and young graduates to fill positions they would historically have been expected to occupy. (Edwards, 2002, p. 30)

Migration is an ever-present stream in the globalization process. Those at the bottom, however, will find themselves in a different relationship to the forces at work from those in business class, and will often be the targets of anti-immigration groups. The dependence of many sectors on low-paid migrant workers is rarely celebrated or acknowledged.

The experiences of globalization can be uneven and often contradictory. People who live in the same space, who encounter each other in the home or the office, will find their access to the 'benefits' of globalization to be vastly different, as between, say, the executive and the cleaner, the financier and the nanny. The movement of people, on which a globalized urban economy depends, is vastly more restrictive at the lower levels.

New demands will be made on urban settlements to accommodate a vast array of groups and minorities within a common space: a process accompanied by competition and conflict as well as new forms of co-operation and co-existence. In an age of globalization, new forces are shaping settlements as new patterns of identity and community make much of the old planning theory redundant. It is often the urban planners who first encounter these demands, often through religious groups wanting accommodation for worship. Similarly, the initial impact of new migrants is often in the local arena of community politics as the focus of incorporation programmes as well as through their own organizations (see the section 'Globalization from below', p. 26).

Security

Globalization changes the way we perceive cities. The rapid flow of information means that we are aware of events in cities elsewhere. We are witnesses to natural and civil catastrophes, to terrorism and financial failure. Low-cost travel also affects us in unexpected ways, such as disease travelling rapidly.

Cities are often perceived as places of danger, even by those who live in them. The creation of safe zones for private and public life has become a new driving force. Public spaces are patrolled by security personnel or surveyed by CCTV. As previously public spaces become privatized behaviour becomes restricted – nowhere more apparent than in railway stations and shopping malls. As threat is perceived, levels of domestic security increase and concierge systems, gated communities and private protection proliferate. Global security firms offer local solutions. What may have been considered a benign security firm will appear in another country as an armed response unit. Considering the New York experience post 9/11, Peter Marcuse writes of the *citadelization* of the city,

> incorporating more and more of daily functions within enclosed and protected spaces in large planned developments accompanied by an increased public investment in security and surveillance and control mechanisms, together with a diminution of the public sector in its social welfare function [and a] disproportionate growth of those industries providing real or perceived or mandated security for daily activities. (Marcuse, 2003, p. 275)

Culture

If those who are profiting from our city centre have global interests this changes the relationship between how profits are distributed and the local community. Richard Sennett notes the changes in urban philanthropy as international cultural events and touring exhibitions are privileged over the local institution (Sennett, 2000).

City centre regeneration has become orientated to new cultural and sporting facilities based on 'big-ticket' events, creating the right environment to attract firms with sports-mad executives and art-obsessed spouses. Inter-city competition and regional dominance is encouraged. 'National centres for . . .' and 'Years of . . .' are eagerly sought. Even 'high culture' has become an essential part of the city whose rationale is now based on consumption rather than production.

Reflecting on the experience of Sheffield, with its bid to be a global 'Sports City' through hosting the 1991 World Student Games, and the cultural ambitions of its doomed National Centre for Popular Music, Graeme Evans and Jo Foord write:

> Linkages, networks and flows of ideas need to be more than one way. A cultural renaissance is not a quick fix. It does mean quality opportunities for everyone – to be entertained as well as enlightened, to create for leisure and pleasure as well as enterprise, to consume culture and to participate in its everyday production. (Evan and Foord, 2006, p. 167)

Similarly, Tristram Hunt describes the move away from the encouragement of local sporting and cultural life to an economically driven culture
with an emphasis on brand and status: 'the culture of today's cities
appears more of a branding and marketing tool than a reflection of civic
identity. It is frequently the work of quangoes and urban regeneration
consultants rather than the organic outcome of any home-grown civic
sentiment' (Hunt, 2004, p. 346).

Globalization from below

As we have seen with migration, globalization is not solely the preserve
of international financiers and information technologists. People who
are not part of the visible international business caste are also moving,
communicating and creating alternative financial flows. Sometimes the
two worlds come into direct conflict, as has been seen in the campaigns
for a living wage among office cleaners in London or hotel workers in
Los Angeles, movements in which churches and other faith groups have
played a leading part (Davey, 2001, pp. 114–25).

Globalization is responsible for the changes we witness on our urban
streets as cheap telecommunications businesses, East European grocers
and West African Pentecostal churches change shop fronts and commercial space. We find it in new demands and expectations placed on
schools and social services, on housing and policing. Globalization
brings with it new urban forms of religion, often first apparent to planning authorities who discover changes of use or breaches of zoning
regulations as meeting and worship spaces are sought and developed.
Satellite television, travelling evangelists and new forms of religious
franchising will often connect these groups across the planet, making
them less dependent on local roots.

The structures of globalization provide a new framework in which we
all live. For many there are forces that operate through these global
structures that need to be resisted, engaged with or diverted. Recent
campaigns on debt and global poverty have taken to the streets.
Demonstrations against the effect of unjust trade agreements are a
regular feature of international financial gatherings. Movements for
'fair trade' have city authorities as well as corporations and retailers in
their sights. We see this emergent informal political sphere growing in
what has been called 'global civil society'. It is apparent in the social
forums that meet in India and Brazil, at the same time as the World

Economic Forums in Davos and New York, under the cry 'Um outro mundo é posibel', 'Another world is possible!' (Forum Social Mundo). A rainbow coalition is emerging of groups concerned with the environment, the fairness of trade, migrant and indigenous people's rights, the destructiveness of war, and cities as arenas for social justice (Albrow, Anheier, Glasius and Kaldor, 2006). Often these groups are involved in very localized struggles but they have begun to understand the connections, and will exploit the possibility of global connectivity. Older members of these groups are often those who were engaged in the struggles of previous decades – the apartheid struggle, nuclear disarmament, and so on. Younger participants are found using new organizing tactics and technologies, with little experience of the formal political arena. The willingness to confront dominant narratives of city have often brought groups into direct conflict with city authorities. Doreen Massey has recently written of the need for 'a more outward-looking politics that seeks to address that wider geography of place and to ponder what might be thought of as the global responsibilities of (some) local places' (Massey, 2007, p. 176).

A globalized city

In the twenty-first century those who 'seek the welfare of the city' need to take its global dimension seriously. Global connectivity is rapidly reshaping urban life beyond the conventional patterns of control and regulation by state or city authority, or social constructs of place such as community or neighbourhood. The contested nature of urban life will mean that those forces will be competing for dominance of the city centre or the high street, as well as our social and economic lives.

Bibliography

Albrow, M., Anheier, H., Glasius, M. and Kaldor, M., 2006, *Civil Society Yearbook 2006/7*, London, Sage Books.

Beaverstock, J.V., Smith, R.G., and Taylor, R., 1999, 'A Roster of World Cities', *Cities* 16(6), 445–58.

Carvel, John, 2005, 'Retail chains "cloning" UK towns', *Guardian*, 6 June. Read online: http://society.guardian.co.uk/urbandesign/story/0,,1500199,00.html

Castells, Manuel, 2000, *The Rise of the Network Society*, 2nd edition, Oxford, Blackwell.

Chung, Chuihua, with Palop-Casado, Juan, 2001, 'Resistance', in Chuihua Judy Chung, Jeffrey Inaba, Rem Koolhaas and Sze Tsung Leong (eds.), *Harvard Design School: Guide to Shopping*, Cologne, Taschen, 633–59.

Davey, Andrew, 2001, *Urban Christianity and Global Order: Theological Resources for an Urban Future*, London, SPCK.

Edwards, Michael, 2002, 'Wealth Creation and Poverty Creation. Global–local interactions in the economy of London', *CITY-Analysis of Urban Trends, Culture, Theory, Policy, Action* 6(1), 25–42.

Evans, Graeme and Foord, Jo, 2006, 'Mall Cities for a Small Country. Sustaining the Local Cultural Renaissance?', in David Bell and Mark Jayne (eds.), *Small Cities: Urban Experience Beyond the Metropolis*, London, Routledge, 151–68.

Hunt, Tristram, 2004, *Building Jerusalem: The Rise and Fall of the Victorian City*, London, Weidenfeld & Nicholson.

Leong, Sze Tsung, 2001a, '. . . and then there was shopping', in Chuihua Judy Chung, Jeffrey Inaba, Rem Koolhaas and Sze Tsung Leong (eds.), *Harvard Design School: Guide to Shopping*, Cologne, Taschen, 128–35.

Leong, Sze Tsung, 2001b, 'Divine Economy', in Chuihua Judy Chung, Jeffrey Inaba, Rem Koolhaas and Sze Tsung Leong (eds.), *Harvard Design School: Guide to Shopping*, Cologne, Taschen, 299–303.

Marcuse, H., 2003, 'The "War on Terrorism" and Life in Cities after September 11, 2001', in Stephen Graham (ed.), *Cities, War and Terrorism: Towards an Urban Geopolitics*, Oxford, Blackwell, 263–75.

Massey, Doreen, 2007, *World City*, Cambridge, Polity Press.

Murray, Warwick E., 2006, *Geographies of Globalization*, London, Routledge.

Sassen, Saskia, 2000, 'The Global City: Strategic Site/New Frontier', in Engin F. Isin (ed.), *Democracy, Citizenship and the Global City*, London, Routledge, 48–61.

Sassen, Saskia, 2001, *The Global City: New York, London, Tokyo*, 2nd edition, Princeton, Princeton University Press.

Sassen, Saskia, 2003a, '"More than CitiBank": Who belongs in the global city?' in *Topic Magazine 3: Cities*, 111–17.

Sassen, Saskia, 2003b, 'Global Cities and Survival Circuits', in Barbara Enrenreich and Arlie Russell Hochschild (eds.), *Global Woman: Nannies, Maids and Sex Workers in the New Economy*, London, Granta, 254–74.

Sennett, Richard, 2000, 'The Art of Making Cities', London School of Economics public lecture, 9 March 2000. Reprinted in *New Statesman*, 5 June.

Short, John Rennie, 2004, *Global Metropolitan: Globalizing Cities in a Capitalist World*, London, Routledge.

Smith, Neil, 2002, 'New Globalism, New Urbanism', in Neil Brenner and Nik Theodore (eds.), *Spaces of NeoLiberalism: Urban Restructuring in North America and Western Europe*, Oxford, Blackwell.

2

Renewal in the Centre of the City and the Churches' Contribution

CHRIS BAKER

On 15 June 1996, a normal and busy Saturday morning, a massive 3,300lb IRA bomb ripped through the central shopping core of Manchester. Thanks to a quick response to a coded warning, 80,000 people were evacuated and no one was killed that day (although several people were seriously injured and some still bear the mental and emotional scars). However, the physical damage to much of the 1960s and 1970s regenerated city centre was devastating, with a third of Manchester's shopping, retail and commercial space destroyed.

Ten years almost to the day, the following article appeared in the *Guardian* on 7 June 2006 entitled 'Reach for the sky':

> From his new penthouse on the 47th floor of Britain's tallest residential building, architect Ian Simpson will soon look down on a city he helped to transform from the rubble of a terrorist outrage . . . A decade on, the result is a city reborn with a completely remodelled city centre embracing new squares, streets, shops, offices, apartments and much more . . . At least 20,000 people have moved into the city's central core since the bombing and . . . today, the partners in the new Manchester . . . are pushing the centre steadily to the more deprived north and to the east – where new communities are being established around old canal basins, redundant textile mills, and warehouses.

Ian Simpson is a Mancunian himself and was part of the successful consortium that won the international design competition held in the immediate aftermath of the IRA bombing to redesign the entire city centre. The building in question is the newly completed Beetham Tower, otherwise known as the Manchester Hilton. It is 171m. tall and includes a five-star, 285-bedroom hotel from levels 5–23, a 'destination sky bar' on the 24th floor (from which one can see the mountains of Snowdonia in north Wales), and apartments up to floor 50. Simpson, in compliance with a growing tradition of architects living in their own designs, has bought his duplex penthouse apartment for a reported £3 million.

The purpose of this scenario is to lay out the key mechanisms that lie at the heart of urban regeneration – namely the rebranding of Manchester and its city centre as a postmodern iconic brand name that will successfully compete within the global economy to attract those new citizens upon which its wealth and future security will be predicated. These citizens will be young and ambitious researchers, managers, designers, cultural and media trendsetters and entrepreneurs who come to Manchester's universities from around the world and who will then be tempted to stay rather than emigrate to London or a new global destination. Manchester and its Beetham Tower thus represent a paradigmatic shift of identity and purpose that has occurred within the last 15 years in all regional cities in the UK.

This chapter will explore some of the key shifts that are driving city centre revitalization in the UK by observing trends within three vital sectors of city centre life – housing, retailing and nightlife. We then conclude this review by asking some strategic questions about both the challenges and opportunities presented to the churches by these three areas of spatial-cultural change within our city centres.

Housing – offering the urban 'buzz' for the new professional class

The restructuring of housing in the centres of our towns and cities has been widely influenced by the 'urban renaissance' agenda aimed at transforming city centres and surrounding inner urban areas scarred by the economic and social blight of deindustrialization from the 1960s to the late 1980s. This 'renaissance' agenda emerged within the UK in the Urban Task Force Report (1999) chaired by Lord Rogers of Riverside, which became the basis of New Labour's Urban White Paper in 2000. Among its many recommendations for creating renewed city centre spaces was a return to high density housing to produce 'pyramids of intensity'. These high density pyramids (not in the literal sense) would combine progressive urban design with well-connected transport infrastructure, but also a sense of a safe public realm – from outdoor eating to street entertainment – along with the re-establishment of the well-maintained, attractive and uncluttered public spaces which would nevertheless be sympathetically constructed to enhance the value of old industrial landscapes (railway arches, canals, warehouses, etc.: see Rogers, 1999, pp. 64, 65).

Rogers reminded the government that a safe public realm also required the presence of a body of people who would live in the city during the weekends and at night (once the offices and shops closed down) and so provide the core market for an expanding night-time and cultural economy (Rogers, 1999, p. 311). Housing therefore is a key component in the repopulation and renaissance of the city centre, and it is being built in a 'niched' and increasingly sophisticated way – that is to say, different types of housing provided and then marketed to attract a number of different populations as dwellers and consumers of city centre life.

Research carried out by the Centre for Regional Economic and Social Research at Sheffield Hallam University (Allen and Blandy, 2004) has identified different typologies of city dweller. The two main types divide along age lines. The younger type of dweller – typically the single young post-graduate – works long hours and lives in the city centre because it is convenient. A survey of city centre dwellers in Manchester (Seo, 2002) revealed that 77 per cent were under 40 with more than half living in single-person households. Over 60 per cent were employed at managerial or similar professional level and nearly one third earned over £35,000 a year. However, further assessment of client feedback provided by estate agents (as well as focus groups) found that this population had not come to live in the city centre only for convenience. They had also come to access the urban *experience* or 'buzz' – a combination of culture, hedonism and 24/7 leisure activities supplemented by the security of living among homogenous professional groups, often within gated or secured environments with gym and health club facilities attached. These new apartments have usually one or two bedrooms and are marketed with a new vocabulary aimed at conveying a sense of postmodern urban chic (e.g., 'uqubes' and 'klustas'). These apartments will be built to higher densities and lower building specifications (such as sound insulation) and will often be bought by the 'buy-to-let' market to meet the demand for reasonably priced short-term tenures in the city centre. In a potentially worrying trend, Allen and Blandy note that in some apartment developments in northern cities up to a third are bought by London-based landlords. Current starting prices for one-bed apartments in Manchester are around the £100K mark (as of August 2007).

This group of young professionals is only in the city centre for the short term – anywhere between 12 and 36 months judging by interviews

(Allen and Blandy, 2004, p. 11; Urry, 2000) – but during that short time is committed to accumulating an ever-lengthening list of new experiences (moving jobs, living in different places, meeting new people) before settling down in the suburbs with a longer-term partner and the possibility of starting a family.

The second type of urban dweller tends to be older and constitutes perhaps 25 to 30 per cent of city dwellers. This segment is a relatively stable community because it is more interested in an 'authentic' experience, rather than the 'buzz' of the hyped-up fashionable urban symbolic imagery or 'brandscape'. This second type of city centre dweller falls into three sub-categories. First is the 'successful ager' who, because of increased advances in health and equity acquired during working life, no longer sees post-retirement as a phase of life traditionally associated with dependency and loss of economic spending power. Rather, they see themselves as active consumers embracing later life as an opportunity to experience the cultural sophistication of urban living. They will therefore be drawn to the high end of the apartment market – usually mill or warehouse conversions whose duplexes often start at around £250–300K. This group of citizens requires 'high-end' cultural activities such as galleries, theatres, concert halls and art-house cinemas.

The second sub-category in the 'authentic' typology is the counter-culturalist – for example, people who ran micro-businesses in art and design and started an authentic alternative grass-roots scene, but who have now graduated into successful cultural entrepreneurs. A classic example of this would be the small network of graphic artists, clothes and jewellery designers and musicians who lived and worked in the decaying industrial suburbs in the north of Manchester's centre in the later 1970s and early 1980s and from whom emerged the influential Factory Records brand that was built on the widespread success of bands like Joy Division and New Order. Out of this record label evolved the Hacienda nightclub (converted from a disused warehouse), which itself became the centre of the ongoing domination of the national dance/acid house/post-punk culture during the 1980s and early 1990s by Manchester-based bands like The Smiths, The Fall, Happy Mondays and The Stone Roses. This 'heritage' has allowed the area to be re-christened as new Manchester's Northern Quarter – a semi-bohemian space of small but often exclusive businesses selling high-end nostalgia products, clothes and jewellery. This space acts as an 'individualized' retailing counterpoint, close by but separated from the branded and mass-market retailing on offer in the city centre. This counter-cultural group of residents also includes those original pioneers of the city's gay scene in the late 1970s and early 1980s, who congregated in a small area of semi-clandestine gay pubs and clubs in the Canal Street area of Manchester, which has now developed into an official Gay Village. Many of these social and cultural pioneers continue to live in the original terraced housing they bought close to the city centre (but now considerably upgraded) as well as locating themselves in the new higher-end city centre apartments.

The third sub-category is referred to as 'lifestyle changers' – those who have either divorced or separated or who have deliberately chosen not to commit to long-term relationships. They are looking to the city centre to provide a sense of the 'non-conventional' as an alternative to the idea of settled monogamy – a space for encountering new and multiple relationships and an overall sense of choice and individuality. This is a rather shadowy group, 'stumbled' upon in focus groups, and they are perceived to be 'semi-authentic' rather than truly committed to the city centre for the long term. They thus produce a higher turnover of people; perhaps closer to that produced by the younger 'experience-seeking' group.

The main point to draw from this analysis (which doesn't include emerging groups such as asylum seekers and students) is that the evidence base suggests that, while city centres are acquiring populations once more (which is good news for churches seeking to re-establish themselves in this urban space), most of this population (possibly 75 per cent) will be highly transient and often living in new residential spaces that are zoned and 'gated' in some way or other. They are in the city centre (so it is suggested) to seek a sense of individual fulfilment and experience rather than a sense of community (in the traditional, gathered sense of the word). This will therefore present a challenge to many churches whose default ecclesiology is still predicated on the 'one size fits all' model of a gathered church congregation of mixed age and socio-economic background all doing the same thing at the same time (what Pete Ward calls 'solid' church, 2002, p. 28).

Retailing – the shopping mall as 'experience' destination

There is little doubt that retailing lies at the heart of the 'rebirth' of the UK city centre. In accordance with the historical precedents identified by geographer David Harvey and the regeneration of the US city of

Baltimore in the mid 1980s, a central component of any successful urban rebirth is the boosting of 'consumer potential' for the city and its region. Harvey identified the following components of the Baltimore recipe for successful rebirth:

> Gentrification, cultural innovation and physical upgrading of the urban environment (including the turn to postmodernist styles of architecture and urban design), consumer attractions (sports stadia, convention and shopping centres, marinas, exotic eating places) and entertainment (the organization of urban spectacles on a temporary or permanent basis), have all become much more prominent facets of strategies for urban regeneration. *Above all, the city has to appear as an innovative, exciting, creative and safe place to live or to visit, to play and consume in.* (Harvey, 1989, p. 14, emphasis mine)

According to Harvey's prescient description, the boundaries between shopping and tourism have now become blurred. Shopping centres are now tourist destinations in their own right and so need to provide those opportunities for both relaxation and stimulation that we now look for when we go on a holiday or short city-break.

Any internet search of shopping malls, particularly in the States where the concept of retailing has been perfected into a seamless shopping/tourist package, will highlight the paramount significance of shopping within our daily lives. For example, in April 2007, Cabela's (a national franchise selling 'hunting, fishing and outdoor gear') will open its first 130,000 sq ft superstore in St Louis, Missouri (the equivalent size of three football fields). This store is the newest attraction within St Louis Mills, 'a 1.1 million square foot retail and entertainment centre in Hazelwood, located just off the I-270, north of I-70 (Exit 22B, Hwy.370)' (see www.fibre2fschion.com/news/), a destination hub which attracts up to 3 million people a year. The Cabela's store, in which it is claimed will draw 50 per cent of its visitors from more than 100 miles away, with customers staying an average of three and a half hours, will have the following attractions:

- Hundreds of animals in museum-quality dioramas, including an African scene.
- Cabela's hallmark two-storey Conservation Mountain, complete with running waterfalls and stream, a trout pond and wild game in distinctive habitats.

- A 50,000-gallon, walk-through aquarium, stocked with freshwater fish and an alligator/snapping turtle tank.
- A 3,300 square foot wildlife museum with an extensive collection of trophy mounts.
- Other highlights including a laser arcade, furniture department, gun library, fly fishing shop and gift shop.

The closest a UK experience possibly gets to this typical US fare is the Bluewater shopping centre in north Kent just outside the M25. It has a total retail floor space of 1.6 million square foot (and car parking for 13,000 cars) and, in addition to the shopping, offers a 14-screen cinema, 40 cafes and restaurants, discovery and fitness trails through its carefully sculptured 240 acres of parkland (from reclaimed chalk pits), a climbing wall, fishing, cycling, boating, miniature golf and an ice-skating rink in winter. But a visit to the centre's extensive website reveals two further features of interest at Bluewater.

First is its overt pitch towards providing a space of healing and spirituality. It provides what it calls 'A Place of Quiet' where 'you can rest the spirit and retreat for solitude and reflection . . . located in the Lower Rose Gallery, between Prêt a Manger and the Carphone Warehouse' (see www.bluewater.com). Included in this Place of Quiet is 'a listening space offering a suitable space for one to one conversations' provided by the Chaplaincy Service at Bluewater – an agreement between Bluewater and Kent Industrial Mission to 'provide support to retailers, staff and guests' via a team made up of 11 members of local faith communities.

Second is the strongly expressed commitment to issues of surveillance and security. Bluewater is a heavily managed environment with strictly enforced rules regarding public behaviour. Over 400 CCTV cameras monitor human activity in both the centre and parklands areas. Here is a selection of 'taboo' activities prohibited by the management of Blueco Ltd, the company that owns Bluewater:

- All groups of more than five without the intention to shop will be asked to leave the Centre.
- The wearing of any item of clothing which restricts the view of one's head/face (e.g., hoods) with the exception of religious headwear.
- Leafleting, canvassing or the conducting of third party interviews or surveys unless authorized by Bluewater Centre management.
- No cycling, roller-blading, using micro-scooters or skating in the centre.

- Alcohol is only to be consumed within the premises that hold a relevant licence.
- No climbing or sitting on any balustrade, barrier, fence or railing.

With these UK and US case studies in mind, the key trends associated with retail development can be summarized. Retailing is now:

- An 'experience destination' incorporating entertainment, education and the opportunity for new thrills and experiences and highly risk-managed physical challenge.
- A space that can aspire to providing a sense of tranquillity, healing and even spiritual activity such as prayer and contemplation.
- A surveilled space that offers safety and predictability, aimed at eliminating any form of public behaviour that can be perceived to be a threat or annoyance to individuals or the sense of the public realm.

In other words, shopping space has become 'private space' in the sense that external authorities (in this case the consortium of pension funds that owns Bluewater) dictate and control appropriate standards of dress, public speech and conduct. To transgress any one of its 18 prohibitions will result in expulsion or prosecution.

While the experience of city-edge retail developments such as Bluewater may be seen as an exaggeration of what happens in newly regenerated city centres, it is in fact only a matter of degree. The levels of CCTV surveillance will be high – in 2002 a state-of-the-art control room was built in Manchester to house monitors from 84 CCTV cameras focusing on one small area of the city centre. The expulsion or prohibition of 'undesirable elements' (e.g., young 'hoodies', homeless adults) will be strongly reinforced with ASBOs and byelaws. Meanwhile the amount of city centre space that comes within the enclosed shopping mall design is increasing (for example, Cardiff's St David's Phase 2 development will expand the city centre retail capacity by nearly a million square feet), thus allowing a greater degree of control over what happens and also who is allowed to enter that space. We shall explore the wider ramifications of these shifts in our concluding section.

Nightlife – imbibing hedonism and fun in the urban brandscape

An influential critique of the increase in the night-time economies of the re-gentrified city centres (see Chatterton and Hollands, 2003) sees a double process of homogenization and commodification whereby a few corporate companies are applying essentially Fordist market mechanisms (namely mass-produced, centrally controlled and corporately marketed brands), but masquerading their products as post-Fordist goods (i.e., goods that focus on consumer choice and cater for individual expression). Thus the big players in the market, namely the largest owners of pub chains, restaurants and nightclubs and casino franchises, are tightening their stranglehold on how our city centres are redeveloped. For example, although the number of UK pubs remained static over a ten-year period from 1990 to 2000, the number owned by national brewers (regional and smaller, independent breweries) fell from 32,000 to 3,300. In contrast, global pub companies (or 'pubcos') raised their share (via a series of acquisitions and mergers) from 16,000 to 48,000. Many of these pubcos have little connection with brewing, and will be unknown to the general public. Thus Nomura, one of the largest pub-chain owners in the UK with 5,500 pubs, is also one of the largest securities firms in Japan with operations in 30 countries and employing over 12,000 globally. Its portfolio includes betting chains, off-licences, international hotel chains, and Ministry of Defence married quarters. It also owns one third of rolling stock used on British railways and won the bidding rights to redevelop the Millennium Dome (Chatterton and Hollands, 2003, p. 35).

The increasing grip of pubcos has a number of implications. As Chatterton and Hollands correctly point out, 'fun, hedonism, socialising, sexual encounter and drunkenness remain long-held motivations for a good night out' (2003, p. 69). However, the mechanisms by which such experiences are mediated and controlled are increasingly 'mainstreamed' and 'gentrified'. This mainstreaming has been largely driven by the rise of the new consumer whose tastes and spending power are more refined and enhanced than that available in the traditional working-class and largely male bastions of entertainment originating in the industrial era – pubs, music halls, working men's clubs, bingo and pool halls, picture palaces, etc. These new consumers are professional women, gentrified members of the gay and lesbian community, and students with higher levels of disposable income and closer access to the city centre thanks to the expansion and relocation of student accommodation nearer to hubs of city centre activity. These consumers have helped shape what has been dubbed the 'brandscape'; i.e. a central urban area dominated by a 'symbolic' landscape of globally recognized images and products that promise a wide variety of themes and 'structured fantasies' (Chatterton and Hollands, 2003, p. 96). These will include sports bars, sushi bars, Moroccan bazaars, Aussie and Irish pubs, beach bars. As Chatterton and Hollands explain, 'The logic of such easy to read themed environments is that their legibility stimulates our propensity to spend. In short, people like to be entertained while they spend money' (p. 97).

However, these brandscapes offer more than entertainment – they also speak of social status and economic spending power in a hierarchical zoning of space. At the bottom end of the market are the large capacity (1,000 plus) themed venues that offer their owners the best opportunities for economies of scale and profit maximization. They appeal to the widest possible audience with design features such as 'bright walls, rock and pop music, legible signage and well-known drink brands'(Chatterton and Hollands, 2003, p. 98). A UK example of such a franchise is J. D. Wetherspoon with its cheap beer, no music or TV, 'just a pub' philosophy. At the more hedonistic end of this market is Brannigans, whose branded moniker contains the 'strap-line' 'Eating, Drinking and Cavorting' and whose main identity is expressed by the words 'fun pub'. At the higher end of the market are the 'yuppie bars' (such as the Slug and Lettuce chain) aimed at affluent young professionals, and offering premium food and quality beers. J. D. Wetherspoon attempts to cater for this market with its Lloyds No 1 franchise. Meanwhile, the Bar 38 franchise (part of the Scottish and Newcastle group) incorporates zones within its premises for eating, drinking and socializing, but all placed in such a way as to increase circulation. They also include cash points and intensive CCTV operations, but all tastefully concealed within an esoteric yet minimalist decor – stripped wooden furniture, metallic walls and glass frontages.

Residual space – home of the flawed consumers

The logical implication of this zoned and hierarchical understanding of city centre space is that the lower down the socio-economic chain you are, the less choice and opportunity you have to participate in the night-time economy. This is especially true of those younger people who are the direct or indirect descendants of the industrial working-class communities who, prior to the deindustrialization of the 1960s, had direct access to the city centre and whose cultural and entertainment needs were met by its many spaces for socializing and discussion (see above, p. 37). Because of a lack of spending power (due to low-paid employment or no employment at all) the best this group can aspire to in terms of participation in the city centre is at the lower end of the brandscape spectrum, where their presence is viewed with suspicion and subject to disparaging labelling such as 'chavs', 'slappers', etc. At worst, when even participation at the lower end of the night-time economy is denied them (in 2001, the average cost of a 'night out' for drinks at a number of venues, food and taxis was £40: see Chatterton and Hollands, 2003, p. 121), the only remaining 'space' open to them for entertainment is their 'home' environment – a few remaining pubs on estates or those parts on the edges of city centres awaiting 'refitting', but more typically street corners, parks, shopping centres and localized gang cultures (Chatterton and Hollands, 2003, p. 189). Homeless people (i.e., those most excluded from participation in what the city centre has to offer) will often be subject to official harassment or attack from other users for whom 'kick the beggar' might be one further addition to the night-out menu (p. 192).

These spaces are what Chatterton and Hollands define as the 'residue' spaces – non-productive spaces (in terms of globalized turnover) lying in the shadow of the 'bright neon of youthful gentrified nightlife consumption' and 'marginalised by new urban brandscapes and the commercial mainstream' (2003, p. 175). Originally useful in the industrial city, these residual spaces are now 'surplus to requirements' (p. 175). Zygmunt Bauman, in one of his most striking sociological typologies, defines two broad categories of citizen in today's 'liquid' modernity (1997). One group are the 'cash rich but time poor' citizens who are broadly affluent and secure, but whose lifestyles and choices are constantly being dictated by the work ethic. Consumption of new products and experiences is the reward offered by the market for their endless flexibility, mobility and hard work.

The other group are the 'cash poor but time rich'; those whose lack of appropriate skills and economic status mean that they increasingly struggle to participate in the consumer economy – these are the redundant and the dispossessed and therefore, by definition, the most stigmatized and potentially most criminalized. However, their greatest 'crime', according to Bauman, is their unwillingness or inability to play their part in the new forms of production – i.e., consumption. The poor, in Bauman's terms, are therefore 'flawed consumers' and thus seen as undeserving of either respect or compassion.

Seeking new spaces of production and alternative spaces of hope in the indifferent city

As we come to the conclusion of this chapter, we can frame some emerging questions and themes which will inform subsequent contributions to this volume. We appear to have reached a consensus that says that, for all the 'buzz' and energy of iconic pride associated with buildings such as Beetham's Tower in Manchester (and the undeniable benefits it brings in terms of enhanced cultural, housing and retailing facilities), there is in fact a growing and worrying polarization between the spaces and opportunities available to productive consumers as opposed to flawed consumers.

The productive consumers appear to inhabit an increasingly protected and isolated 'bubble'. The new city is laid out as an entertainment zone for their enjoyment while the housing they choose to buy is increasingly homogenized and gated. This has led to the emergence of a variety of theoretical terms regarding the city centre and its role. In the early 1990s the American theorist Michael Sorkin (1992) referred to the growing influence of large corporations on cities as a 'Disneyfication' process. In a similar vein Thomas Bender, a social historian, refers to contemporary Los Angeles as City Lite. Any product that has 'lite' attached to it is one that approximates to the real thing, but has all the nasty and unhealthy bits taken out. By applying this brand indicator to cities, Bender is emphasizing the way the historic and cultural identities of urban spaces (which helped define a unique sensibility and sense of *polis*) are now repackaged as consumerist items offering an a-historical experience based on safety, convenience and standardized elements for individuals to partake of. He writes:

> For a millennium, cities have carried history and sustained our cultural traditions through their universities, museums and libraries and in their physical fabric, with its traces of social succession . . . The complexity of that history, like the social and physical complexity of the city more generally, nourishes the human spirit, even as it tries it. Life in the Lite City reveals no passage of time, no history. The City Lite does not age; it is consumed and replaced. It is any time and any place – it no longer holds culture nor provides an orientation to past and present for its residents. (Quoted in Soja, 2000, p. 47)

This steady erosion of historical public spaces of shared memory, which are enjoyed and even contested by a wide variety of diverse groups, in favour of the emergence of scripted, surveilled and therefore essentially privatized space (controlled ultimately by private corporations rather than publicly elected and accountable civic authorities) has led to other similarly dystopian theories. Fincher and Jacobs (1998) devise a concept of 'cities of indifference', in which urban areas, constantly evaluated for their *exchange* value rather than their human use value, do little to proactively create humane and meaningful public spaces. Then there is Smith's notion of the 'revanchist' (or revenging) city (1996) – red in tooth and claw as it ruthlessly purges its city centre and financial districts of undesirable and 'unproductive' elements via aggressive economic and social gentrification.

But at the heart of the Christian gospel is the imperative to proclaim alternative messages (or *kerygmata*) of forgiveness and salvation through reflection upon the example and symbolic commemoration of Jesus' life, death and resurrection. There is also the message of *metanoia* – the turning around of one's thinking, leading to new life and transformation. These messages of hope lead to the production of alternative spaces of hope (i.e., the 'church') – spaces where people and their communities are believed and invested in and narratives of present courage and future fulfilment are interwoven with both sober and joyful evaluations of the past.

In practical terms these alternative messages and spaces of hope involve celebrating the presence of the iconic, the bold and the innovative that undoubtedly exists within the postmodern city centre, especially when these buildings or spaces provide a sense of what Philip Sheldrake (2001) defines as the 'sacred'. By this he means any building or public space that has something of worth or value invested in it that allows us to transcend our daily life and reflect upon the wider dimensions of human existence, as well as what the human geographer Ash Amin has called, at a colloquium on Faith and Spirituality in the City held at Durham in 2007, the 'embedded ethics' of hospitality and healing that underpins any 'good' *polis*.

But it also means celebrating the *everyday*; what the Jesuit philosopher Michel de Certeau understands as the daily process by which the superstructure of consumerism is subverted and adapted in a myriad of small but significant ways. Thus a 'simple' church initiative in running an advice centre and a clothing and food store for destitute asylum seekers, or providing a homely and welcoming (and brand-free) space where one can buy a cheap but locally sourced and homemade meal and converse with a neighbour at leisure, becomes at more complex levels deeply counter-cultural because it represents the importance of valuing people for who they are, not for what they can spend or consume.

Physical spaces can also be subversive. Chatterton and Hollands devote a chapter in their book to the description of alternative 'free' spaces such as illegal raves and community squats that take over old redundant buildings such as churches, large residences, even banks. These alternative spaces exist for a range of purposes; from the *pragmatic* (the saving of community resources such as community centres, allotments, childcare centres, places of local memory and symbolic significance from redevelopment), through to the more *visionary* and *utopian* (co-operatives based on organic food production, alternative energy, demilitarization, etc.).

Popular culture as well as physical spaces can be subversive. Popular culture is the means by which citizens use the symbols and spaces on offer to their own ends. De Certeau refers to it as the age-old art of 'making do' – of 'constructing *our* space within and against *their* place, of speaking *our* meaning with *their* language'. He reflects, 'The consumer cannot be identified or gratified by the commercial product he [or she] assimilates: between the person (who uses them) and these products . . . there is a gap of varying proportions opened by the use the consumer makes of them' (de Certeau, 1984, p. 32). This gap consists of the concrete uses to which the consumer or citizen puts the products on offer; what John Fiske calls 'the individual acts of consumption-production, the creativities produced from commodities' (Fiske, 1989, p. 36). By way of an example, Fiske identifies those small acts of resistance exhibited by teenagers in an Australian shopping mall in the mid 1980s.

> With no money, but much time to spend, they consumed the place and the images, but not the commodities . . . They would cluster round store windows, preventing legitimate consumers from seeing the displays or entering; their pleasure was in . . . provoking the owners to emerge and confront them, or call in the security services to move them on . . . drinking alcohol was forbidden in the mall, so the youths would fill soda cans with it and, while consuming the rest places provided for legitimate shoppers, would also drink their alcohol under the surveillance of the guards. (Fiske, 1989, p. 38)

This may seem a quaint and perhaps outdated form of 'guerrilla warfare' to our experience now, although more recent media portrayal in the UK has suggested a more random, violent and dangerous culture associated with public alcohol consumption by young people. However, the point being suggested by de Certeau and Fiske still stands; namely that a city centre without a sense of everyday contestation and subversion is a city centre driven by synthetic experiences, but without a complex, gritty and human core.

In conclusion, perhaps we can say that in the rapidly evolving city centre of gentrified brandscapes (as expressed in housing, retailing and nightlife) the Church will be called upon to create alternative spaces of meaning-making. These alternative spaces may be *physical spaces* (such as night-shelters, youth projects, fair-trade retailing outlets), *symbolic spaces* (spaces of public worship, prayer, silent witness, public art), or *political spaces* (demonstrations, single-issue protests). While affirming all that is good in the buzz of the regenerated city centre, the churches' role will primarily be to remind the wider community that for a healthy, balanced city centre we still need to provide spaces of *production* rather than merely passive consumption – spaces where people generate stories and visions and a sense of meaningful identity as well as contributing culture, enterprise and a public sense of the common good to the spaces in which they are located.

Bibliography

Allen, C. and Blandy, S., 2004, *The Future of City Centre Living: Implications for Urban Policy*, Sheffield, Centre for Regional Economic and Social Research.
Bauman, Z., 1997, *Postmodernity and its Discontents*, Cambridge, Polity Press.
Bender, T., 1996, 'Opinion' section, *Los Angeles Times*, 22 December.
Chatterton, P. and Hollands, R., 2003, *Urban Nightscapes: Youth Cultures, Pleasure, Spaces and Corporate Power*, London, Routledge.
de Certeau, M., 1984, *The Practice of Everyday Life*, San Francisco, University of California Press.
Fincher, R. and Jacobs, J., 1998, *Cities of Difference*, London, Guildford Press.
Fiske, J., 1989, *Understanding Popular Culture*, London, Routledge.
Harvey, D., 1989, 'From Managerialism to Entrepreneurialism: The Transformation of Urban Governance in Late Capitalism', *Geografiska Annaler* 71B, 3–17.
Rogers, Lord, 1999, *Towards an Urban Renaissance*, London, Spon.
Seo, J. K., 2002, 'Reurbanisation in Regenerated Areas of Manchester and Glasgow: New Residents and the Problems of Sustainability', *Cities* 19(2), 113–21.
Sheldrake, P., 2001, *Spaces for the Sacred: Place, Memory and Identity*, London, SCM Press.

Smith, N., 1996, *The New Urban Frontier: Gentrification, and the Revanchist City*, London, Routledge.

Soja, E., 2000, *Postmetropolis: Critical Studies of Cities and Regions*, Oxford, Blackwell.

Sorkin, M. (ed.), 1992, *Variations on a Theme Park: The New American City and the End of Public Space*, New York, Noonday Press.

Urry, J., 2000, *Sociology Beyond Societies: Mobilities for the Twenty-First Century*, London, Routledge.

Ward, P., 2002, *Liquid Church*, Carlisle, Paternoster.

3

Power in the City:
How to Get Things Done

HUW THOMAS

This chapter will discuss how things get done in the city. It will focus on the way that important dimensions of the city's life are shaped, such as the city's physical development (what gets built where), its educational system, its transport system, and the like. These are dimensions of life that affect to varying degrees almost every citizen and visitor to a city, and they warrant attention. But it should be borne in mind that there are many circuits of power in the city besides those that feature in orthodox discussions of local politics, and these other circuits can sometimes be crucial for bringing about change. For example, within social housing estates – often the forgotten spaces of the city – it may be the rhythm and values of the ways of life of groups of unemployed, typically feckless young men, that dominate (Campbell, 1993). Achieving change in such areas involves recognizing this and devising strategies for neutralizing that power.

Here, however, attention will be given to more wide-ranging exercises of power, particularly those that involve public policy. These are the kinds of activities of which the formidable local politician quoted by the student of American city politics, Clarence Stone (2005, p. 311), was talking when he said: 'Nothing just happens. Everything is *arranged*.' The intimations of conspiracy in the quotation are, perhaps, a little strong. Harold Macmillan famously conceded that even experienced politicians are at the mercy of events. On the other hand, what gets done in cities is hardly accidental, for the most part. How is it, then, that power and influence are exercised in cities? How might churches, or others, work for the common good, as they see it?

One aspect of getting things done is mundane, but no less important for that. It is that dimension which involves making the machinery of governance work. Much of the chapter discusses how we might under-stand that machinery. In many cities, though, there is another important aspect to the way power works. It is the existence of a dominant way of seeing, and understanding, the city – as it is, as it could be, and as it should be. Many terms are used for this kind of understanding of the city – 'vision', 'policy discourse' and 'city imaginary' are among the more common. This varied vocabulary is gesturing at a vital aspect of how power operates in at least some western cities; namely the way that a certain way of thinking about (and understanding) the city can have a grip on popular and political imaginations. Such a discourse or vision, when well established, can be shared across social and organizational divides, providing a broad basis for identifying priorities, allocating resources, and mapping the future. This sounds very positive – unless one's particular concerns happen to fall outside the vision that is so dominant. These kinds of shared visions are not to be found in all cities. In many places there is no coherent, focused debate over local issues, because there are no shared terms of reference. For many scholars, a key task of effective governance is generating such shared visions (e.g., Healey, 2006); others suggest that a more conflictual, almost anarchic, situation has its advantages if it avoids the suffocating intolerance that can too often accompany an allegedly broad consensus on 'what's best for our town' (e.g., Sennett, 1973).

Whatever the ideal, the reality is that in some places there are hegemonic visions/discourses. Where they exist, a key objective for any person or group wishing to change a city for the better is to work towards developing a more 'fitting' vision or discourse about that city. We will discuss how this might be done. We begin, however, by reminding ourselves that the world beyond its boundaries inevitably impinges upon a city's life. It would be misleading to suggest that such influences are brought to bear in a mechanical fashion. The interaction between a city and the world beyond its boundaries is influenced by the nature of social relations within the city and how these relate to the wider world. Those who work and live in cities are not passive victims of external forces. Rather, they actively relate to, and sometimes help constitute, those forces. The Roman Catholic Church, for example, is, in an obvious sense, a force beyond any given city, and one that impinges upon it (e.g., through Papal pronouncements); yet in an equally clear sense the Church is partly constituted by the activity of its members 'on the ground', including (on occasion) their networking across city (and national) boundaries on specific issues and concerns. Consequently it is important to think about the way specifically urban social and organizational structures help shape how things get done in the city.

It is a commonplace of discussions about contemporary cities that they are part of a 'networked' world. Whatever may be meant by the term, it certainly underlines the continuing, and perhaps increasing, importance of a city's connections with the rest of the world in explaining what goes on within the city. More pertinently for this chapter, it reminds us that understanding power in a city requires a grasp of the way the city interacts with the rest of the world.

The world beyond the city can impinge upon it in very straightforward ways. The closure of a manufacturing plant in south Wales in 2006 by the South Korean company LG was a consequence of a decision made in Asia, in response to problems that LG shared with other Korean companies. It had serious effects on the cities of Newport and Cardiff. When companies flourish, on the other hand, those who run their local operations may well have influence in the city related to the importance of the company they represent. The manager of a successful department store, or the local M&S, for example, will likely have readier access to the office of the chief planner for a city than will a small newsagent. On the other hand, the newsagent may have more at stake in the city and its future than the store manager, and may translate this into active membership of an interest group like the Chamber of Trade or even a local political party. Usually, the more a business is dependent on its fortunes in a particular town or city for its overall financial health the more likely it is to want to influence what happens in that town or city.

As well as economic conditions, administrative and governmental structures beyond the city's boundaries can also influence decisions within it. In England, the latest national advice on the planning of town and city centres is contained in *Planning Policy Statement 6: Planning for Town Centres* (PPS 6, 2005). This advice has to be considered by local authorities when they make any kind of planning decision related to town and city centres. But beyond that, it helps create a kind of shared sense, at least among professional planners, developers and councillors involved in planning, as to what centres are for. This can feed into a vision of how a specific city should be. In *PPS 6* the government emphasizes the importance of creating town and city centres that have the appropriate kinds of facilities and activities in them, and that constitute a hierarchy of provision (so that city centres, say, provide a greater range of, and more specialized facilities than, a town centre, and so on down the hierarchy to local centres). Naturally, the advice states the kinds of activities that centres might be expected to contain. Shops and offices are mentioned often. So is housing, increasingly promoted as part of so-called 'mixed-use' developments. Leisure is also regarded as an important activity in town and city centres, especially as part of the 'evening and night-time economy'. But churches, or places of worship of any kind, are not mentioned at all. So it is that an influential government statement on how city centres should be planned in effect writes churches out of the life of the centre. It does not *oppose* churches and church activity. But it ignores, and hence devalues, the idea of there being a spiritual dimension to the city centre.

Context impinges upon, constrains (and enables) what can be done in a city. But what more can be said about how things get done? And for those working within cities, what kinds of structures – formal and informal – might shape the detail of how things happen, including how the city's links beyond its borders have particular effects within the city itself?

In Britain the starting point must be local government, 'the council'. There is no uniformity in the detail of British local government: Scotland, Wales and Northern Ireland have developed their own systems of unitary (i.e., 'all-purpose') councils. In England, piecemeal review has left a two-tier system of county councils and district councils in many areas (especially rural ones), with each tier responsible for its own set of services – counties for education and social services, districts for most planning functions, and so on; in the English conurbations there are unitary authorities, except in London, which has an elected Greater London Authority with strategic powers for some services such as planning, alongside the London boroughs. There are also unitary authorities in some parts of England. In a few places – notably London – there are directly elected mayors, who have a limited, but in London's case increasing, range of powers and responsibilities.

This confusing institutional patchwork should not obscure some important points: that elected local government disposes of big budgets (English local authorities received close to £3.5 billion from national government in 2006–7), and that since the Local Government Act 2000 local authorities have had a statutory duty to promote the well-being (economic, social and environmental) of their areas (as well as specific duties with respect to education, drainage, etc. under other legislation). The combination of money and responsibilities for important aspects of quality of life make local authorities big players in their localities. In addition, local councils can still make a plausible claim (and most are happy to do so) that they are the single best representatives of their localities: the best 'voice' for Bognor, Bradford, or wherever. For most citizens, and urban voluntary organizations, the possibility of gaining the support of, or forcing action from, their local council will be the first thought in any aspirations and plans they have to make something happen in their city.

Local government itself has been in a state of almost perpetual change – some might say crisis – since the late 1970s. The changes have been both internal and contextual. The internal changes began with the imposition by (Conservative) central government of the kind of crude managerialism that was also introduced into other public services in the 1980s and 1990s. The contracting out of services to the private sector, the introduction of performance indicators, and the promotion of 'efficiency' by budgetary discipline were the key initiatives. Conservative antipathy towards (sometimes mellowing to a mere suspicion of) local government was palpable, and 'reform' seemed sometimes to have a punitive edge. There were two important consequences of the Conservative distaste for local government. First, they did relatively little radical rethinking of it. Typical of this was the way that abolition of the Greater London Council in the mid 1980s – in order to stifle a seemingly popular left-wing alternative to Thatcherite policies – was not accompanied by any serious thought about London-wide governance. Administration of services was achieved by a series of co-ordinating measures involving the London boroughs, and that was that. It was left to the Labour administrations of the late 1990s to devise a new system of government for London as a whole, which involved – inter alia – a directly elected mayor. A second consequence of the hostile shaking up of local government in the 1980s was the creation in many authorities of a desire (sometimes among councillors, sometimes senior officers, sometimes both) to make sure that local government (or at least their part of it) was seen (by the public, the press and other commentators) to be doing something useful. In adversity, there were many officers and councillors willing to try something a little different. So it was that many councils began to experiment with economic development initiatives. Some of the more left-wing councils tried to develop clear alternatives to the radical right-wing prescriptions being promoted by central government; far more were simply pragmatically 'wanting to do something'. Overall, the effect was to begin to change some of the local government activities that had become well established in the post-war heyday of state expansion.

The Labour governments since 1997 have been more sympathetic to local government, if suspicious of the possibility of councils being havens of unreformed 'Old' Labour ideas and practices (with a tendency, at its worst, to hierarchy, cronyism, and patronage politics). In England especially, Labour has not let up on the drive for efficiency and effectiveness, and has retained a faith in new public management. Its particular contribution in this respect has been to devise ways of sidelining the majority of councillors (and, behind them, local political parties) by devices such as insisting on executive cabinets of senior councillors to 'streamline' decision making, and offering the possibility of directly elected mayors. Nor has Labour reversed the trend of public services being delivered by organizations other than the council: private companies and voluntary organizations are more important than ever, while some services that remain within the public sector – notably schools – have more independence from local councils. But unlike the Conservatives, Labour has gradually developed a positive agenda for local government. This revolves around the idea that councils must be more responsive to the distinctive needs, challenges and aspirations of their localities, and must organize their work (and internal organization) accordingly. Efficiency remains important; but purpose is also central. And, gradually, it has come to be accepted (at least in principle) that in important respects the purpose of local government can be defined locally.

This idea leads us to the great changes in the external environment of local government in the last 20 years. Put simply, the local authority as a sole (and insular) deliverer of a collection of important public services has been replaced by a shift to the council as being a key player in a network of 'stakeholders' in the future of a locality. On this view, the council is supposed to be both more and less than a local delivery mechanism for a bundle of services and activities defined by various laws. It is more than this in the sense that it is allowed to devise (in 'partnership' with 'stakeholders') a vision and accompanying strategy for its locality that is sensitive to local needs and aspirations. Such a vision and strategy will be unique to that place; it will not have been transmitted from a higher level of government. Moreover, its requirements will dictate the priorities, and (to an extent) the organizational form, of the council and all other organizations that have been involved in its development. This is a vision of a council as a responsive, and responsible, body, flexible and efficient in its desire to make its town or city a better place in which to live and work. The term 'place-making' has come to be used to describe this aspect of a council's work.

Yet, in some ways the new expectations of local government may be perceived as having diminished it. For there is no doubt that, important as it is, the local council is certainly not the only player in town. If a town or city is to be changed in any significant way then the council will not be able to 'go it alone' because it will not have all the relevant responsibilities nor the necessary finance. Multi-agency initiatives are common in our cities because a complex institutional landscape has developed as local authorities have lost responsibilities, and new initiatives have more often been given to non-governmental organizations. One consequence is a plethora of strategies, plans and partnerships. In a smallish city such as Swansea, south Wales, a search of its website in March 2007 using the term 'strategy' generated hundreds of hits, including in the first 30, the following: Economic Regeneration Strategy, Domestic Abuse Strategy, Children's Play Strategy, Waste Management Strategy, Empty Property Strategy, Local Housing Strategy, Homelessness Strategy, Inclusion Strategy, Tourism Strategy, Strategy for People Aged 50+, Accessibility Strategy, BME Strategy, Learning Policy and Strategy . . . the list could go on.

Since 2000, the Local Strategic Partnership (LSP), which produces a Community Plan/Strategy, is supposed to pull this complexity together by providing an overall vision and direction. LSPs contain the major stakeholders in an area, and the membership of their boards gives a good idea of who might be regarded as the local 'movers and shakers'. The board of the Leeds LSP (the Leeds Initiative), for example, has 36 members, of whom only four are associated directly with the local council. The Chamber of Commerce provides four members, and the council of voluntary services provides five. There are two members specifically representing black and ethnic minority communities, and another two 'faith representatives'. Among nine co-opted members is someone from the *Yorkshire Post*, and another from ITV Yorkshire. The city's universities are also represented, as is the police. The Leeds LSP works through 14 partnership groups and seven strategy groups. Inevitably, within this kind of complex institutional terrain, the effectiveness of LSPs in producing a coherent overall strategy for the city as a whole varies considerably. What should be clear is that anyone wanting to influence the direction of any given city will need to become familiar with relevant strategies and initiatives, the 'partnership' or forum that has produced them, and – beyond that – the kind of ethos in local governance that is being promoted (with variable success) by national government.

Familiarity with the institutional landscape of city governance is a necessary, but not sufficient, condition for influence. Clarence Stone, referred to earlier, suggests that politics is the art of arranging how things get done in cities, and that is as plausible a description of the UK as it is of the USA. His own contribution to explaining modes of arrangement is the idea that in many cities the important decisions and the mobilization of resources behind them (what gets done) is determined by agendas developed by long-standing coalitions of public and non-public sector organizations (with businesses often prominent) which are put together, and maintained, in a multiplicity of formal and informal ways. He terms these coalitions 'regimes'.

The idea that to get something done in a city you need to put together a coalition of support is widely accepted by political scientists (though the idea of the urban regime is questioned – especially in its applicability outside the USA). The bite in Stone's analysis is that it recognizes the importance of embedded social and economic inequalities in limiting the development of any kind of political 'perfect market'. He suggests it is implausible that any persons (or groups) have pretty much the same chance as anyone else to put together a coalition to influence local politics if they can just make their goals attractive enough to others. Getting things done in cities is not some kind of classroom exercise in democracy. There is always a great deal at stake for someone (and usually for many), and it is to be expected that most organizations, groups and individuals will deploy any social and economic advantages they have to get their way. Privileges associated with class or gender, membership of restricted groups like Freemasons (or in some cases golf clubs), are among the resources that are unequally distributed in the urban population, but will be drawn upon by those who can do so. Economic leverage is particularly potent. This can be exercised in a crude way – direct threats to pull out of town if such and such is not done; but in the cases of major employers it is usually undertaken more subtly. A famous study of the 'un-politics' of air pollution in the USA made the point that in some cities like Gary, Indiana in its steel-town heyday the agenda of local politics simply didn't include an issue such as air pollution. That would threaten the interests of the steel company that employed so many in the town. The issue was organized out of local debate without the company needing to take any overt action. But this was surely an exercise of power of a kind by the company (Lukes, 2005, pp. 44–8). Agenda-setting is a key technique in the exercise of power; and a widely accepted view of the world, or discourse, can be an effective way of focusing attention on certain issues and simply not defining other things as issues at all, as we shall see later.

A moment's reflection reveals that the businesses of a city do not have identical interests (though they may share some, of course). For example, regeneration proposals in inner city areas are often supported by major landowners, property developers (including house builders), large construction companies and businesses that are likely to develop new facilities in the area; in today's cities these are likely to be larger hotel and leisure companies, and national retailers. These all stand to gain from the kind of property-led regeneration that has become so common in British cities over the last 30 years. But that kind of regeneration often displaces small manufacturing and warehousng businesses. These are businesses that have less economic leverage individually, and are often poor at networking. On the other hand, like the newsagents mentioned earlier, they have a greater incentive to try to wield influence because, as a small firm, their future is far more bound up with what happens in their home city than is the case with national companies. Of course, the Tescos of this world try very hard to have their way (and often succeed) but failure in any one place doesn't jeopardize the company. For a small firm forced relocation is a great challenge to the firm's future, and as mentioned earlier such local dependence may be a spur to involvement in local politics.

No one organization – not even the elected local council – has the resources or authority to simply dictate what will happen in a city; indeed, some urban problems are not ones where dictating will work. For example, how are we to increase the amount of waste that residents recycle? It is obvious to most that it will be by a judicious use of stick (sanctions), but also mixed with carrots (incentives), and genuine changes of heart and habits brought about by argument, persuasion and example. What mix will do the trick in any given place at a given time is much harder to know. But it is going to need co-operation, co-working, dare one say it 'partnership'. So, it is plausible to think of getting things done in cities as involving the mobilization of the resources of (sometimes complex) networks or coalitions. Perhaps there are slightly different, overlapping coalitions/networks involved in different policy fields; often there will be organizations or groups – the local council will be one – which are heavily involved in coalitions and networks in many areas of urban life. These few institutions (and key individuals or groups within them) will often be recognized as those who 'run the city'. Meanwhile, the populace in effect exercises a power of its own by its daily recalcitrance in abiding strictly by the rules laid down by those who supposedly run things – by parking cars where they shouldn't be parked, by not recycling as much as it might do, and so on. In considering power in cities we need to bear in mind these daily, often mundane acts because they can be very significant indeed in relation to the realization of some ambitions to get things done.

Members of coalitions or networks have to earn their place in them; they have to have something to offer their fellow members. Local councils typically offer resources (such as property, funding, personnel). Often they also offer a stamp of democratic legitimacy as the elected voice of an area (it is surprising how the well-rehearsed limitations of local electoral politics are not dwelt upon when it serves the interests of 'getting things done' to downplay them). Voluntary organizations – such as churches – tend to offer channels of communication between those who administer and govern and those who are on the receiving end of governance (the poor, the homeless, young people, and so on). Churches may sometimes emerge as grass-roots leaders of communities. A great fear of anyone involved in governance or management is getting out of touch with the 'sharp end', and hence misjudging what is happening and what needs to be done. So organizations that can offer an authoritative window on the 'real world' have something to offer. Increasingly, church-related organizations deliver services as agencies of the council or some local partnership (for example in relation to housing, or counselling), and can offer experience based on that. One of the problems, however, that councils have is to know with whom to work. Which are the most representative and authentic groups? This can be an acute problem in relation to churches and other faith groups. There is inevitably a plethora of religious organizations, many very small and often ephemeral, some with somewhat dubious beliefs and practices. There are two usual solutions to this dilemma. The first is to marginalize religion and keep it at arm's length. But at a time when government policy is to draw faith groups into community building processes this is not viable. The alternative is to work with the larger and more established structures that seem to offer reasonable collaboration. Among the churches this means the so-called mainstream denominations, especially the Anglicans and Catholics, or some well-established ecumenical structure. Similarly there are often recognized bodies in the Jewish and Muslim communities with which to relate. But for many, not least churches and other groups from ethnic minorities, there can be a sense of frustration and isolation.

But even if an organization or group has something to offer, where does it offer it? Getting things done in cities involves working within networks. How does an organization insert itself into networks? They operate in part in formal arenas (the multifarious organizations and partnerships that constitute the terrain of local governance). Getting involved in these is a matter of introducing oneself formally to those who are central to the networks: for example, who is it that convenes, or chairs, or acts as secretary to, particular forums or partnerships? For reasons mentioned earlier a sensible place to start is the council. Increasingly faith groups are playing a part in the voluntary structures (like Voluntary Action committees and organizations) which are enabled by the local authority and have a subscription membership, and which provide training, information and meeting points.

There are also informal arenas in which networking occurs. How important is that? In most areas there are voluntary activities such as Rotary clubs, religious groups, and sports clubs of various kinds whose workings are – in practice – heavily influenced by the great social cleavages of contemporary society: class, gender, age and ethnicity especially. These activities can be influential in facilitating contacts and cementing relationships between those who want to wield power in cities; but perhaps we should beware of overestimating their significance. On occasion one might come across a case where an influential local councillor is clearly influenced by his or her ties to a local 'interest' – a church, sports group or what have you. But the issues involved are rarely major – they amount to the political equivalent of the kinds of 'perks' that people in authority in any sphere of life come to expect, such as a dedicated car parking space, or someone to phone one's dentist to postpone an appointment. On big issues, ties based on sentiment take second place to the exigencies of keeping coalitions and networks together – as many of us have found as we are disappointed by friends and colleagues who find it impossible to honour friendship or shared histories of ideals and struggles by pressing our case in some local political dispute. This is an important and harsh lesson for those who would press for change from outside influential networks: don't expect too much of old contacts and friends. On the other hand, these informal contacts can be extremely useful for keeping up to date with important developments – if one has a nose for rooting out the reliable gossip from the rest!

Getting things done requires resources but when it involves collective action then it also requires co-ordination and a sense of purpose. It is here that what was referred to earlier as a discourse or vision can be influential (occasionally the term 'policy discourse' is used). We may think of a discourse as a way of thinking about and understanding the world, a way that is, of necessity, selective. A policy discourse provides a way of looking at the world (including any given city) that identifies certain aspects of that urban world as issues and problems requiring attention, and attention of a particular kind. It frames what constitutes a policy area, identifying a set of priorities, what constitutes appropriate intervention and by whom. It provides a way of understanding how policy of whatever kind makes a difference to urban life. Typically, this kind of discourse will be set out as broad descriptions or aspirations that encode the key elements of the discourse. 'Cardiff: Europe's youngest capital city' is a slogan which encapsulates political priorities that have dominated local politics for decades across party lines. It sums up the significance in the politics of Cardiff of promoting development that is said to increase the city's profile nationally and internationally; it lays claim to a disproportionate share of public resources within Wales (as it is a capital city); it does this within a view of the nature of the global economy that is, broadly, neo-liberal capitalism.

It is within this view of the world, this discourse, that the city council in Cardiff has worked with national government, property developers and organizations such as the Welsh Rugby Union to redevelop the city centre (more than once in the last 30 years), develop the Millennium Stadium and redevelop Cardiff Bay. Making things happen in Cardiff is easier if you can present what you want to do as fitting within this view of the world. So voluntary groups may try to present a proposal for a local arts centre as a potential tourist attraction, for example. The influence of the capital city discourse will stretch, to a greater or lesser extent, to all aspects of urban life, though of course in some areas – housing policy or social services – there are likely to be other more significant discourses related to the specialized concerns of those with a direct interest in what is at stake.

Power in cities is diffuse, operating through networks and loose coalitions, which in some places may persist for many years. Developing the agenda around which a coalition can form is easiest done within a shared frame or discourse, which presents an understanding of the world (the city), its problems and potential. In the short tem, influencing city politics is more likely if you present your ideas within this discourse.

Yet the discourse itself is something that is created and sustained; over time, it can be modified (or even destroyed). What are the mechanisms through which this might happen? In relation to the public expression of key aspects of a vision, undoubtedly local media play a part in constructing ideas of what kind of place a city is and might be. This is why the local press is often brought 'on board' when major redevelopments are in the offing (Thomas, 1994). But the role of local media extends beyond simply banging the drum in editorials and news items. The kinds of items featured, and the tone employed, and the popular historical features of local newspapers also play a part in developing a picture of a city or town. Our conception of a city as it is today includes some notion, some understanding, of how it has come to be what it is; and this understanding of a city's history is built up from silences and exclusions as much as from inclusions and celebrations. Official publications and reports also present, if in a crude way, a discourse about the city: one might expect planning documents to do so, but general corporate 'bumf' (including the ubiquitous corporate newsletters), of which there appears to be an increasing amount also plays its part. Even simple slogans – such as the path-breaking 'Glasgow's Miles Better' – can play a modest role. Often they are intended to jolt the city's population to see the city differently as much as they are intended to impress outsiders to the city. These perspectives or discourses or visions can also be useful for other organizations associated with the city. So, a university or a hotel may find it useful to 'piggyback' on the identity/vision of a city when presenting its public face; and in so doing it will, of course, help strengthen the vision of the city as a whole.

These are some of the mechanics of how a particular understanding of a city is generated, sustained and disseminated. But where does the content of the discourse arise? Where do the values come from? Why is there a broad consensus among the movers and shakers in Cardiff, for example, that being known for having a Millennium Stadium is worth more (in any and every sense of 'worth') than if the city were known as an exemplar of care for the elderly? Here it is only possible to point to where I believe we must look for an answer. The starting point, I am convinced, has to be the day-to-day organization of people's lives – in work and in the home, especially. It is in the experience of the routines, disciplines and vicissitudes of the day-to-day that sets of values and particular perspectives on the world begin to make any, or no, sense. So it is the economic and social structure of a city (including the way house-holds are formed and organized) that provides the material base for the constellation of political and moral values that are significant in that place. In addition, the social and economic organization of a place will require certain kinds of collective activity and discussion, encourage other forms, make yet other forms virtually impossible. So we begin to have an explanation as to why union activity, or Freemasonry, may be significant in one city but not in another.

Those who would understand power in any given city must understand the machinery of local administration, the networks of local governance, local political values and discourses, and the economic and social structures within which they make some kind of sense of the world. The way the city runs from day to day will then make more sense, as will the reasons for occasional eruptions of direct action, even violence. No essay on power in the city should overlook the reality of (and sometimes necessity for) occasional straightforward direct action to stop something happening, and, if planned carefully, its effectiveness. For those outside the networks and coalitions and with few of the resources and attributes needed to penetrate and flourish within them, life can be frustrating. The power to halt things, or to draw attention to one's plight through a howl of rage, is at best a small step on the road to the better city, but for those without access to networks and coalitions it can sometimes seem the only course of action on offer.

Bibliography

Campbell, B., 1993, *Goliath: Britain's Dangerous Places*, London, Methuen.
Department of Communities and Local Government, 2005, *Planning Policy Statement 6: Planning for Town Centres*, London, Department of Communities and Local Government.
Harvey, D., 1989, *The Urban Experience*, Oxford, Blackwell.
Healey, Patsy, 2006, *Collaborative Planning*, Basingstoke, Palgrave Macmillan.
Lukes, S., 2005, *Power: A radical View*, Basingstoke, Palgrave Macmillan.
Savage, M., Warde, A. and Ward, K., 2003, *Urban Sociology, Capitalism and Modernity*, Basingstoke, Palgrave Macmillan.
Sennett, R., 1973, *The Uses of Disorder*, Harmondsworth, Penguin.
Stoker, G., 2004, *Transforming Local Governance: From Thatcherism to New Labour*, Basingstoke, Palgrave Macmillan.
Stoker, G. and Mossberger, K., 1994, 'Urban Regime Theory in Comparative Perspective', *Environment and Planning C: Government and Policy* 12(2), 195–212.
Stone, Clarence, 2005. 'Looking Back to Look Forward: Reflections on Urban Regime Analysis', *Urban Affairs Review* 40, 309–41.
Thomas, Huw, 1994, 'The Local Press and Urban Renewal', in *International Journal of Urban and Regional Research* 18, 315–33.
Warde A., 1988, 'Industrial Restructuring, Local Politics and the Reproduction of Labour Power: Some Theoretical Considerations', *Environment and Planning D: Society and Space* 6(1), 75–95.
Zukin, S., 1991, *Landscapes of Power*, Berkeley, University of California Press.

PART II

Theological Reflection on the Church at the Centre of the City

Introduction: Being in the City

The city has been a constant theme in Christian thought. It has been an image through which the great doctrines of sin, salvation and providence have been woven. There has been a constant ambiguity towards the city, not least in the Bible.

Positively the city is the stronghold (Ps. 46, 48), the market place for the exchange of goods and the source of justice. The well-ordered city is, indeed, an expression of God's care for the nation. Indeed, in the Davidic tradition, Jerusalem is the place where God has chosen to place the divine footstool. The Temple draws to itself the tribes to celebrate their covenant relation with God (Ps. 122).

There was, however, always a deep suspicion of the city. The nomadic people saw the city as the seat of evil. Riches and power corrupt and the unscrupulous take advantage of the poor (Amos 5.10–13, 8.4–8; Jer. 5.1–5). Even the sanctuaries were polluted (Amos 4.4–5). Indeed it was Cain, the murderer, who founded the first city (Gen. 4.17). It was the great cities that were the enemies, warring against God, the people and creation itself. Voracious, seeking power, consuming the world, a succession of cities, Tyre, Nineveh, Babylon and Rome, were the face of evil (cf. Ezek. 26—28; Dan. 4). In Revelation, Babylon, standing in for Rome, is the great whore (18). Even Jerusalem cannot avoid the stigma, betraying its calling to be the city of God (Lam. 1.8–9).

Nevertheless it is the city that is the image of salvation, of journey's end. Jerusalem is the hope for the future, the place where God will fulfil the promise and where community, justice and peace will be found (Isa. 24.23; 40.9; 65.19). Abraham is said to have sought for a city (Heb. 11.10), that is, the new Jerusalem (Rev. 21—22), where the nations will find their healing and the Lamb is enthroned in the midst. As Paul says, 'our citizenship is in heaven' (Phil. 3.20), the country to which we are journeying.

To live in hope, however, does not mean abandoning the present city. Jeremiah, in a much-quoted passage, bade the exiles make a home in

Babylon and pray for the welfare of the city (29.7). This means that we have to live in the ambiguity of the present, not just as those who are strangers and refugees but as citizens, as those who see the city as potential gift, the place where community and purpose can be found, believing that the city can echo its source and potential.

The classical theological expression of all this is, of course, Augustine's *City of God*. The two cities, the human construct and the City of God, are simultaneously present in history, though the City of God is hidden beneath the everyday appearance. But it is this city that is the true source of the human city that it strives to emulate. So in the midst of the fallen world it is possible to glimpse the reality of the ultimate city. We can, therefore, serve God by being in and for our city, even as we wait patiently for God's city to be revealed. Our task is, in faith, to dwell here in prayerful watchfulness, in loving service and prophetic living. These are the parameters of our ministry and mission as the people of God.

It could be argued that the modern metropolis bears almost no resemblance to the cities of the ancient world or, indeed, to any city prior to the industrial revolution. In what way, then, can we appropriate today images and metaphors of an earlier epoch? The differences must be acknowledged, in terms of size if nothing else. There are, however, close similarities. We would recognize many of the characteristics found today in the cities of an earlier time. Ancient Rome, for example, had its slums and commuter problems, its markets and workshops, its civic government and public amenities. It is, too, perhaps, in the city centre, which after all is often the site of the original settlement, that the similarities are most obvious. It is still the heart of the urban complex, the seat of power, commerce, law and order.

Against this background the three following contributions take up particular themes. John Inge asks the Church to be true to its essential calling in Christ as a priestly community, an alternative presence in the city. Paul Ballard picks up on the characteristics of the city centre and puts them into a missiological context. Geoff Cornell, dwelling in the centre of the city, draws on the experience of urban living and the Christian tradition to delineate some of the marks of an urban spirituality.

4

The Church in the City

JOHN INGE

What is the place of the Church in the city? The prior question of what a city is might not be as simple to answer as one might think. I lived in the city of Ely for 12 years. Before that I lived in the 'inner city', ministering as a parish priest on Tyneside. These are two very different environments indeed: Ely has a population of some 15,000 and, though its city status is jealously guarded by the City Council, it is more like what most people would think of as a market town – except for the presence of a vast cathedral in its midst. Such contrasts have existed for some centuries in England: in 1688 the only provincial cities with a population of more than 10,000 were Bristol, Exeter, Newcastle, Norwich and York. The largest was Norwich with about 30,000. Only London bore, in terms of population, any resemblance to what most people would nowadays think of as a city, with a population by 1700 of over 500,000 (Thomas, 1991, p. 1). Hence very different sorts of city have existed side by side for a considerable time: it is just that larger cities, having been in a minority of one, are now the overwhelming majority. Over a longer period, the nature of cities has changed very substantially: it hardly needs saying that the difference between any contemporary city and a city in biblical times would be immense by any standards.

Timothy Gorringe (2002) asks the question 'What is a city?' and, in answer, argues that cities 'gather' their regions by virtue of their tradition, of their activity, and 'thereby have a degree of creative spirituality which other places lack. It is this which constitutes their place in the economy of redemption, and this which the Book of Revelation means by the "angel" of a city, indicated by the fact that they are often addressed as corporate personalities in the Scripture' (p. 140).Gorringe reminds us that cities, by definition, civilize and that Aristotle thought of cities as nurseries of the virtues. He concurs and suggests that a city 'is purposive in a qualitatively different way to the village or the town. It represents a corporate attempt to fashion the human future. It is

63

"larger than life"; the buzz of its diverse trades and conditions stimulates both art and ideas' (p. 148).

Cities certainly, whatever their size, should be 'nurseries of the virtues' but, if this is the case, how is it that such virtues are nurtured in them? Some creative reflection on this is offered by Jonathan Sacks, the Chief Rabbi (2002). He asks us to imagine that we are explaining to someone the basic institutions of society and decide to do so by taking a walk through the centre of London:

> You pass the Houses of Parliament, home of politics, and you say that these buildings are the seat of government, the home of politics, and that politics is about the creation and distribution of power. You enter the city proper, passing streets of offices and shops, and seeing in the distance the Stock Exchange building. You say that these are the homes of the market, the domain of economics, and that economics is about the creation and distribution of wealth. As you are walking, your companion points to the steeples and spires of London's churches and the great dome of St Paul's Cathedral. 'And what', she asks, 'do houses of worship create and distribute?' You might be inclined to say that they are not that sort of thing at all, but you would be wrong. Houses of worship, congregations and communities do create and distribute something, but it is significantly different from wealth or power. (p. 148)

Sacks suggests that political and economic relationships are contractual, involving arrangements between self-interested parties who will benefit from the exchange. This is self-evident with economics. In politics, he explains, 'it turns on what Hobbes, Locke and Rousseau described as the social contract – that process, explicit or implied, whereby individuals give up certain of their powers and freedoms to a central body, the state, which in return undertakes to secure the rule of law and thus the security of life and personal property'. He points out that there are, however, other relationships more fundamental to human beings than the contractual. He cites the family and suggests that, as its members eat, drink and play together, they develop an 'unconscious choreography of mutuality' in which they help one another and depend upon one another, and this giving and taking promotes their identity and growth as individuals. There will be disagreements followed by rituals of reconciliation – the saying of 'sorry' which enables forgiveness. This microcosm of community and its everyday transactions, he tells us, demonstrates something significant: the 'making and sustaining of the moral life'. Beneath the surface of this family, Sacks reminds us, lie some basic concepts of love, loyalty, responsibility, authority, obedience, fairness and compassion. It is these virtues that hold the family together and define their relationships. The latter are not contractual, having nothing intrinsically to do with exchange of power or wealth. They are, rather, covenantal. 'Whereas contracts are about the self, covenants are about the larger groupings in and through which we develop our identity. They are about the "We" in which we discover the "I". Covenantal relationships are those sustained by trust' (2002, p. 151; cf. Volf, 1996 on covenant).

Sacks suggests that it is in covenantal relationships that we develop what he calls 'the grammar and syntax of reciprocity', and we might add that this is the basis of the virtuous life. It is in such relationships that trust is born because we help others and they help us without calculations of relative advantage. Such trust is necessary for the proper functioning of the markets and the state, of course, but the crucial point is that it is not where it is born. As Sacks puts it, 'markets depend on virtues not produced by the market, just as states depend on virtues not created by the state'. They are created, rather, in families and in other voluntary associations – communities, friendships, congregations – wherever people are brought together 'not by exchange of wealth or power but by commitment to one another or to a larger cause they serve in common'. These virtues are not only more fundamental to our humanity than the contractual, they are also essential to the latter. As Sacks puts it, 'without them, not only do markets and states begin to falter':

> Social life itself loses grace and civility. The bonds that connect us to one another begin to fray. The sense of identity and belonging become ever more tenuous. We begin to feel vulnerable and alone. We can now say what houses of worship and their attendant communities once created and is now in danger of being lost – the covenantal dimension of life that generates trust. (2002, p. 152)

Sacks is right, I think, both in his analysis of the role of what he describes as 'houses of worship and their attendant communities' and in his perception that what they create is in danger of being lost. There is much evidence that most western societies function today in what might be described as the individual–state–market grid. Between them the market and the state have weakened trust-creating institutions and, as I have suggested elsewhere (Inge, 2003, p. 16), there are strong forces that serve to weaken such mediating institutions by depriving them of the social environment they require to flourish. It is not only the Church and other faith groups that are at risk: it is the family itself which, as we observed above, is central in the generation of trust. It is, perhaps, sensing the importance of the family in this regard but not quite being able to articulate it that makes the Church sometimes appear shrill or reactionary in defending it. Even more insidious than the erosion of an environment in which they can flourish is the attempt by the market or the state to refashion intermediary institutions in a way that brings them into conformity with priorities very different from those of the institutions. This latter problem as experienced by the Church is examined by Luke Bretherton who observes that, after many years of being marginalized by the state, a new openness on the part of the latter to work with churches can appear a welcome development, but that 'close analysis of the impact of partnership with the state, under present conditions, suggests that the church should be cautious about receiving money from the state. Involvement with the state often exacerbates social division and forces the church to mimic the state in its form and practices' (2006a, pp. 389–9). He points out that a variety of theologians as varied as Stanley Hauerwas, John Paul II, Oliver and Joan Lockwood O'Donovan and Radical Theologians such as John Millbank all emphasize the importance of the Church being the Church and refusing to allow the state to set the terms and conditions of entry into the public sphere since 'the church fails in its vocation if, when it speaks or acts, it is no more than a ventriloquist's dummy, mouthing the ideologies and mimicking the practices of someone else' (p. 385). Such theologians do not speak into a vacuum. Rather, they perceive that it is all too easy for churches, sensing their influence to be diminished, to abandon their central vocation in a desperate attempt to be 'relevant'. Archbishop Rowan Williams bids the Church remember that its calling is to be on another level from that of various bodies struggling for dominance and access and warns that 'it must simply offer a radically different imaginative landscape, in which people can discover possibilities of change – and perhaps of "conversion" in the most important sense, a "turning around" of values and priorities that grows from trust in God' (in Walker, 2005, p. 17). Churches are about generating a covenantal way of living, about generating trust in God and, flowing from that, trust among people and the promotion of human flourishing. Only thus will they play the part they are called to play in enabling cities to become nurseries of the virtues.

The importance of what the Church has to offer in this regard is crucial to both cities and society at large. Moreover, the urgency of it doing so faithfully could not be greater. Jonathan Sacks tells us that 'we have at our disposal a resource of unparalleled power with which to confront the problems of a new age. That resource, neither mysterious nor difficult to understand, is morality, specifically the Judeo-Christian tradition. For several centuries it has been under attack. There are intellectual, political, economic and social reasons why this should have been so.' All is not lost for, as Sacks points out, Britain is 'still a powerfully moral nation. Our sense of connectedness, one to another, remains. But our self-knowledge has become temporarily obscured. We have lost the habit of telling the story that explains us to ourselves as a moral nation. The result is that we see the bad more clearly than the good' (Sacks, 1997, p. 13). Our society is an amnesiac one that sometimes prefers to forget the importance of its history, particularly its Christian history (Inge, 2007). It is the Church that has provided its ethic, has trained its people in virtue, and the Church still does an enormous amount that is sometimes obscured by negative publicity from the media. As the report *Faithful Cities* (2006) puts it:

> [F]aith-based organizations make a decisive and positive difference to their neighbourhoods through the values they promote, the services they inspire and the resources they command . . . The value of civic and communal commitment is unparalleled by any other agency and the church need have no embarrassment in presenting it more clearly. (p. 76)

In fostering virtue the Church is called to put before the rest of society a radically different perspective from that which is prevalent in our society. Concentration is nowadays generally centred on economic notions of flourishing and these, as Sam Wells (2003, p. 18) points out, give precedence to the importance of the autonomous individual. In contrast, the Christian vision of the human person sees relationship as integral and interdependence as desirable. This is because we are all dependent upon God for whom, as Trinity of persons, relationship is of supreme importance. Further, rather than being entirely captive to the here-and-now, the vocation of Christians is to understand themselves as being poised between the salvation of God's creation in Christ and the consummation of God's purposes on the last day. This does not mean that Christians are to be any less committed to the welfare of humanity than anyone else – quite the reverse: Christians identify with others, particularly with the poor and heavy laden, because they are to see in them Christ's face and expect to share eternity with them. The Church shares with all those of good will a desire for human flourishing – to see the glory of God in human beings fully alive. These various factors, as Wells suggests, combine to produce a freedom:

> The gift of the Christian story is freedom. That freedom is a release from having to secure one's own salvation, freedom from having to make one's own and the world's story have a happy ending, freedom from having single-handedly to conquer the limitations and intimidating oppressors of life and to institute a commonwealth of love and peace all on one's own. It is a release from the burden of having to be effective, and an opportunity instead to be faithful. (Wells, 2003, p. 22)

Here we encounter a paradox: that in order fully to enable the city to become a nursery of virtue the Church and its members must be aware of their own limitations. They must place faithfulness to God and trust in his plan before any strategy of their own to improve the world. What will such faithfulness entail? First, living out that freedom by recognizing that past, present and future are in God's hands: 'God alone has created; he alone, in Jesus, has died for the sake of his people; he alone has taken away the ultimate power of sin; he alone has empowered his people with the Holy Spirit, the living presence of Christ; and he alone will end the story when and how he sees fit' (p. 22). There is a glorious liberation in accepting that no individual or human agency can solve the problems of the city and the world; nor do they have to since the future is in God's hands. Their role is to exhibit that trust which undergirds and fosters virtue.

In determining what such faithfulness and trust will entail in practice requires attention to the person of Christ. The Church is, after all, the body of Christ and is called to imitate him in its faithfulness. In the life and death of Christ we see, first, a radical submission to the will of God and, second, a complete self-giving which is understood in the New Testament in terms of sacrifice. The understanding of the death of Christ as a sacrifice is clear throughout the letters of St Paul and the Letter to the Hebrews; it is pre-eminent in Jesus' discourses and the account of the last supper in the fourth Gospel and the crucifixion in the other three. Christ's sacrifice, as Alec Graham puts it, 'is understood to be unique in its effect of bringing reconciliation, forgiveness, peace, liberty and fulfillment to needy humanity':

> His priesthood is understood to be unique in that it is the expression on earth of the eternal self-offering of the Son to the Father. Even as He was coming into the world, the Epistle to the Hebrews tells us, He said, 'Lo, I have come to do Thy will, O God'. Consonant with that is the prayer to the Father on Jesus' lips in John 17 that it was for our sakes that He consecrated Himself. (Postscript in, Bowering, 1994, p. 175)

Graham goes on to argue that this is the foundation upon which any understanding or doctrine of the Church and its ministry must be built since the Church is composed of those who are in Christ: if Christ is the High Priest of our confession, and if his life and death were marked by sacrificial obedience and self-consecration for the sake of others to his heavenly Father, then we should expect the life of those who are in Christ to be marked by precisely the same characteristics:

> The Church must understand its vocation in terms of obedience priestly and sacrificial (in the words of the Eucharistic prayer, by, with, and in Christ). Further, we should hope, expect and aim to be agents in our time of conveying and promoting the reconciliation, peace, forgiveness, liberty and fulfillment which Christ's own offering made once for all set forward as no one else and nothing else could. (Postscript in, Bowering, 1994, p. 175)

This, then, is the aim of the Church – in the city and elsewhere: to witness to that Christ in whom, for the Christian, all virtue is grounded and to point to him in order to promote such virtue. As Miroslav Volf puts it:

> A genuinely Christian reflection on social issues must be rooted in the self-giving love of the divine Trinity as manifested on the cross of Christ; all the central themes of such reflection will have to be thought through from the perspective of the self-giving love of God. (1996, p. 25)

As it seeks to embody the self-giving love of God the Church must, first and foremost, be attentive to its own life and vocation based on repentance, forgiveness, worship, proclamation, holiness of life and a sense of coming judgement (Wells, 2003, p. 3). In reflecting on the role of the Church in regeneration, Sam Wells reminds us that God has given the local church a number of particular practices to shape, sustain and characterize its life. It may well, he tells us, 'think these unremarkable – unless it realizes that they constitute its most significant gift to a community-led regeneration process'. He points us to four among many: the first is baptism, which witnesses to God's sovereignty in Christ and the need for change in the face of that sovereignty. Christians who know about change of heart, Wells tells us, can encourage a community that is experiencing it. The second practice is the Eucharist, at which 'reconciliation is made, a story is recalled, gifts are presented, all are fed, and are then sent out with renewed purpose'. These happenings are crucial ones for society at large: there is desperate need for the reconciliation and renewal which the Eucharist symbolizes and enables. The third is Scripture. As Wells puts it:

> Reading Scripture is the way the Church recognizes that others have sought to follow and serve God before. There is wisdom to be found, experience to be shared, truth to be learned. People struggled with poverty and oppression long before we started to, and God showed his grace and glory as much through their failures as through their successes. So he will today. (Wells, 2003, p. 23)

Lastly there is prayer: 'The community of faith wonders at God's choosing to include them in his story, are thankful for what seems like chance but they realise is providence, and offer all that is still beyond their strength, wit and power' (p. 24).

The primary task of Christians, from which they must not be distracted, is to witness to the sovereignty and love of God, and if Christians fully understand and trust God to do what only he can do, they will better be able to do what only they can do; if Christians are able to trust with all their hearts that all things are safe with God, they will be set free to give themselves to the community as Christ has given himself to the Church. Immersing themselves in the practice of baptism, Eucharist, reading of the Scriptures and prayer they will continuously be drawn back to the self-giving love of Christ and so be given power and strength to emulate it. Lesslie Newbigin makes proposals similar to those of Wells, pointing out that Jesus did not write a book but formed a community:

This community has at its heart the remembering and rehearsing of his words and deeds, and the sacraments given by him through which it is enabled both to engraft new members into his risen life and to renew this life again and again through sharing in his risen life through the body broken and the blood outpoured. (1989, p. 233)

He suggests that any such community true to its calling will have six characteristics: it will be a community of praise, a community of thanksgiving, a community of truth, a community that does not live for itself but is deeply concerned in the concerns of its neighbourhood, a community of mutual responsibility and, finally, a community of hope. If Christians hold firm to this vocation under God they will 'recognize that they exist for the sake of those who are not members, as sign, instrument, and foretaste of God's redeeming grace for the whole life of society' (p. 233).

It might be thought that such an approach will lead to pietism and withdrawal on the part of the Church but if the practices above are entered into faithfully this should not be the case. It is true that in the western Church there has developed, on the one hand, a pietism that does not encourage engagement with society and, on the other, an embrace of the 'social gospel' which can easily become divorced from the core practices of the Church referred to above. Newbigin himself warns of the danger that

the congregation may be so identified with the place that it ceases to be the vehicle of God's judgement and mercy for that place and becomes simply the focus of the self-image of the people of that place. Or it may be so concerned about the relation of its members to God that it turns its back on the neighborhood and is perceived to be irrelevant to its concerns. (1989, p. 299)

It is worth noting that this kind of polarization is not at all evident in the Church in other parts of the world – south India, for example, where Newbigin ministered so effectively. There one can experience a proper balance between attention to God and attention to neighbour, the latter enabled by the former. Immersion in its core practices should enable the church, as Newbigin himself puts it, to 'be the church for the specific place where it lives, not the church for those who wish to be members of it – or, rather, it will be for them insofar as they are willing to be for the wider community'. He argues that when it is true to its calling the church becomes 'the place where men and women and children find that the gospel gives them the framework of understanding, the "lenses" through which they are to understand and cope with the world' (p. 227). The Christian congregation become something like God's embassy in a particular place – one which enables, we might add, the fostering of virtue.

In so doing the church in the city will be the servant of the society in which it finds itself. Its task, according to Timothy Gorringe, is that of 'the contemporary equivalent of the Isaianic theology of the Servant. The Servant, whether an individual or a community, was not called to garner honour for him or herself but to be "a light to the nations, that my salvation may reach to the end of the earth" (Isa. 49.6). If Church inherits that task, then it is first and foremost called out, imagined community for the sake of the earth which sustains us' (2002, p. 249). How the church serves the city and the society in which it finds itself will differ according to circumstances. Ann Morrisey gives examples of two churches that engage with the pain of their community in imaginative ways: one, in west London, opens its doors every evening for those who are concerned about young people in the area in the grip of drugs: 'Mums and grandparents and fathers come in and light a candle and, on occasion, in that holy place, sob for the sake of their children.' Another, near Guildford, is left open for drug addicts to enter during the day:

> [T]he power of the holy in that place has the potential to enable the addicted to rekindle the lost hope of being able to free themselves from their addiction; the sense of the holy in that place helps the addict to rehearse continually putting their hand in the hand of their God, as they grapple with their captivity to drugs, searching for the moment when they can say no to drugs and do say no, again and again. (in North and North, 2007, p. 130)

Such initiatives are perhaps best thought of, in an increasingly multicultural environment, in terms of Christian hospitality. Luke Bretherton proposes that the practice of hospitality both describes and defines the manner in which the church should relate to its neighbours in ethical disputes in a way that 'enables it both to be a guest and host of the life of its neighbours':

> Christian hospitality is inaugurated at Pentecost, bears witness to the eschaton, and corresponds to the tension at the heart of the eschaton,

whereby it is established but not yet fully manifest. As an eschatological social practice, hospitality is inspired by the Holy Spirit, who
enables the church to host the life of its neighbours without the
church being assimilated to, or colonized by, or having to withdraw
from, the life of the world. (Bretherton, 2006b, p. 146)

He argues that hospitality should be central to shaping relations
between the church and its neighbours and suggests that 'care for the
sick and the poor, hospitality to strangers, educational initiatives, and
peacemaking endeavours are all examples of ways in which the church
hosts the life together of its neighbours and enables that life to bear
witness to its eschatological possibilities' (p. 150). Similarly, Rowan
Williams tells us that 'If the Church is there to tell people that God is
hospitable, that Jesus's company can be shared now, and that this trans-
forms the world of sinful and divided humanity, what it must, above all,
guard against is the temptation to think of itself and present itself as a
human association offering benefits on the same level as other leisure
activities. It has to remember that it is trustee of a divine initiative and
invitation' (in Croft, 2006, p. 55).

The mention of eschatological possibilities and the offering of hospitality in order to witness to them can serve to remind us of what is
perhaps the most important role of the Church in the city: to bring hope,
a central Christian virtue. Writing from a South African perspective,
John de Gruchy suggests that Christian eschatology is 'not simply about
hope for justice in the future but about the impact which God's future
has on our present experience' (2002, p. 210). God's future will be
brought to bear upon present reality partly through practical ministry
but also by virtue of presence and God-centred character – in other
words, by faithful witness. St Paul speaks of 'the God of hope' (Rom.
15.13) and in so doing refutes the hopelessness of the present time.
When Swan Hunter shipyard, in which so much of the identity and
sense of self-worth of the local community was invested, went into the
hands of the receivers in the early 1990s, I was vicar of the shipyard
parish in which it is situated and it seemed to me then that the distinctive contribution of the church was to offer hope in a situation that
seemed hopeless.

That faithful witness will often, though not always, be centred on
buildings and such buildings have an important part to play in that
witness. Not only can buildings be useful in practical ways, such as in
the example cited by Anne Morrisey, they can, in addition, be a power-

ful symbol of the values for which the communities that worship in them stand and which have been the bedrock of our culture for generations. As Jonathan Sacks implied in his writing about the role of churches in the city of London cited above, the buildings themselves have an important symbolic function. Churches should be a reminder to all those who see them of the holiness of those to whom they are dedicated and of values and virtues crucial to human flourishing.

In conclusion, churches and the communities of worship associated with them have a crucial role in enabling cities to be true to their vocation to be nurseries of the virtues. If churches are to succeed in this, their primary focus must be on Christ: they must place their hope and trust in him and be characterized, like Christ, by the self-giving love of God. As they await the coming of the consummation of all things in the new city of Jerusalem (Rev. 21.1) in which they hope finally to dwell, it is by concentrating their attention upon him who is the Alpha and the Omega and being faithful to him that they will be empowered by God's Spirit to serve the cities in which they are presently situated.

Bibliography

Bowering, M., 1994, *Priesthood Here and Now*, Newcastle-upon-Tyne, Diocese of Newcastle.

Bretherton, L., 2006a, 'A New Establishment? Theology, Politics and the Emerging Shape of Church-State Relations', *Political Theology*, 7(3), 371–92.

Bretherton, L., 2006b, *Hospitality as Holiness: Christian Witness Amid Moral Diversity*, Aldershot, Ashgate.

Commission on Urban Life and Faith, 2006, *Faithful Cities: A Call for Celebration, Vision and Justice*, London, Church House Publishing.

Croft, S., 2006, *The Future of the Parish System: Shaping the Church of England for the 21st Century*, London, Church House Publishing.

de Gruchy, J., 2002, *Reconciliation: Restoring Justice*, London, SCM.

Gorringe, T., 2002, *A Theology of the Built Environment*, Cambridge, Cambridge University Press.

Heslem, P. (ed.), 2004, *Globalization and the Good*, London, SPCK.

Inge, J., 2003, *A Christian Theology of Place*, Aldershot, Ashgate.

Inge, J., 2007, *Living Love: In Conversation with the No. 1 Ladies' Detective Agency*, Peterborough, Inspire.

Martin, D., 2005, *On Secularization: Towards a Revised General Theory*, Aldershot, Ashgate.

Newbigin, L., 1989, *The Gospel in a Pluralist Society*, London, SPCK.

North, P. and North, J., 2007, *Sacred Space: House of God, Gate of Heaven*, London, Continuum.

The Pontifical Council for the Pastoral Care of Migrants and Itinerant People, 1999, *The Shrine, Memorial Presence and Prophecy of the Living God*, Rome, The Vatican.

Sacks, J., 1997, *The Politics of Hope*, London, Jonathan Cape.

Sacks, J., 2002, *The Dignity of Difference: How to Avoid the Clash of Civilizations*, London, Continuum.

Thomas, S., 1991, *Religion and the Decline of Magic*, Harmondsworth, Penguin.

Volf, M., 1996, *Exclusion and Embrace*, Nashville, Abingdon Press.

Walker, A. (ed.), 2005, *Spirituality in the City*, London, SPCK.

Wells, S., 2003, *Community-Led Regeneration and the Local Church*, Cambridge, Grove.

5

Towards a Missiology for the City Centre

PAUL BALLARD

Missiology is reflection on the theological understanding of the relation between God, the world and the Church. It asks about the place and task of the Church in the creating and saving providence of God in the history of God's dealings with the world. Missiology, therefore, is always specific, addressing particular historical, cultural or geographical contexts. As part of practical theology, it holds the great themes of Christian understanding, found in Scripture and tradition, in critical correlation with the challenges and opportunities of a given situation. This chapter, in the context of a study of the Church at the heart of the city, seeks to outline the salient features of a missiology that should inform that concern.

It also draws on the discussions of the nature of the city today found in the first part of the book, offering a missiological response which, together with the other chapters on the Church in the city and spirituality in the city in this second section, provide a theological backdrop to the examples and stories of Christian witness and service found in Part III.

There are three sections to this chapter. The first sets the enquiry against the background of the broad sweep of contemporary missiology; the second pays attention to the ways the city centre shapes theological understanding; and the third looks at some marks of the Church that are specially relevant to its city centre mission.

Themes from the contemporary theology of mission

It is widely agreed, and set out most clearly by David Bosch (1991), that the second half of the twentieth century saw a significant 'paradigm shift' in the understanding of mission. This process, still being worked

out, marked the end of Christendom and the decline of western hegemony in an age of turbulence and violence. This is the background of
any contemporary discussion of mission and it provides a number of key
perspectives, summarized below, for our general theme.

The missio Dei

This is, perhaps, the normative perspective for modern mission, which
emerged decisively at the International Missionary Council's meeting at
Willingen in 1952.

Mission is rooted in the person and activity of God. God is the sending, seeking one, working out the purposes of the Kingdom in creation
and salvation. What is true for the economy of God is also true of the
very nature of God. The Triune God is revealed as a community of
giving and receiving. It is this life into which we are caught up by faith
and which gives meaning and substance to human existence.

One of the key implications is that the Church is the servant of
mission, not the sole instrument and object of mission. Her task is to
witness to the reality of the Kingdom, pointing to what Christ has done
and is doing in the world. But this is a complex relationship that has
many levels. First, the Church is the servant of God in and for the world.
In solidarity and judgement the Church seeks to work for the Kingdom
in every aspect of life, looking for and strengthening signs wherever they
are. Second, however, the Church, at the same time, is part of the
ambiguous and broken world, caught up in and reflecting its short-
comings. It can, therefore, can only point away from all false hopes and
expectations, in the world and in itself, to the hope of the world in Jesus
Christ. God alone is the place whence our help comes (Ps. 121.1). But,
third, the Church is the community of faith that names the name and
begins to find in Christ, by the Spirit, signs of the Kingdom in its own
life. It is a priestly presence, mediating the things of God to the world. It
is the visible presence of the Christ who is hidden in the concrete reality
of history, awaiting the fulfilment of the promise. As witness, therefore,
the Church, like John the Baptist, points away from itself and to the
crucified and risen Lord, the source of all grace and strength, yet invites
all to join in the pilgrimage of faith, in the fellowship of the Spirit.

The cosmic Christ

The emphasis on the *missio Dei* also reconfigures our perception of the person of Christ. There is a tension in Christology between the historical particularity of Jesus of Nazareth, born, crucified and risen, and the eternal reality of the Word. Not unreasonably our imagination and devotion tend to focus on the Gospel story, the more so in a secularized cultural environment. But the New Testament equally, if not primarily, sees Jesus in terms of the eternal will of God, bound up with the Father as the creative Word in and through whom all things were made (John 1.1–5; Col. 1.16). He is also the consummation towards which all things press (1 Cor. 15.24–28; Eph. 4.15–16; Phil. 3.16). In Christ all things are reconciled in the peace of the Kingdom (Col. 1.20). The Gospels, too, echo this in the way they weave, most explicitly in John, the story into a cosmic context, of Jesus as the Lord of creation and mediator of God's grace.

This claim carries important consequences. First, there is the affirmation that Jesus reveals for us the very heart of the universe (Col. 2.1–15; Eph. 1.20–23). All things are under his aegis. This suggests that Christ's authority, though hidden and challenged from our point of view, runs throughout the cosmos and across history. His reign is not confined to the Church, over those who happen to accept him. It is part of the mystery of existence itself. So, second, we must expect to find Christ beyond the boundaries of the community of faith. There is nothing, no one and nowhere that is beyond his presence. This can be seen in the dynamic of Scripture. On the one hand, it is the diversity of the nations that come into the city and enrich it (Rev. 20.26; cf. Isa. 60). On the other hand the gospel is sent out from Jerusalem to encompass the whole world, taking root in every tribe and nation (Acts 1.8; Matt. 28.18–20; Rom. 9—11). Indeed the New Testament can be read as the story of the transition of the faith out of Judaism into the Graeco-Roman world, a process that has, down the years, continued, until today the Church is established in almost every culture and takes many diverse forms. This is important in our own time of massive social mobility and changing social and economic patterns. We are thus learning, in a pluralism that is new to the West, to find Christ coming to us through strange and unexpected ways, as we enter into dialogue with other cultures that incorporate other faiths. This is not indifferentism or relativism. We are called to seek the truth, which for Christians sets Christ at the centre.

Third, however, there is an eschatological dimension. We are in the midst of a process of which we do not know the end or how it all is going to work out. We are living between the times. In this sense we know only in part, but then face to face (1 Cor. 13.12). Hope is founded on Christ in whom God has been made known as Creator, Saviour and Sustainer, but the future is also open, allowing fresh gifts to be bestowed. Whatever the strains and threats that seem to pervade our times the final reality, the Kingdom of God, calls us forward. Our calling is to journey in faith, witnessing both crucifixion and resurrection, paradigmatically in Jesus, but also in the rest of the world.

The pilgrim people of God

This leads to the third mark of contemporary missiology, the pilgrim people of God, brought on to centre stage through the work of the Second Vatican Council (1962–5). For our present purposes there are two aspects that need to be underlined.

First, the Church, journeying with God, is 'on the way', on a voyage of discovery. It is a matter of discerning where God is leading. The journeying Church should be mobile and adaptable, responding to the challenges of time and place. Nowhere is a final resting place, because God moves ahead into the unknown. The Church lives by the dynamic of hope, relying on the promises of God and the vision of God's future. This is the eschatological reality of the already and the not yet, of living between the times (Phil. 3.12–14).

Second, the emphasis is on the corporate fellowship of the Church, a band of pilgrims travelling together. There is a shift from the institutional and hierarchical to personal belonging to the company of faith. Perhaps this has been most vividly symbolized by the rediscovery of the Eucharist as the focal form of Christian worship. Here the whole people of God gather round the table. There has been a move away from the priest facing away from the people in the Catholic context and the stress on preaching in Protestantism. Rather, the emphasis is on the common shared life of communion in Christ. It is, however, not simply a coming together to meet the Lord; though there is need to be found in the Father's house. It is also a sending out. The offering of our lives is caught up into the life of Christ, then broken and poured out, given to us as life indeed, to be seen through our witness in the everyday world. Thus the eucharistic fellowship spills out into the recognition of the priestly ministry of the whole Church through each member in their place and through the diversity of specific and authorized ministries, both within and beyond the Church, that are increasingly being recognized. Hereby use is being made of the talents to be found in the body of Christ within the broad and general affirmation of, in Catholic terms, the recovery since Vatican II of the lay apostolate and the traditional emphasis among Protestants on the priesthood of all believers as that of each believer.

Justice, peace and the integrity of creation

This phrase, taken from a longstanding programme of the World Council of Churches, points to a major dimension of mission that has become more and more central to the life of the churches. Globally, nationally and locally the issues of poverty and wealth, social cohesion and conflict and the rapidly emerging ecological crisis are key to where the struggle for the Kingdom lies in a turbulent and broken world. The age-long concern for human welfare has taken radically new forms in a post-western, technologically innovative and globalized world. This has happened in different ways in almost every major tradition. It finds expression, for example, in the rapidly evolving Catholic understanding of 'the common good'; in the recovery of responsibility for the poor among evangelicals; and in the political and liberation theologies of both the West and the Third World, together with those addressing special concerns such as black, feminist and, more recently, gay theologies.

This has worked itself out in many ways. There is the prophetic activity of critically engaging with the social, economic and political realities and advocacy of the poor and oppressed. There is, also, the service of the poor, from relief in times of acute hardship to community development. This happens on the world stage through the work of such agencies as Christian Aid, CAFOD and Tearfund; and more locally as groups and congregations seek to address the needs of their neighbourhoods, whether by working with asylum seekers, mitigating family breakdown, fighting unemployment or in community regeneration. Increasingly this has become the norm for church life and, in a pluralistic society, it creates bridges for working with others in the community.

The summons to faith

The call to serve God by serving the world can bring with it a tension in contrast with the dominance, in a previous age, of evangelical conversionism. In the 1960s, in the hey-day of the secular gospel, the contrast became particularly acute. Many evangelicals felt that those referred to as the 'ecumenicals', the mainstream denominations, had allowed social concerns to oust the divine mandate 'to make disciples' (Matt. 28.19). Perhaps this was part of the trial and error of moving into a new era. However, subsequently there was a process of convergence towards the recognition that Christian witness was both an invitation to faith and responsibility to the neighbour. Evangelicals, as we have just noted, found it impossible to walk away from social concern and the World Council of Churches rediscovered the evangelistic dimension of serving the Kingdom in the world. This was further strengthened by a call to evangelism from Pope Paul VI, where the emphasis was on the continuous process of being called into God's new life. The call to conversion is seen as part of belonging to the pilgrim people of God, journeying with Christ in his passion and entering into his resurrection in the service of the Kingdom in the world. As the Church in the West moves out of Christendom, and Christian allegiance becomes both more tentative and yet more deliberate, so there is a need to discover how people can be drawn into faith and supported in discipleship.

Contextuality

Christian witness has always been embedded. This is the thrust of the incarnation – 'Emmanuel, God with us' (Matt. 1.23). But this contextuality has been forcibly rediscovered in radical ways. The decline of the West and the globalization of the Church has meant the recognition of its cultural diversity. To participate in the *missio Dei* is to relate the gospel to the particularity of time and place. Faith has to be inculturated.

This gives rise to a number of issues. How far can this go without losing the distinctiveness of the gospel? To be inculturated means to accept a wide range of differences. This can threaten the cohesion of the Christian community and raise questions of catholicity, the relation of the local to the universal. Yet Christian believing, practice and witness must start and grow out of the given situation as much as from the foundation in Scripture and tradition. All have to 'work out their own salvation' (Phil. 2.12), faithful to the Lord who has called them.

The city centre

We move from some of the major themes that have dominated missiological thinking over the last decades to the more specific context of our enquiry. This section, therefore, will look at some key aspects of the city and set them into theological and missiological perspective. There is thus a conversation between social context and faith. There has always, of course, to be a note of caution here lest the signs of the times are read too glibly and unwarranted assumptions are made. The spirits have to be tested (1 John 4.1). It is too easy to set our own agenda, mirroring our own prejudices and fears. Moreover, the twists and turns of history tend to upset any nice calculations. Nevertheless we are committed to the exploration. Indeed it is necessary because human beings are hermeneutical creatures, always seeking for meaning, trying to make sense of the world. What Christians are trying to do is to discern that process in the light of the gospel.

The city centre as history

The Central Business District, normally found at the heart of any large town or city, generally delineates the historic core of the settlement. This may be a medieval city, or the early effects of industrialization, or a combination of both. It will also include the signs of the religious history that has been woven into the urban fabric. Here are the roots of tradition and identity.

The city has traditionally been at the creative edge of civilization. It has been the location of power and culture and human progress. Christianity took root and developed in the cities of the Roman Empire and for 1,500 years was present at the heart of learning and authority. It is the city centre that still remains the location for civic, economic and cultural power. If the Church is to relate in any meaningful way to modern culture it must be visible and actively present there. It may not be the whole story but that aspect of the city is abandoned at its peril. The churches, in modern times, have too easily allowed themselves, both physically and culturally, to drift out into the suburbs. The temptation in an age of individualism and consumerism is to remain in this 'suburban captivity', becoming a domestic, personal and marginal activity. At the centre of the city, however, the Church can witness more readily in and to the social, economic and structural reality that is modern urbanized life.

Now, however, more or less isolated from the normative suburban setting, the Church of the city centre has to look afresh at its purpose and task. So often older ways do not seem to fit any more. Located at the hub of city life, and at a time of urban renewal, this is a formidable challenge: to become once again engaged with all that the city centre holds and represents. Much can be learned and adapted from earlier patterns and practices, some of which have been forgotten and could do with reviving. Often the churches still retain a place in the public life of the community, even if it seems simply symbolic; but this too can be a basis for renewal and fresh initiatives. Also, at a time when, slowly, revived interest is being taken in 'faith communities' and their potential contribution to 'social capital', there are more and more openings for Christian participation in the life of the city. Those in authority are often only too glad to welcome into partnership, albeit in critical solidarity, those who have the welfare of the city at heart (Jer. 29.7). City centre churches or city-wide church groupings, such as ecumenical councils, can provide a visible point of connection with the somewhat scattered reality that are the churches. The point being made here is that the Church in the city centre has the potential, in each setting, to take up the historical witness of working for and in the heart of urban life. It is in the city centre that 'public theology' must be practised through engagement with 'the powers that be' (Rom. 13.1).

The city centre as sector

One of the marks of modern society has been the separation and dispersal of functions. This is most visible in the split between the domestic and the world of work. However, other functions too have clustered and scattered, such as shopping and medical care. Urban life has been split up into activity-specific zones, connected by an intricate web of public and private transport. The Central Business District can be seen as one of these sectors, a zone that has its own peculiarities and patterns, even though it can also be characterized as being a conglomeration of a number of 'sector' functions, such as retail, office and leisure activities, each with their own ethos.

The churches have partially responded to this phenomenon of modern life, slowly recognizing special spheres of ministry. The obvious example is the emergence of industrial mission after the Second World War. The failure has been not to recognize that this is the pattern for the whole range of ministry. This includes parish or local congregational ministry as being as much of a sector ministry (i.e., the domestic sector) as any. It should not be regarded as the normative and almost exclusive expression of Christian belonging. To operate in this restrictive fashion suggests that large areas of life are of no interest to the Church. The report *Faith in the City* (1985), fortuitously, brought attention to the plight and poverty of the inner city. This has now begun to be accepted as a special field of ministry, with its own demands and skills. This should be true of the city centre also, with its very different and crucial tasks. The vision that underlies such an approach is one of complementarity. The Church is present in the whole city and in each part of the city. This makes the diocese, or its equivalent, the strategic unit through which all the different local ministries interlock, contributing to the whole.

In this the city centre is crucial, being where so much that shapes and controls the city in all its variety is forged and controlled. This is where city centre ministry is placed. Within that ministry there may well be, for some, sub-divisions and specializations of function, such as working with the retail trade, in the council offices, among the clubbing population, or in the entertainment world, each of which has its own demands and opportunities. Nevertheless the city centre is a very special place. To minister here should be seen as a particular calling for which adequate induction, training and support is offered. So much more care needs to be taken over strategic planning for the city centre both locally and nationally, with job descriptions specific to the situation, and appropriate networks and back-up structures developed.

The city centre as crossroads

In the city centre is the market place. There the business of the city is conducted and the crowds jostle in their coming and going. The city is a magnet that draws into itself the great diversity of humanity, a melting pot of new and old, of the familiar and the strange, of comfort and threat. There is the cosmopolitan Babel of the competing and clashing sounds of those who are anxious to gain attention, sell their wares and create a space for their concerns. Not least is this a market place of ideas and cultures. The city is the exemplar of modern cosmopolitan pluralistic society. Here is one of the crucibles where the Church has to recover its voice in a post-Christian world.

The city, too, is the hub of the region. The roads go out into the hinterland, into the region that the city serves. They form a web that links the scattered communities and concerns together. The city provides both a sense of identity and a place of shared experience. For the churches at the centre there is the challenge to be responsive to and ready to offer a ministry in and for the whole region. This can perhaps be seen as, first, a place for those functions and celebrations that are wider than the local parish or congregation. The classic example is that of the cathedral. But, second, there are those ministries that of their nature are best situated centrally, such as educational courses or pastoral counselling. Often the city centre church is well placed to house a specialist institute or service.

Power in the city

The city is the focus of power. Often located in the city centre, the marks of the city become visible: the civic centre, banks and corporate offices, department stores, theatres and libraries. Here the transactions, corporate and personal, which create the wealth of the city are executed. From here the city is governed. But where does power really lie? Clearly there are the movers and shakers, those whose decisions and opinions count. But they operate as part of a wider nexus of connections and are dependent on others to respond. They are also dependent on the wider structures of law and custom, of what is acceptable and allowed in society. Behind all this, deep-rooted and often invisible, there are the basic assumptions and models that inform and drive the kind of society within which we all operate. Culture, and therefore power, is a complex and deep-rooted, if ever-changing, reality that seems to control and drive us along; yet it is also the expression of human activity and choice.

This comes very close to what the New Testament has to say about 'the principalities and powers'. Sometimes the reference seems to be to the ruling authorities (Rom. 13.1). At other points they seem to be 'spiritual' realities that govern and shape society (Eph. 6.12). With Walter Wink (1992), it is possible to assume that these dominant powers are embodied in representative people. The powers can be beneficent or malignant. Above all, however, they are part of the order of creation, serving God's purpose, shaping human society. It is when they break loose and serve their own ends, usurping their limitations under God, that they are evil. So part of the redemptive act of Christ is to bring them once again into the service of the Kingdom (Col. 1.16). When they are fulfilling their proper task they should be accepted; but resisted when rebelling against God. If this is so, then the Church's task is to engage with the powers, both in their institutionalized and cultural forms, in critical solidarity, strengthening them and co-operating with them where they serve the good of society, challenging them where they are a threat. This is the prophetic task in the city. It is not easy to discern the wise from the destructive in the complexity of modern life. It demands patience and understanding, standing alongside those who are engaged in difficult decisions, especially if they are there as part of their Christian calling, always setting out the vision of the just and peaceable city.

Theologically, power is understood in terms of Jesus Christ, who is the power and wisdom of God (1 Cor. 1.24). This can be illustrated from John's Gospel, when Jesus confronts Pilate. Power may be unequal, but it is always shared. When Jesus told Pilate that he would have no power unless it had been given him (John 19.11), he was making five points. He was reminding Pilate that he was dependent on the Emperor, serving a wider authority. This is power exercised within the constraints of law, legitimized by due process. But for John, second, God is the primary giver of power. This is fundamental to all power. It is not exercised in its own right but as a steward or agent of God. This is the prophetic touchstone, for power serves a greater good: justice, peace and reconciliation. But, third, God also yields power, withdrawing, as it were, in order for Pilate to exercise his power. Pilate had responsibility. He was involved, willy-nilly, in the mess that seems to have been a constant feature of Judean politics. Limited though his options may have been he had made his own decision. There is, however, a fourth dimension. Jesus, too, conceded power, that is, to Pilate. He could have refused. Pilate's only recourse then would have been either to concede or to have destroyed Jesus arbitrarily, which would have destroyed his power to exercise power. Yet Jesus, fifthly, retained power. He kept his integrity. Even though submitting to his decision, Jesus did not allow Pilate, or the Sanhedrim, or the soldiers to take him over. There is a subtlety in this exercise of power that, hard though it is to sustain, nevertheless is stronger than all power, for it is the power of love and not anger or hate or resignation, which power is God's power. Power, therefore, is not simply the ability to coerce. It is about legitimacy and authority, means and ends, and the morality of community and service. Pastorally it is important to keep all these levels in mind because they are always in play. Perhaps some appear to be strong and others weak, but there is a gossamer web of relationships that link us to each other. In this way the strong can be reminded of their weakness and dependence and the weak be given hope, dignity and an ability to exercise a greater power. This is the model of power that should both inform its own exercise of power and shape its engagement with the principalities and powers.

It may be true that the Church does not have the clout it once had, which was, perhaps, not always exercised with good judgement. But the Church still has a voice and can exercise influence, seeking to obey Jeremiah's advice to seek the good of the city where it is placed (Jer. 29.7).

People in the city centre

Alongside the prophetic task there is always the pastoral need; people for whom there is a mandate to care, as they work, live in, and visit the city with its promise and dangers. The city centre has its own rhythms, setting up a diverse pattern of need and opportunity.

We can discern, perhaps, five groups of people. First, each weekday there is the influx of those who come to work. These include those who exercise considerable power with all the pressure and responsibility that entails. But there is also the far greater number of those who keep the wheels of modern life turning, serving across the counter, sitting in front of the computer in the office, administering public services or managing teams of people and ensuring productivity. There is also the invisible army of cleaners and night workers without whom the city would soon grind to a halt. Second, there is the night scene of cafés, clubs, theatre or cinema. Third, the city centre is the place of the stranger. People come and go, passing through, hurrying about their business, shoppers, tourists and business persons. For most this is enough, but for some there is tiredness and loneliness. Fourth, in recent years there have been moves to live in the centre of the cities, in converted warehouses and new apartment blocks, but mostly cut off behind secure entrances from the bustle of the streets around. Fifth, and perhaps most important, there are those attracted by the anonymity, not least of the bus or train station: the poorest and most destitute in society, the homeless on the streets, the refugees and asylum seekers, the alcoholics and the druggies, each seeking refuge, warmth and some sign of recognition.

The life of the Church

The Church is present in the centre of the city in a number of ways. Most visibly it is in the church building and the congregation that gathers there and the worship that is offered throughout the week. Then there is the representative ministry of chaplains in shops, offices, clubs and town hall, signs of the concern of the Church in and for the workplace or on the street. There are also more hidden expressions of Church, often in unexpected places and developing their own patterns of discipleship and worship. What, however, are some of the marks of the Church that are important for mission in such a situation?

The Church as gift

At the heart of the gospel is the acknowledgement of our dependency on God. All that we have and are is gift, to be received in wonder and love. Therefore the Church is a gift, the gracious means whereby God calls us to himself and sustains us in our discipleship. More that that, however, the Church is a gift to the world, a sign of God's saving care for humanity. This is perhaps strange to both Christians and those outside the Church for it is too often assumed that Church is the possession of the Christian community. But if it were seen as gift, something that does not depend on us and is not for our benefit, perhaps it would be easier to be more open and less possessive. It is God's Church, to be used as God wills, in prosperity or dearth.

Second, the Church has gifts to give to the wider community. Importantly there are buildings. But there are also people who, in work or at home, offer their daily living as a gift to others. There is also the gift of hospitality, welcome and fellowship. Finally there is the gift of the gospel, God's encompassing love in Christ. One of the current concerns of government is to build 'social capital', to increase the sense of community. The William Temple Foundation has recently extended this idea to 'religious' and 'spiritual capital'. Religious capital is the way the Church, and other faith communities, through their structures and social participation, contribute to the general quality of communal life. Spiritual capital is that contribution that Christians make through their faith and discipleship, through their quality of personal life and the quality of church life, offering the beliefs and wisdom drawn from the Christian faith to the world around.

Worship in and for the city

The Church is a priestly people (1 Pet. 2.5), offering praise and prayer to God on behalf of the world and seeking God's blessing on the world. At the heart of Christian worship is the ministry of intercession. This is a sacred obligation, whether others recognize it or not, a privilege to be taken seriously. Being engaged with the life of the city vitally allows prayer to be informed and articulate. This is part of the Eucharist and will spill out into other times and places.

Second, the Church is often in a position to enable others to offer prayer by articulating for them the often unformed longings of their hearts. This may be at civic or other formal occasions. It may be at more private moments and gatherings.

Third, we live in an age that is seeking a spirituality and many are travelling paths of exploration, attracted by the need for silence and meditation. In the business of the city the quiet place can allow escape from the pressures of everyday living. In this quiet place it is possible to begin to introduce people to Christian contemplation and the vision of God in Christ.

The fellowship of the Holy Spirit

In the anonymity of the city there is often a desire for a sense of belonging. This can be offered through the openness and hospitality of place and group. It is more, however, than strong bonding and togetherness. There needs to be both a freedom and respect as well as a willingness to be brought into the group. The need is for a safe place where the stranger is respected and listened to and is supported in his or her own pilgrimage and exploration. It is the Holy Spirit that creates communion or fellowship. Moreover there is a fellowship of faith which is greater than ourselves and those immediately around. In Christ it is possible to embrace and be embraced by a Church that transcends time and space. Through the Spirit we participate in the life of the Trinity which is the source and model of fellowship, a pattern of mutual giving and receiving, of welcome and response, of responsibility and recognition. It is here that the stranger and even enemy begin to be accepted and received as gift. It is part of mission to create means whereby people can find the recognition that gives them identity, that stays with them as they stumble, and to deal appropriately with those who have acute needs or who are vulnerable. This almost impossible task will grow out of already existing activities as well as demanding new projects and experimental ventures.

Another issue arises here. Modern pressurized and mobile life creates new patterns of living. The old rhythms, such as regular Sunday worship, are not holding up and close ties with a particular local community are much harder to maintain. To counter this there is a need to develop mechanisms whereby Christians, though scattered, are united in praise and prayer. This could be a simple rule of life that all share wherever they are. There are several models that can be explored: the Franciscan Tertiaries, the Iona Community, the Northumbrian Community or the Taizé offices. It would be equally possible to draw up a simple local scheme whereby Scripture readings and simple prayers were sent out on a regular basis by e-mail or newsletter. The other side of this is to have key times and seasons, around special events, when there is a large celebration. For some the annual gatherings like Spring Harvest provide such a focal point for spiritual development.

Catholicity

The Creed includes an affirmation of 'one, holy and catholic Church'. This clause has been the focus of much controversy in separated Christendom; yet it is even more crucial for our own time when the shape of Christian belonging is going through such far-reaching changes. It is essential that this claim and aspiration be the focus for any missiological action when the impetus is to explore new ways of being Church, lest there be complete fragmentation in the coming diversity. Here three points will be made.

First, because the almost inevitable trend has been for the city centre, until recently, to lose population, compounded by a reluctance to travel in to the centre, traditional congregations have lost ground. Thus, with the exceptions of cathedrals and other historic places, the Church finds itself in a weak position. Yet, it has been argued, the city centre is a vital arena for witness and mission. This would strongly suggest that new patterns of ministry be devised that maximize the use of restricted resources, ecumenically planned and supported. This would also provide another workshop of practical catholicity, an exploration of a renewed and enriched Christian existence, where diversity goes hand in hand with collaboration, so that 'the world might believe' (John 17.21). But this is dependent on the various ecclesiastical bodies not only co-operating but also seeing, once again, ecumenism as essentially missiological in nature. How it would be worked out would vary from situation to situation. Here is a particular type of ecumenical project, of which there are comparatively few at present.

The second example develops the first further. Recent years have begun to see the emergence of new ways of being Church, often in small and tentative ways. It is not clear what the long-term prospects are. What is clear is that there is an ever-greater diversity among Christian communities, some in contrast to traditional expressions and others growing out of the mainstream structures and complementing them. This could lead to an even greater fragmentation of Christian witness and, as people become settled into their new ways, a hardening of these divisions. There could be a radical weakening of the ties that draw different Christian congregations together in churches and across churches, together with a loss of the sense of belonging to the Church catholic. There needs to be, among such groups, a sense of belonging to the universal Church that both informs their inner life and is suitably structured.

Third, this sense of belonging to the fellowship of Christ across the world and down time is especially relevant to the churches in the city centre. It is here that the reality of globalization is most acutely felt. The Church must affirm its global existence, alongside and yet different from and counterbalancing the economic forces that mould the world. One of the tasks of the Church is to be the voice of the people, like the poor and oppressed, who are so often the victims of social and economic changes. This is true both of the immediate locality, in the inner city and rural hinterland, and across the world. To be a member of the community of faith is to be a world citizen, reaching out to those across the continents but also radically responsible for those who are here in the immediate neighbourhood. This can only be done when one is rooted in the particularity of one's own time and place and yet sees them as part of the universal whole.

Bibliography

Allen, John, Massey, Doreen and Pryke, Michael, 1999, *Unsettling Cities*, London, Routledge.

Archbishop of Canterbury's Commission on Urban Priority Areas, 1985, *Faith in the City*, London, Church House Publishing.

Ash, Amin, Massey, Doreen and Thrift, Nigel, 2000, *Cities for the Many and not for the Few*, Bristol, Policy.

Ash, Amin and Thrift, Nigel, 2002, *Cities: Reimagining the Urban*, Cambridge, Polity Press.

Avis, Paul, 2003, *A Church Drawing Near: Spirituality and Mission in a Post-Christian Culture*, Edinburgh, T&T Clark.

Bevans, Stephen B. and Schroeder, Roger P., 2006, *Constants in Context: Theology of Mission for Today*, Maryknoll, Orbis.

Bosch, David, 1991, *Transforming Mission: Paradigm Shifts in the Theology of Mission*, Maryknoll, Orbis.

Bridger, G. and Watson, S., 2002, *The Blackwell City Reader*, Oxford, Blackwell.

Byrne, David, 2001, *Understanding the Urban*, Basingstoke, Palgrave Macmillan.

Carter, Harold, 1981, *The Study of Urban Geography*, London, Arnold.

Davey, Andrew, 2001, *Urban Christianity and Global Order: Theological Resources for an Urban Future*, London, SPCK.

Kirk, J. Andrew, 1999, *What is Mission? Theological Explorations*, London, Darton, Longman & Todd.

Le Gates, R. T. and Stout, F., 2003, *The City Reader*, London, Routledge.

Mission and Public Affairs Council of the Church of England, 2004, *Mission-shaped Church: Church Planting and Fresh Expressions of church in a Changing Context*, London, Church House Publishing.

Murray, Stewart, 2006, *Changing Mission: Learning from the Newer Churches*, London, Churches Together in Britain and Ireland.

Newbigin, Lesslie, 1978, *The Open Secret*, London, SPCK.

Oborji, Francis Anekwe, 2006, *Concepts of Mission: The Evolution of Contemporary Missiology*, Maryknoll, Orbis.

Orum, Anthony M. and Chen, Xiangming, 2003, *The World of Cities: Places in Comparative and Historical Perspective*, Oxford, Blackwell.

Pile, Steve, Brook, Christopher and Morney, Gerry, 1999, *Unruly Cities?* London, Routledge.

Scherer, James A. and Bevans, Stephen B., 1992, *New Directions in Mission and Evangelisation I*, Maryknoll, Orbis.

Shenk, Wilbert R., 1999, *Changing Frontiers of Mission*, Maryknoll, Orbis.

Stevenson, Deborah, 2003, *Cities and Urban Culture*, Maidenhead, Open University Press.

Taylor, John V., 1972, *The Go-between God: The Holy Spirit and Christian Mission*, London, SCM.

Warren, Robert, 1995, *Being Human, Being Church: Spirituality and Mission in the Local Church*, London, Marshall Pickering.

Wink, Walter, 1992, *Engaging the Powers: Discernment and Resistance in a World of Domination*, Minneapolis, Fortress Press.

6

Spirituality for the City Centre

GEOFF CORNELL

Every morning, as I walk round the corner to buy a newspaper, I pass a place concerned with promoting well-being through the spiritual. Tasteful window displays of aids to meditation lead into a shop whose basement is a spa, for massage and the like. As I go down the street I pass shops catering for a balance to the frenetic pace of city life, selling perfumes, essences, expensive unguents. I pass other shops that simply cater: the lavish restaurant, the café providing the all-day breakfast, a plethora of pubs. Others offer what they consider is needed for life to be full: two specialist cookware shops, a fine bookshop, dress shops, dry cleaners, travel agents, banks, post office. My office is at Hinde Street Methodist Church, at the foot of the High Street. It has a significant ministry among the Twelve Steps Movement, Alcoholics Anonymous and the like, a programme of recovering that sees a reliance on 'a higher power' as crucial to well-being. Opposite sits the grand, expensive headquarters of a New Religious Movement, the School of Economic Science, which proudly announces that its philosophy 'works'. Looking back up the street I see the gilded tower of the parish church at its head, a place dedicated to health and healing, from the concerns of its liturgy through to the Health Centre and counselling services in the crypt. I seem to encounter signs of an urban concern for the spirit everywhere. But it is elusive, hard to describe, let alone categorize.

Leonie Sandercock, the distinguished urban theorist based in Vancouver, began her Ferguson Lecture, 'Spirituality, Urban Life and Urban Professions', at Manchester University in 2005, by remarking that when she grew up she was told to keep conversation away from money, politics and religion. But in her work on cities she had discovered that it was all about money and politics – and now she was realizing that it was all about faith too. She offered a definition of spirituality that she, an atheist, was comfortable with. It was 'the diverse ways in which we respond to the heart's longing to be connected to the largeness of life'. This does not seem a million miles away from Rowan Williams' 'the human self in tune with the truth of its own nature and with God' (in Walker, 2005). I am intrigued by the elusive concept of spirituality explored and expressed within a city centre. I am convinced that it is more than a series of techniques to enable people to feel better about themselves, massaging the human spirit to enable it to survive the city. Somewhere it engages, unbeknown, with the Spirit of God. This encounter offers perspectives on a Christian spirituality of the city centre and this in turn both affirms and critiques urban spirituality.

Wonder

There are days when I pinch myself that I am living and working where I am. My grandfather was a truant officer in London's East End. Two generations later I am surrounded by the magnificence of the West End. To get around I often cycle – past historic landmarks, alongside the Thames, through the diverse and delightful back streets. There is a deep sense of wonder and of privilege. The built environment connects me to the largeness of the past and to the wide global purposes of the city. There is an ease, a comfort here, with shops to hand and entertainment a stroll away. The young delight in this: one of their current voices, Lily Allen, whose infectious rhythms and smart lyrics made her 2007 single 'LDN' hugely popular, wonders why we would want to be anywhere else. In an acclaimed slim volume of poetry, Tobias Hill (2006) encourages this sense of wonder. In 'To a Boy on the Underground' he urges a youngster, immersed in his iPod, face in his laptop, to 'disconnect' and so to engage with the vibrancy of the city that is so easily taken for granted or ignored through the sheer effort of trying to survive:

> and here and there green hanging gardens,
> sunken gardens, roof gardens,
> yards like cesspits, and everywhere carnivals
> of people, the crowds embracing their collision.

There is an intoxicating thrill about living in the centre of a city. It is particularly embraced by the young, who come, often after study, for a couple of years here. The best-represented age in my part of the West End is 27. The sheer energy of the city is partly accounted for by its age profile!

Christians are slow to see the built environment as a holy place. Hymn books are crammed with all things bright and beautiful but few are urban. In September 2006 the Methodist Church re-organized its work in London into a single district and ran a hymn-writing competition to celebrate. The winning entry, 'The cloud of witnesses', contains not a single reference to London or the city or urban life! The feeling among the young people who were adjudicating was, perhaps, that speaking of the city was not seemly, not worthy of offering to God.

Some trace this ignoring of the city back to Augustine's distinction between the City of God and the Earthly City, claiming that it linked the spiritual with the other-worldly and ignored the ways God works in the human place. Philip Sheldrake (2001) argues against this, showing how Augustine sees two dimensions, the divine and the human, within the one history. However, his subsequent exploration of the Christian understanding of place centres on religious buildings before asking, only in conclusion, whether the city can be 're-placed'. John Inge (2003) enlarges on this by observing that a cathedral so dominated a medieval city that every place within the walls had a kind of holiness by association. But this is a long way from celebrating the man-made built environment as something influenced by the divine Spirit. In Hinde Street Church, during Lent 2007, we exhibited Mark Cazalet's *West London Stations of the Cross*, a series of paintings in which familiar places in West London became part of a Jerusalem where Christ was taken and where Christ died. The holy city was re-placed around Wormwood Scrubs! Tobias Hill has a sense of reverence and wonder in his poem appreciating a pumping station. He uses religious imagery, the church, the baptism – 'Inside its nave, the reservoir casts slatted ripples upon the walls' – and captures through his collection a strong sense of wonder at the city. It's one I share: to stand on Hungerford Bridge and gaze downstream is to delight not just in the rounded assurance of St Paul's Cathedral but also in the impish erection of the 'Gherkin', the winking, shimmering bulk of Canary Wharf, the bridges spanning the river, the snaking, lumbering trains and, a hidden and little-known wonder, Bazalgette's sewage system under the granite of the Thames Embankment. The 'largeness of life', touching the history and the wonder of a city's existence, is felt.

The human response to wonder is so often to fall silent, as description fails. I sense such stillness in the city, even with its continuous noise. You will come across people just standing and staring, meditating on its beauty. You will find quiet in the gardens, in the churches. My local

Baptist church has recently begun times for silent prayer – and has discovered such a response that they are creating further opportunities: the inner quiet staying with the one who prays into the sounds of the city, the more to wonder at it and to thank God for it.

Pilgrimage

A city is a gathering of nomads. Some are migrants of long standing. My ancestors moved from near Newmarket in Suffolk around 150 years ago as agricultural depression bit deeper and they sought work and betterment in the East End of London. That same East End has welcomed waves of Huguenots, Italians, Jews, Irish, Poles, Punjabis. More recently, others have come to flee political oppression or to seek economic advancement from within the enlarged European Union. London now has over 300 first languages and currently 29 per cent of its population was born outside of Britain. On my streets the ubiquitous traffic wardens are from west Africa and the street sweepers from eastern Europe and overhearing people on mobile phones reveals a plethora of languages. An indication of this was being stopped by a van recently and the driver asking for directions in French – presumably expecting not only to be understood but to be replied to in the same language. The shops and restaurants announce food from every part of the world. Tobias Hill's volume contains a series of 12 poems on London, one for each month of the year. Many celebrate the contribution of people of different cultures, be it an Afghan café (January), Algerian chess players (April), single migrant labourers (June) or a Chinese fishmonger (July). Such people are seen not as threat to the city but as gift.

City centres are places of passage. Great tidal flows of people sweep through them: those arriving, those leaving, those with a foot in Britain and a foot overseas. There is also the daily tide of people in and out of the centre of the city. The City of Westminster has a resident population of a quarter of a million, a working population of a million and a nightly entertainment population of half a million. The fact that transport is a perpetual topic of conversation reveals a nomadic mind-set. But there is other movement too. Zygmunt Bauman argues that modern life is 'liquid', characterized by uncertainty, reshaping endlessly, precarious. It is a life of a succession of new beginnings, where the old is discarded without processing and learning from endings. The art, he says, is to 'learn to walk on quicksand' (2005).

All this movement connects city centre dwellers to the largeness of life. The neighbour may well speak a different language and the city is networked to events in other countries, whether discussions about elections in Ghana or cars noisily processing through the streets waving national flags when a football competition is under way. Young people who are raised through multi-ethnic and multi-cultural schools and employees who work alongside people from different backgrounds, cultures and faiths invariably engage with wider horizons. Some may retreat into a narrow, mythical Britishness, but the overwhelming majority do not. As the *Guardian* proclaimed in a supplement, in London we have 'the world in one city' (21 January 2005). Migrant festivals mark the life of the city. The fireworks for Diwali have long outclassed the limp efforts for Guy Fawkes Night. My daughter decided to join her Muslim friends fasting for Ramadhan. Oxford Street strung lanterns to celebrate the Chinese New Year. Trafalgar Square fountains gush green in honour of St Patrick. And everyone parties to Carnival in Notting Hill. Leonie Sandercock (2003) gave her book *Cosmopolis II* the subtitle *Mongrel Cities*: a largeness open to the complex vitality of the world.

Christians sometimes forget how central movement is to the Bible. From Exodus, to Exile, to Diaspora, the Jewish story is one of wandering. The tension between the settled and the nomad runs through Scripture and is explored in the Genesis myths, in particular the story of Cain and Abel in Genesis 4. At the end of that story the blood-stained Cain, the rich farmer, is himself turned into a wanderer, a fugitive, but one marked by the grace of God. In the New Testament Jesus journeys with 'nowhere to lay his head' (Luke 9.58). The good news of the resurrection is taken by the early Church from Jerusalem to Rome via the major cities of the eastern Mediterranean. From its outset the Church has been a community of migrants. In a lecture Rowan Williams (2002) explored the origins of the word 'parish'. Surely nothing could be more settled, more geographically defined? But parish comes from the word *paroika*, which, originally, was the area in the town where the migrant workers lived. City centre churches now live this truth out – from Polish migrants transforming surprised Catholic parishes, to the strength of Orthodox or black-led Churches. The London Methodist District is now majority black. Ten per cent of Methodists in London come from Ghana. A significant task facing church life in our age is to discover an ecclesiology for the migrant movement rather than continuing to base it on the settled neighbourhood.

City centre spirituality takes movement seriously. Many people use their lunch hour to head out of the office for a walk. Journeying to be with friends and family, sustaining networks that criss-cross the city, is an evening activity for many; as are youngsters in cars, windows down, music volume up, parading the streets. It might remind Christians that prayer and pilgrimage go together. Latin American theology is born out of the *caminata*, the walking. So for me, walking or cycling the city is very important. It's a deliberately slower movement than the traffic, a more active engagement with the surroundings than a commute. There is eye contact with people, often leading to the courtesies without which city life would grind to a halt. Walking, you notice the beggar, the window displays, the perspectives that open at every street corner. At times there is contact, there are conversations – often across cultures and at times across languages. The diversity of the city is encountered and God is given thanks. And pilgrim people need shrines, stopping places. Westminster began with its Abbey, containing the bones of St Edward the Confessor, a shrine for pilgrims. It's part of the unseen ministry of the Church to be such places for the urban pilgrim, with open doors to welcome those who perhaps have but a distant under-standing of the Christian faith but who know the need to stop in a place of continuous movement.

Sanctuary

I started work here on 1 September 2001. Soon events in New York changed the way we see the world. The city became a precarious place to be. Scroll forward four years to 7/7 when London had its taste of urban terrorism. My wife was on the Edgware Road tube train that was bombed. The city is an exposed and dangerous place to be. The relent-less media repeats of those events, the investigation and trials only serve to underpin an acute sense of vulnerability. Fear is a feature of the centre of cities, whether in the threat of terrorism or in the violence that accom-panies drink and drugs. Concern for security dominates the political agenda. Sandercock (2003) explores the implications for urban plan-ning. On our High Street, the new Victorian-style street furniture dis-guises CCTV cameras. Police and support officers are joined by street wardens. Above, a helicopter often hovers. Emergency vehicles regu-larly scream their way along the crowded roads. 'Largeness of life' now appears threatening. What is being said in the language I do not understand? How much diversity can we sustain? Was I truly reassured, when travelling on the underground after 7/7, to encounter a young man, foreign and turbaned, with an orange T-shirt proclaiming 'Don't freak, I'm a Sikh'? Richard Rogers' 1995 Reith lectures lamented that 'cities are increasingly polarising society into segregated communities' and argued for the recovery of what he called 'open-minded space'. London has retained this better than some other cities where the central shopping centre locks its gates at the end of the day and leaves the remaining streets as a battle ground for disorientated youngsters out on the town. But it still has its police searches, its blast protection around buildings under threat. There remains a wariness and a desire for safety.

Tobias Hill's second poem in his collection captures the downside of 'liquid life'. Entitled 'Repossession', it begins with bailiffs violently securing a building:

> they frogmarched metal shutters from the van
> and bolted down the door and the windows.

And the building, thus secured, dies, is taken over by neglect. It ends hopefully with a young couple buying the property and setting about its restoring:

> the two of you scything the bittersweet,
> hopeful and very young, pulling up weeds . . .

Robert Putnam's seminal study *Bowling Alone* (2001) explored the breakdown of social capital. His plea for its restoring has underpinned government strategies to promote social cohesion. But Putnam's analysis exposes the tensions in such strategies. He distinguishes between 'bonding capital' and 'bridging capital'. The former is like linking with like. The latter is like linking with unlike. The response to threat is to encourage bonding capital. Putnam does not dismiss its importance, better bonding than no social capital; but social cohesion requires bridging capital, not tribal groupings. The secular state, unsure whether religion coheres society or fragments it, has struggled with this, not perhaps understanding how to encourage the development of secure identities with a reaching out. Individuals have equally moved in different directions: for some there has been a firming of religious affiliation and for others a distancing. Interestingly, a Tearfund report (2007) found that, whereas at the Census (2001) 71 per cent had defined themselves as

Christian, now only 53 per cent would give the same answer. The spirituality of safety connects with the largeness of life through deepening of known ties and rooting in particular places. Ethnic groups give particular attention to the preservation of their way of life. Alienated young people find refuge in the gang or their territory. The popular music scene has a tribal component, even extending to particular clubs for specific genres. Faith communities, particularly those that are clearly defined, probably within a conservative tradition, flourish.

Within Christian spirituality there is a concern for safe space, for sanctuary. It understands the sense of being small in a large world, perhaps just how much effort it takes to remain self-confident in the modern city. It knows of the need for bounded space within which to safely grow, to contain hurt, to develop trust so that healing may come. Spiritual survival in the city requires places and people where someone is held and accepted, where they can face who they are and what life is doing to them. Soul friends are key. But Christian tradition also knows of the need for those boundaries to be somewhat porous, to allow comings and goings. The monastery welcomes visitors and allows people to leave. The enclosure is for growth. It is less a sanctuary of refuge than a sanctuary for holiness.

Exile

A totally built environment is in many senses unnatural. I now live surrounded by brick and stone, the hard man-made surfaces, the sharp edges of rectangular buildings. I work in an office surrounded by taller buildings, where the sun makes a late-afternoon entrance through my windows. The house that comes with the job is similarly confined. Having grumbled about gardening, I now find myself bereft when all I have is a roof with a few pots. Even weather seems tamed here. A few months ago I ventured out to the far extremes of Walthamstow for a baptismal visit and was caught, between station and house, in a huge downpour. I arrived soaked, to the consternation of the host who rushed off for towels. And I shared with him just how good it was to be drenched, to be aware of rain and wind once again. For the most part, nature does not touch me.

There are of course signs around me of the natural world. I live near the glory of Regent's Park, with its heronry and where, last year, the RSPB set up telescopes so that you could watch a brood of peregrine falcons hatching on a nearby tower block. It is a short bus journey to Hampstead Heath and a colleague of mine swims every day, year round, in one of the outdoor ponds there. Trees blossom and bud, crocuses flower and there are baskets of geraniums. Every Sunday the farmers' market arrives and our vegetables are fresh and reasonably priced. But it is all tamed. It is nature-lite. The skies are small, the grass manicured, the streams in culverts. Marylebone, a locality in London's heart, is named after a shrine by a river, the Tyburn, which is now completely hidden under Marylebone High Street. The only time I sense nature in the city is in the tidal flow of the Thames where, even within secure banks and managed channels, there is a dangerous energy, affecting light, weather and mood. I need to escape, to experience, whether by the sea or in the hills.

Many people survive the city only through escaping from it at regular intervals.

A second home, in England or abroad, is a goal for many and a reality for a large number of people. Holidays, aided now by cheap flights to the sun, or taking a weekend skiing, are considered essential. The crowds in the clubs, filling with alcohol or other drugs, are seeking to reconnect with their sensual selves. Part of the spirituality of the city centre touches this feeling of exile from the real world, from our true selves.

The sense of exile is explored in Scripture in the tension between Jerusalem and Babylon, the two archetypal cities. The Jews in exile are encouraged to make their home in Babylon, to set up businesses, to marry and settle down – but all the time to wait for the moment of their return home (Jer. 29.1–23). But of course their return and the rebuilding of Jerusalem does not end the sense of dislocation; rather, it brings a growing recognition that, in the words of the New Testament, 'here we have no lasting city' (Heb. 13.14), that we are all exiles. Jerusalem, the true Jerusalem, the holy city becomes, in Revelation (21.1—22.7), a gift from God at the end of time, and in its perfection nature is restored to the city, the river flowing down the centre of the street, the trees for the healing of the nations.

Mary Grey argues that 'sacred stones are not just pebbles on the beaches of Holy Islands, the Druidic memorials like Stonehenge, or even the city's Cathedrals. They are the ground where city dwellers are nourished by healing earth connections, cairns not on mountain sides, but waymarkers for redeemed city space' (2002). Part of a spirituality for the city, then, involves a recognition of this exilic condition and a readiness to connect with the land wherever possible.

Struggle

William Blake's poem 'London' sees the city as a place of oppression, enslavement, whose streets are roads to fortune for only a few and hard surfaces to trudge through or even sleep on for many. He wrote:

I wander thro' each charter'd street,
Near where the charter'd Thames does flow
And mark in every face I meet
Marks of weakness, marks of woe.

'Charter'd' means 'bought up', 'claimed' 'commercially managed', and so the city is hard to access; it excludes you. Such a system scars the inhabitants and reduces them to lives with the 'mind-forged manacles' and vice of later lines in the poem. Life for many in the centre of the city is a struggle to survive. In the course of a year over 1,600 people sleep on Westminster's streets. Those on low incomes have multiple jobs. Paying the mortgage requires both parents to be employed. Children are raised by grandparents, whether in this country or overseas. There are many barely existing in the black economy, or in the modern equivalents of the slave trade. The wealth of the city depends on the low-paid worker rising before dawn to start work. Such voices are often not raised and are often hard to hear.

Ian McEwan's novel *Saturday* chronicles an affluent and contented man's sudden encounter with those who struggle. Set in the very streets where I live, it is a disturbing read! The Saturday in question is the day of the demonstration in 2003 against the then impending war on Iraq that disrupts his routine. The shouts of struggle disturb his hard-won comfort. A minor car accident brings him into contact with a menace that invades his family, a disturbed individual whom McEwan describes as an 'unpickable knot of affliction'. The novel explores the different kinds of stories that the streets can tell and suggests that in the collision of those stories lies life, even if it comes with its partner death. The city is multi-layered and people can engage with the largeness of its life through listening to those who struggle.

For the Christian, the prayer is for the Kingdom of God, that God's will 'be done on earth as it is in heaven' (Matt. 6.10). It is in struggling for this that people of faith not only come alive but can come together. London Citizens is an increasingly influential community organization. It brings together people and organizations, those of faith and those of no faith. Christians and Muslims and atheists find themselves working together – on simple matters like the local provision of rubbish bins, or on larger issues like a living wage (as opposed to a minimum wage). A key approach involves cutting through the layers and bringing together stories: the Chairman of Barclays being brought face to face with the cleaner who comes in before dawn to make his room ready for the day and earns in a year less than the executive earns in a day. The current campaign centres on refugees and illegals in the city, promoting an amnesty for those in Britain for longer than four years: turning 'Strangers into Citizens'. Of course faith organizations are uniquely placed to hear these different stories because they comprise people from across the wealth spectrum and from across the world.

The good of the city needs to be fought for or else the powerful will just divide it up and sell it off to the highest bidder. Such struggles bring new companions and insights into the God who asks us, simply, to 'do justly, and to love mercy' (Mic. 6.8 AV). It is significant that the leading agencies working for the homeless in my city are church-based. They struggle against a local authority that wishes to remove those sleeping rough, not least because the homeless are seen as bad for the tourist trade. But getting alongside those sleeping rough is to see the city differ-ently, to hear new stories. To challenge the city with a vision of inclusion and care energizes the spirit.

Imagination

Throughout this exploration of spirituality in the centre of the city I have quoted from the arts. These offer words or images that connect to the largeness of life and nourish the city dweller. Major art galleries wel-come thousands, quietly walking through or sitting and reflecting in a manner close to prayer. Such galleries hold blockbuster exhibitions that many thousands more jostle to visit. The musical life of a city is deep. Add together formal concerts, gigs in clubs or pubs, the profusion of choirs or amateur ensembles and the street buskers and it is a formidable feature of city life. Some places attract the status of secular cathedrals: the Turbine Hall in Tate Modern or the Olivier Stage at the National Theatre. Here people are challenged, invited to reflect on themselves and what living today means through speech and image, the secular word and sacrament.

Walter Brueggemann's perceptive analyses (1993) of contemporary life speak of the necessity to 'fund the imagination', and this so often comes through experience and engagement with a larger canvas for life. The pulsating pleasure of an Arctic Monkeys gig, the thrilling transport of the Verdi *Requiem*, spending time in the company of a Velasquez, even the defiant singing of 'I'm for ever blowin' bubbles' at Upton Park are part of a city centre spirituality. These energize, give life, create story, fund imagination. Travel on the underground and you will invariably see people, perhaps seated, but as likely standing and strap-hanging, reading a book: and often not a trivial page-turner but a work of some seriousness. The imagination is being touched, nurtured.

Brueggemann considers the central task of the Church today, a Church in many senses in exile, apart from the mainstream of a secular society, to fund the imagination of those it encounters. He urges engagement with Scripture, an exploration of the vision that sustained and energized people of distant generations but which contains fundamental truths for today. He asks for poetry and paradox, for depth and discernment to mark Christian spirituality. While the exuberance of a fine music group and worship songs may both attract the outsider and energize the commitment of the regular, Brueggemann's thesis suggests that it will not provide sufficient depth or sense of the mystery of God to sustain Christian spirituality in the city. He suggests there is a deep hunger for words beyond the sound-bite, for preaching that is deep and courageous, for encounters with the numinous in silence or in art. The marketing skills of Alpha and the like tell of success and numbers. But Brompton Oratory, next door to Holy Trinity Brompton, attracts higher numbers with its Latin and other masses. Cathedrals are bursting with visitors. In Advent 2006 Lucy Winkett, Canon Precentor at St Paul's Cathedral, collaborated with Peter Moreton in a series of Evensongs that focused on jazz and the blues, with reflections on the songs. It attracted hundreds – simply by word of mouth.

The spirituality of the public square

I can walk to Trafalgar Square in 15 minutes. If any place is the heart of this sprawling city, Trafalgar Square can lay claim to it. Crowds flow through it, and demonstrations fill it. Enlarged through the northern side being pedestrianized, it is a meeting place for Londoner and for tourist. From it the eye stretches down to Westminster, or to Hungerford Bridge, or to Buckingham Palace. At the centre, newly restored, is

Nelson's column with the lions and the fountains below. Along with other statues it reminds us of an imperial past, of the British stamp upon the world. The buildings around it remind us of struggle, most notably South Africa House, scene of vigils during the apartheid years, or walls echoing to the shouts of protesters against nuclear weapons or the Poll Tax. On its northern side sits the National Gallery, a place for refreshing the spirit in stillness and safety. To the east we find St Martin-in-the-Fields, the name a reminder of a rural past from which it is now separated, its renovations uncovering a Roman Christian sarcophagus, astounding archaeologists, as it revealed a Christian burial site here centuries earlier than previously thought. Now St Martin's hosts concerts – the joke is that the walls are so impregnated that if they are knocked down they would release the strains of *The Four Seasons* – and follows in the footsteps of its Patron through care to beggars and the homeless. And, on one corner of the square, the vacant plinth. This has housed Mark Wallinger's *Ecce Homo*, a life-size figure of Christ fragile and small against the bluster and pace of the city but persistently asking the question, 'What is truth?' Recently it has been graced by Mark Quinn's *Alison Lapper Pregnant*, the stunning challenge of a disabled woman in white marble inviting us to view the world through her eyes and to recognize her story and right to be heard. She looked slightly away from the square, as if her eyes were fixed on something more important, as if her courage and her vision lifted her to a new way of seeing. Here is the city in its public square – here is the spirit engaging with the largeness of life, seeking the truth of its own nature – and here is the dialogue between the human spirit and the divine. The Spirit of God invites us to enter the conversation.

Bibliography

Bauman, Zygmunt, 2005, *Liquid Life*, Cambridge, Polity Press.
Brueggemann, Walter, 1993, *Texts Under Negotiation: The Bible in Postmodern Imagination*, Minneapolis, Fortress Press.
Grey, Mary, 2002, 'Even the Very Stones Cry Out! An Eco-spirituality for City Dweller', unpubl. Hugh Price Hughes Lecture, Hinde Street Methodist Church.
Guardian, supplement, 21 January 2005.
Hill, Tobias, 2006, *Nocturne in Chrome and Sunset Yellow*, Cambridge, Salt Press. (Quoted with permission.)
Inge, John, 2003, *A Christian Theology of Place*, Aldershot, Ashgate.
McEwan, Ian, 2005, *Saturday*, London, Random House.

Putnam, Robert, 2001, *Bowling Alone*, New York, Touchstone.

Rogers, Richard, 1995, *Sustainable City*, Reith Lectures, BBC, London.

Sandercock, Leonie, 2003, *Cosmopolis II: Mongrel Cities*, London, Continuum.

Sheldrake, Philip, 2001, *Spaces for the Sacred: Place, Memory, Identity*, London, SCM.

Tearfund, 2007, *Religion and Church in the UK*, London, Tearfund.

Walker, Andrew (ed.), 2005, *Spirituality in the City*, London, SPCK.

Williams, Rowan, 2002, *What Kind of Church?*, unpubl. Hugh Price Hughes Lecture, Hinde Street Methodist Church.

PART III

Witness and Service in and for the City

Introduction: Congregation and Ministry

This third section is a series of snapshots of different aspects of ministry and mission in the city centre. It would be impossible to cover the immense diversity and richness of the Church's presence and activity. One of the impressions that has come strongly out of the whole project, through meeting people and listening to stories from across the country, not least in the conference in Cardiff in 2005, has been the sheer range and energy of what is being done, often with few resources and against considerable odds. All that can be done here, in this part of the book, is to take up some key themes and to see how, in particular places, they have been worked on. Inevitably the contributions impinge on each other, but thereby they illuminate each other. And there are other concerns, mentioned in passing, that would deserve greater attention. The contributions stand in their own right. However, what this Introduction will do is to pick up on a major theme that runs through the various chapters but which might well deserve consolidating, namely the place and nature of the Christian congregation in the city centre.

Peter Macdonald sets the scene from Edinburgh (chapter 7). A primary concern for the churches has been the impact of the changes in the city centre on congregations, both the old parishes and chapels and the special plants of the industrial city, such as the Methodist Central Halls. These churches, until the middle of the twentieth century, were able to sustain the Victorian tradition of the 'preaching station', which was at the heart of their traditional congregational life. For a student in London in the 1950s, it was possible to choose between going to hear Leslie Weatherhead at the rebuilt City Temple, W. E. Sangster at Westminster Central Hall, Donald Soper at the West London Mission in Kingsway, or Martyn Lloyd Jones at Westminster Chapel. But even then the pattern was dissolving as membership drifted outward. So the emphasis has tended to change, stressing instead the other aspect of their work, social service and weekday activities when people were in the city. The story of St George's West, Edinburgh, will therefore be familiar in its own way for many who have trodden the same path.

The city centre congregations, however, will not go away, even if there are fewer of them and redundant churches have found alternative avenues of service. What, then, are the nature and function of a city centre congregation that differentiate it from its suburban or rural counterpart? There are no model solutions. Each situation is unique. Nevertheless there are a number of themes that are relevant. They can, perhaps, be summarized by saying that it is a matter of recovering a tradition that has always been there and remoulding it for the new circumstances.

First, there can be a tension, especially if it is expected that all the usual marks of the dominant pattern of the suburban congregation be present. This can divert the energy needed for the wider community ministry and even end up with a split between the two sets of activities. A church in a smaller urban context may be able to work creatively with this tension, but where the congregation is scattered across the city and perhaps the region a normal pastoral ministry is next to impossible. In any case it is important to have clear priorities. Howard Williams, when he first went to Bloomsbury Central Baptist Church, insisted that the congregation accept that it was there primarily to serve its ministry in the West End of London. It took several years, but when accepted it was found to be invigorating and liberating. The church's reason for being there was to welcome the stranger.

This leads to the second mark of a city centre congregation. The stranger is always present. They have taken the bold step to come in, perhaps by chance, perhaps because they were looking for familiar ground. These are people staying in the city for a few days or even a few years and who will then pass on: the student or tourist, businessman or professional. Many may be from overseas, seeking welcoming faces in an unknown land. One minister reckoned that a third of his congregation changed every service. The stalwarts were thus a small proportion of the congregation. Their openness, therefore, was essential. It demanded what he called 'instant fellowship'. This is the 'jet age' and the city centre church is part of the global network, a place where it is possible to find refreshment on life's mad journey.

Nor, third, has the large eclectic congregation of former years totally disappeared. It is alive and well, among others, in the cathedrals, which report large numbers of worshippers. There is also another, more obviously postmodern, entrepreneurial phenomenon. Charismatic leaders, wired up to the internet, often with Pentecostal roots, can gather large crowds, mostly of young adults, for various forms of experiential pop worship. Elaborately staged, these may meet in theatres or cinemas or public halls, moving on as needs must drive. Both these patterns, in their own way, appeal to those who seek 'faith without belonging', grateful for anonymity and cherry picking in their beliefs. The evangelistic and pastoral problem is how to make disciples and build up fellowship.

A similar issue, fourth, is posed by the phenomenon discussed by Ben Edson (chapter 8) and hinted at by Barbara Glasson and John Bradbury (chapter 9). New Expressions is an initiative sponsored by the Church of England and the Methodists to stimulate and support the growing desire for alternative patterns of Christian worship and belonging. At the same time there are often new independent or sponsored groups, usually called 'emerging Church', endeavouring to work out models of contemporary discipleship. These are often fragile and sometimes ephemeral, though it is clear that some will go on to establish themselves. They tend to form around particular shared social or cultural activities, such as professional or leisure interests.

This clearly relates to the problem of making contact with the new city centre dwellers, living behind their secure entrances and independent lifestyles (Willis and Simmonds, chapter 11). Such blocks of apartments cannot be treated like new housing estates, where residents at least meet in the street and have common domiciliary interests. The city dweller is only readily accessible through his or her work or leisure interests.

Fifth, the city centre and the churches situated there are at the hub of the city region. Jonathan Meyrick (chapter 13) explores this in relation to his experience in cathedral ministry. Churches in such a position, which must include major city centre parish churches and Nonconformist churches as well as cathedrals, are able, according to circumstances, to exercise a regional ministry. There is, however, another dimension. It is possible to provide at the centre specialized resources and activities that would not be viable in the local parish or district. Some of these can be dependent on skilled professional competence, such as a counselling centre. This was the vision of Bill Kyle who set up the Westminster Pastoral Foundation. Across the country there are other counselling centres affiliated to the Association of Christian Counsellors. Or it may be a specialized resource, such as an educational programme, whether specifically for training various levels of ministry or for what is called 'education for discipleship'. Two examples are the Cardiff Adult Education Centre and the cathedral library in St Albans. Or there may by a special pastoral or cultural need. The Catholic

Church is currently having to provide ministry to those migrating into the UK from countries of Catholic Europe, such as Poland. In Cardiff, one of the functions of a number of the city centre churches is to serve the Welsh-speaking community of the city region.

Sixth, the city centre congregation is a conduit. It is responsible to both the city and the Church to interpret the one to the other. The project that lies behind this book presupposes that the city centre is a vital arena for the Church's mission and ministry. Cate Adams (chapter 10) refers to her task, as City Centre Chaplain, to be a link between the world of work and the Church. There are many across Britain who are engaged in such city centre sector ministries: to the retail trade, to the world of business, in the city hall, to entertainment and among the night-time youth culture. It is often the city centre congregation that provides their Christian base. They need to feel that their fellow Christians both support and understand their work and that they can be relied on to explain and commend their ministry in the wider Church. At the same time members of the Church are in the city, alongside the chaplains, representing the gospel to those around.

Moreover the city centre congregation and its leadership are often those with whom the council and its officers have most immediate contact, placed as they are at a key point in the urban pattern. This places considerable responsibility on them as representatives of the Church as a whole. It is a pity, as too often happens, that the only impression given is of a group of people simply concerned with their own prestige and needs. The Church needs to show that it is there, in critical solidarity, for the city as such, offering its own particular and yet valuable slant. This will best be done ecumenically, or perhaps through urban chaplaincy structures. It is easier for the authorities to deal with a co-ordinated structure. In these days there is also the added dimension of working with other faith groups. Mary Cotes (chapter 12) tells the remarkable story of Milton Keynes which, from its planning stage as a new town, was a major ecumenical project. Other stories could be told, large and small, of similar endeavours.

Lastly, worshipping communities occupy buildings. These are often historic or architecturally significant. They can also be expensive to maintain. But they also signal a presence and offer a place in the city which is apart. In the bustle and frenetic pressure there is an alternative reality that must not be forgotten. A church building can provide an oasis for the heart and mind, a still point in the storm of existence. This is hinted at in many places, not least in Leslie Griffiths' overview of

London (chapter 14). Such a gift can take many forms, from the formal reflective time of worship to alternative patterns of meditation, from music and art to silence. With it can go simple pastoral provision: the open welcome, simple tools for meditation such as candles and images, the listening ear, suitable and accessible printed material and the opportunity to request prayer. For all this the church is steward, keeping the gates of the Temple open for all who want to come in. After all it was Jesus that declared, 'My house shall be called a house of prayer for all the nations' (Mark 11.17). Rooted in such provision can arise the priestly act of intercession for the city, the place where the incarnate, crucified and risen Lord dwells with his people.

7

The 'Tall-steeple' Church: Adapting for the City Centre

PETER MACDONALD

Our heritage is our power

St George's West is a dying church, its elderly membership a remnant of what was once a leading Church of Scotland congregation renowned as one of the great preaching stations of Presbyterianism. St George's West is a product of the Disruption of 1843, which divided the Church of Scotland over the issue of who appointed parish ministers to a charge. Under the Patronage Act of 1712 such appointments were the right of landed proprietors, but the right of call through Presbytery i.e., through the appointed courts of the Church, was a fundamental tenet of the Scottish Reformation and, with increasing democratic reform within society, opposition to patronage grew within the Church of Scotland. The issue finally came to a head in 1843, when the Westminster Parliament refused to repeal the Patronage Act and to support the Church's 'Claim of Right' to spiritual independence. Several hundred ministers and elders marched out of the General Assembly of the Church of Scotland to form 'The Church of Scotland – Free'. On Sunday 14 May 1843 the minister, Robert Candlish, and a sizeable section of the congregation walked out of the old St George's Church, which still stands on Charlotte Square. They marched out penniless, leaving everything behind them, for conscience sake, except their Bibles and their principles (Seth, 1931, p. 23).

Free St George's thrived, its ministers renowned for their intellect and preaching, its membership comprising many members of the Edinburgh establishment. They were city people, members of the new professional middle class, leaders in their respective fields, who were shaping society and reshaping the Church. The urban church became unlike the rural one in that it became less 'laid on' by the state and the elites. Building a church and inculcating the gospel truths had to be undertaken by voluntary effort and Christian liberality. The effect was to turn the cities into the vibrant focus of aggressive Christianity: churches were no longer institutions of the state but 'free societies of believers' (Brown, 1997, p. 102).

Free St George's responded enthusiastically to the challenge, raising large sums for foreign and home mission. By 1931 membership exceeded 2,000. However, around this time it was noted by the minister, James Black, that increasing numbers of families were moving out of the parish to live in the growing suburbs. The combination of suburbanization, changes in social behaviour and the development of biblical criticism in the light of modern science resulted in the waning of evangelical zeal. Modernity and urbanization fuelled the growth of congregations like St George's, before beginning to hollow them out.

For several decades St George's West continued to attract large congregations drawn from all parts of the city and beyond. This was particularly true of students and other young people, eager to hear a gospel of hope for peacetime, who packed the church at Sunday evening services. The congregation responded by appointing youth ministers and developing a number of innovative projects for young people including one of the first coffee bars in the city. As one of our members recalls:

> Moving to Edinburgh to study, I gravitated towards St George's West, which, even then, had a reputation for reaching out in a much more open way. This manifested itself in the youth café concept but with a totally different approach to the one I had been used to, involving open discussion about matters of faith and relating it to the realities of the world around us. All this changed my whole outlook from a 'right or wrong' disciplinary approach to life to one which tries to focus on the guidance offered and demonstrated by Christ himself through reaching out to others in a non-judgemental manner.

As the 'modern' church par excellence, St George's West seemed to have the magic formula, but within a generation, in common with many congregations of its kind, it was drastically reduced; the congregation became an ageing remnant. Today only trace elements of Presbyterian culture remain in Scottish society. Edinburgh is a global city and amid the many voices and languages of the city there is one story, and that story is inclusive, tolerant and pluralist, or at least it tries to be. The old Christian story, as told by Presbyterians, puritans and priests, is perceived as exclusive, intolerant and sectarian. This cultural shift has shaped a new generation who have internalized the 'city story'. As the influence of the institutional Church has declined, so that generation has been free to reject prescribed religion and to explore the new inner territory of 'spirituality', a development which has been described as 'the massive subjective turn of modern culture' (Taylor in Heelas and Woodhead, 2005, p. 3) and explained as 'a turn away from "life-as" (life lived as a dutiful wife, father, husband, strong leader, self-made man etc.) to "subjective-life" (life lived in deep connection with unique experience of myself-in-relation)' (Heelas and Woodhead, 2005, p. 2).

Where once young people patiently queued to attend worship hanging on the every word of a middle-aged clergyman, today the aim for the young person is: 'not to defer to a higher authority but to have the courage to become one's own authority. Not to follow established paths but to forge one's own inner-directed, as subjective, life' (Heelas and Woodhead, 2005, p. 4).

As the pace of this cultural change quickened the Church, including liberal, socially engaged St George's West, fell out of step with the emerging culture and seemed to become increasingly detached and irrelevant. Instead of being a 'shaping agency' within society the Church became an 'agency of resistance', perceived as judgemental, old-fashioned and unconcerned about the contemporary search for authentic spirituality.

> The old apologetic was effective when it was helping nominal Christians, who assumed biblical authority, discover a vital faith. It has been losing its effectiveness as nominalism . . . gives way to secularism . . . as biblical authority is either questioned or unheard of rather than assumed. (McLaren, 2000, p. 75)

Responding to the changes in the city centre during the early 1970s, imaginative use was made of the building to create 'The Centre' in which a small staff team and an army of volunteers served refreshments and light lunches to office workers, shoppers and various others including a significant number of people recovering from alcohol and drug addictions, suffering from homelessness and mental health problems. Under the banner 'The Open Church', ministers and congregation provided pastoral care and assistance in times of crisis. It was for many needy people 'a place of acceptance . . . a place to find human contact, to be valued as an individual and where one can find peace away from the rush of the city' (St George's West Parish Profile).

In 1997 there was a ministerial vacancy at St George's West and, though initially deterred by the steep decline in membership, the congregational demographics and pessimistic financial projections, I could not resist the challenge, especially after reading the following in a history of the congregation:

> Any Church . . . that lives complacently upon the inheritance of accumulated experience we call its tradition is already dead; however rich and splendid its past may have been. But without that past and without a clear and just appreciation of its meaning for us, our future must be feeble, lacking in impetus and wavering in direction. (Seth, 1931, p. 7)

So I was inducted in April 1998 and from the beginning had the sense that the key to our future lay in understanding the past, particularly as St George's West had such an illustrious history. Around this time I came across a quotation which helped us to unlock our story: 'tradition is the preservation of arguments about what is true . . . it is the continuation of this same enquiry, together with evidence from our own times, that makes us members of a particular community of truth seeking' (West, 1995, p. 92).

Tradition, I realized, should be an inspiration and a guide. When we treat tradition as something static, rigid, unchanging, we betray the legacy of those who have gone before us. We honour them by making that tradition our own. Tradition is a living thing to be re-interpreted by each succeeding generation in the light of its context.

At St George's West we concluded that our tradition was one of acting on principle no matter the cost, of risk-taking and embracing change, of intellectual rigour and passionate faith. These were qualities which we would need as a congregation to address the challenges that faced us.

At my second meeting of the Kirk Session (because I would have been too scared to say it at my first) I asked the assembled elders, if they loved their church so much (and they clearly did), why it did not look cherished. The comment stung them, for they knew it to be true. Signs of neglect were all around. Flaky paintwork, faded notice boards, worn carpets, fraying curtains, a cold, dark basement and vaults full of junk, all said 'Our best years are behind us.' We had to see our building, our worship, our congregational life through the eyes of strangers. What were we saying to them? Something like this?

A building with grass growing from the gutters and with walls still damp from the last time it rained; last month's porch notices flapping in the wind fixed by a single rusty drawing pin to a rotting notice board; a stack of battered books, spines missing, announcing that God is prayed to in the language of the seventeenth century and sung to in language of the nineteenth; every inch of floor space taken up with an over supply of pews, and row upon row of choir stalls defended every Sunday by two blue-robed ladies with processional handbags; a liturgical focus stuck to a wall behind a fence in another room at the far eastern end of the building; brass plaques on everything that does not move; no room to swing a cat let alone a censer; all these things SPEAK. (Giles, 1999, p. 59)

Things were not quite that desperate, but somehow we had to believe that God still had work for us to do and that we could be part of what God was doing in the city centre with us or without us.

We sought to recover our calling in worship. Biblical stories of Abraham and Sarah, of Exodus and exile, of fishermen and the faithful followers in the early Church propelled us on our own journey of faith. Biblical themes of creation, liberation, reconciliation, conversion and resurrection convinced us that we are called to be change makers. Parables about mustard seeds, buried talents and poor but generous widows dared us to be risk takers for the sake of the Kingdom.

A Vision Statement, of sorts, had been drawn up and included in the Parish Profile produced during the search for a new minister.

To maintain, develop and extend the seven day mission and worship: to those living and/or working in this city centre parish; and to disadvantaged, homeless and passing by, taking advantage of a prominent city centre site to offer outreach and caring in different ways to meet the requirements of each group. To maintain and develop the worship and fellowship of the congregation, not only for itself but also to advance the work of The Open Church.

Though entitled 'Vision Statement', this remit did not envision a new approach for St George's West. Rather, it saw the future as a continuation of what had gone before, doing the same thing only harder. It was soon apparent that it did not take into account the profound changes happening in the city centre and within the congregation.

Edinburgh had become one of the most prosperous cities in Britain, second to none for quality of life. The financial sector in particular was experiencing a boom and new offices were being built around the city, including the West End, with derelict sites being transformed. The city's population of 430,000 was growing by 20,000 a year and property prices were booming. Edinburgh has had a long history of city centre living but, as elsewhere, was experiencing living in the heart of the city as an exciting, attractive lifestyle choice for students, young professionals and 'empty nesters'. Edinburgh had become a global city with increased ethnic and religious diversity, and a growing disparity between rich and poor. The desperate social need to which the congregation had admirably responded, with St Cuthbert's and St John's Episcopal Church, our partner churches at the West End, was now largely being met by statutory and voluntary agencies with expertise and resources located in other areas of the city.

The Vision Statement appeared to limit our ministry and mission to two groups; those who lived and worked in our parish and those disadvantaged groups who frequented the Centre. While parish boundaries may aid church administration they are meaningless when it comes to reaching out to people in the city and the nature of our future engagement with disadvantaged groups was unclear.

Our members (most of whom do not live within our parish boundaries) exercised, I came to realize, a 'dual citizenship'. They were concerned about the neighbourhoods in which they lived but also committed to maintain an ecumenical witness in the city centre. We believed that a city centre church in a prime location like ours, with its membership drawn from across the city and beyond, was in a unique position to reach out to people from increasingly varied backgrounds and circumstances by offering hospitality, care, opportunities for worship and a programme of activities seven days a week. It was also clear that, financially, an ageing and dwindling congregation could not sustain the work of 'The Open Church'. The work of the Centre and the use of the building would have to become income generating in order to maintain the presence of the worshipping community and to resource future development.

The building had tremendous potential, especially in its location on one of the city's main arterial routes, on a busy corner site. However, its potential was not being realized because much of the existing use was of low input and low impact. Buildings do speak. Neglected, empty churches may splutter a negative message but vibrant, well-maintained, well-used church buildings proclaim good news to their surrounding communities. I am not totally convinced that we do have too many church buildings in our towns and cities but I am sure we have too little imagination about how they might be used. As a recent report from the Commission on Urban Life and Faith found, 'our buildings may present us with opportunities for outreach: buildings owned and used by faith communities can form the basis for effective contributions to social capital, especially through providing opportunities for bridging and linking across boundaries' (*Faith as Social Capital*, 2007, p. 22).

The church is more than a building but it is surely negligent stewardship and discipleship not to recognize this wonderful resource. We decided to redevelop our building and to manage it strategically. Our plan was to spend around £500,000 on our building and then to give it away, thus providing city centre office space for voluntary sector organizations and conveniently located meeting rooms for a wide range of community groups. We hoped these tenant groups would act as 'multipliers'; their combined activities and client groups would transform our building into a busy hub, thus making it more attractive to others.

Our redevelopment plans began with the worship space though it was to be the last area completed. The worship space, especially, tells a lot about how a congregation views itself; how it understands the nature of the community of faith and what it believes about God. Re-ordering our worship space would be the key to the redevelopment of our whole building and the renewal of our congregational life, therefore it was a 'gospel issue not an architectural one' (Giles, 1999, p. 59).

Worship is what makes us distinctive as a faith community. It is central to our life and witness. The renewal of our congregational life is about more than the refurbishment of our building; that was the easy bit. It is about the transformation of every one of us, of what it means to belong to the Church of Jesus Christ and of how we understand our engagement in the world. Our worship would be the primary locus of that transformation and would, we hoped, be itself transformed in the process.

Our worship should be focused on God as revealed in the life of the man, Jesus of Nazareth. It should be incarnational not other-worldly. It should focus on discipleship not membership, love not guilt, blessing not judgement. We want our worship to be a celebration, both inspirational and aspirational, a sign of the open, inclusive, loving, generous, outward-looking, forward-thinking, dynamic and progressive community of faith that we long to be. Our conviction as a Christian community is that through worship we are changed, as another member testifies:

'I was once content to sit through the standard Reformed hymn-and-prayer-sandwich service where the preacher stepped up into the pulpit and delivered his sermon. This after all was church as I had known it since childhood, where the role of the congregation was to be the passive recipient of the word and sacrament. Although intended to be reassuringly authoritative, it does not speak to me any more. It is excluding of those who don't go along with what is said unquestioningly, and may have contributed to the decline in numbers. Depending on my mood, it either annoys me to death or simply leaves me cold.

'Worship which is inclusive, where there is openness, an encouragement to think and a freedom to question, and not the expectation of blind acceptance, is what strikes a chord with me now and I am certain has the potential to speak to those who are seekers in a way that the old way of doing things cannot now do.'

The purpose of the original design of the sanctuary was to ensure that as many people as possible could see and hear the preacher, who occupied not a pulpit but a grand preaching platform. Though a number of changes had taken place over the years, the layout was basically unchanged, with most of the congregation seated in pews, facing the front, seeing only the backs of the heads of other worshippers, primarily watching what was happening on the platform. This detracted from the worship of a small congregation scattered throughout a large auditorium. We needed to 're-pitch the tent' to reflect the kind of worshipping community we wished to become. Our guiding principles were community and participation, space and flexibility, light and colour, movement and beauty, Word and Sacrament.

The aim was to create a version of the medieval 'collegiate chapel' or Scottish 'hillside conventicle', with the worshipping community seated in refurbished and repositioned pews gathered around the communion table which occupied a central space. We lowered the chancel area and commissioned an 'ambo', or platform, from which worship would be led. We would abandon the old preaching platform pulpit. Using the same colour scheme throughout the building stressed the unity of our worship and work, of our Sunday and weekday activities. The new arrangement works very well by giving the desired flexibility, enhancing the sense of fellowship and highlighting the architectural beauty of the building.

'It is different,' commented one of our older members, 'but it is still St George's West.'

Success!

For non-liturgical reasons four sections of pews are removable to create an even larger central space, and three-phase electrical cabling was installed in the hope that we might become a venue for music and drama events, particularly during the Edinburgh International Festival Fringe held in the city each August. The result has exceeded our expectations. We have formed a long-term partnership with Assembly Theatre, one of the major promoters on the Fringe; welcomed over 150,000 people who have attended performances in our building in the past five years; hosted British comedians, American actors, Russian clowns, Japanese drummers, Zimbabwean dancers; and formed an ongoing relationship with the Soweto Gospel Choir. And in 2003 we were presented with an award for being 'the most welcoming venue on the Fringe'.

Some words of Henri Nouwen, which inspired the creation of 'The Open Church', continue to guide us:

> Hospitality is not to change people, but to offer them the space where change can take place. It is not to bring men and women over to our side, but to offer freedom not disturbed by dividing lines, where strangers can enter and discover themselves as created free: free to sing their own songs, speak their own languages, dance their own dances; free also to leave and follow their own vocations.
>
> Hospitality is not a subtle invitation to adopt the lifestyle of the host, but the gift of a chance for the guests to find their own. (Nouwen, 1975, p. 71)

When I first encountered St George's West and 'The Open Church', though worthy it seemed dated and paternalistic in its approach. The Centre too was showing its age, very 1970s, and had a 'hostel' feel that deterred many potential customers and did not honour those who already used the building. Great care, therefore, was taken when refurbishing the Centre and café, now called The Olive Tree, to broaden its appeal without excluding those who had been regular customers in the past, particularly the elderly, the disabled and those on low incomes. We sought to maintain the sense that this was a safe place for many disadvantaged people but also to promote St George's West as an open place for the sharing of ideas and gifts. We wanted to offer a creative space for people, Christian and non-Christian, searching for an authentic spirituality, to encounter one another, to tell their personal stories alongside the Christian story and those of other faith traditions, to discover places where those narratives weave together giving meaning and purpose, and so to find a story to live by.

A project was established in 2002 called 'Creative Space' to develop a programme of events and courses exploring creativity, spirituality and justice and the 'healthy' faith which, *Faithful Cities* suggests, 'enlarges the imagination . . . teaches and encourages the practice of holiness and wisdom . . . opens us to the new . . . deepens our sympathies' (2006, p. 84).

One of the first events, organized in partnership with the Edinburgh Justice and Peace Centre, was a series of public meetings about the treatment of asylum seekers in Scotland. Several hundred people attended over the three meetings and this has resulted in the development of a course in collaboration with the Edinburgh Inter-Faith Association and certificated by the City of Edinburgh Council as part of its Diversity training, entitled 'An Introduction to the Heart of the World's Faiths'. Other interfaith collaborations include public forums, for example on the Civil Registration of Unmarried Partnerships, and the formation of the Edinburgh Inter-faith Choir, which has performed in a number of religious and civic settings including the Scottish Parliament.

Partnership working has also been the key to a series of workshops exploring the relationship between the arts and spirituality, organized jointly with the Edinburgh International Centre for World Spiritualities and led by some of Scotland's best-known poets, playwrights, musicians and artists. The Make Poverty History campaign provided the opportunity to work with Christian Aid to offer a series of monthly educational events for young people. Since 2006 'Creative Space' has been a joint project with St John's Episcopal Church and the Festival of Spirituality and Peace.

Under the direction of my colleague Fiona Bennett, 'Creative Space' has made a distinctive contribution to the soul of the city, establishing strong links with other faith communities, with the arts and with a wide range of social and cultural groups. It is reaching out to increasing numbers of people who do not look to institutional religion to meet their spiritual needs.

This has been a wonderful learning experience for all of us, including Fiona who writes:

> Often in worship I found myself contorting my spirituality, perception and experience and that of the people around me, to fit into Christian doctrine which felt hollow.

St George's West has offered me opportunities to listen closely to the rich spirituality and experience of people of other faith traditions and none, to see how this could re-shape Christianity but more than this a community in which it is safe to ask questions.

As a result we have replaced the rather tired format of lunchtime prayers with a more holistic, 'subjective-life', programme of Pilates, Tai Chi and Christian meditation which is very well attended by office workers, café regulars and members of the congregation.

In the course of these adventures we made three largely symbolic gestures:

(1) We replaced the existing church logo featuring our tower, which suggested establishment, solidity and permanence, with a stylized scallop shell; a Christian symbol of pilgrimage, to emphasize the journey of faith, movement and provisionality.
(2) We referred to our worship space as the Sanctuary to draw attention to it as a safe space to be, a place of quiet and beauty, of prayer and meditation set back from the clamour and confusion of crowded city streets.
(3) On the suggestion of our signage designer, we made use of our glass entrance doors to offer 'welcome' in five languages, Arabic, English, Mandarin, Spanish and Swahili, to show that our hospitality was not restricted.

We have discovered how important such gestures can be. Those words of welcome, for example, were suggested before any of our user groups were in residence. How appropriate that they are in a building which hosts the Edinburgh Refugee Centre, a Palestinian Fairtrade Shop, and many multi-cultural and interfaith events. All that was needed was for us to show the sincerity of our words through our actions to enable lasting relationship and partnership to be formed. We have learned that if our hospitality is conditional it is not really sincere. For the exclusion of one group of people communicates to other marginalized groups that they might not be welcomed or acceptable either. If we claim to be an open, inclusive and progressive community of faith we must have the courage to practise what we preach and to preach what we practise. Thus we play our part in the global city. 'Cities must be seen as key sites, perhaps *the* key sites, for nurturing the tolerances, diasporic mixings and multi-cultural spaces that are needed to push fundamentalist fantasies of all sorts to the lunatic fringes where they belong' (Stephen Graham in *Faithful Cities*, 2006, p. 65).

Redeveloping our building as a community resource has, as one retired minister commented, 'put St George's West back on the map again'. It has raised our profile and presented countless opportunities for partnership working with our neighbouring churches and other faith traditions, with the arts community and the voluntary sector. It has brought us into contact with thousands of people from all backgrounds, all over the city and all over the world. It continues to change and challenge us as part of Christ's Church, yet we know we are one generation from extinction.

St George's West is a dying church. Thank God we believe in resurrection.

Bibliography

Brown, Callum G., 1997, *Religion and Society in Scotland since 1707*, Edinburgh, Edinburgh University Press.

Brown, Callum G., 2001, *The Death of Christian Britain*, London, Routledge.

Chesnut, Robert A., 2000, *Transforming the Mainline Church*, Phoenix, Geneva Press.

Chicago, Judy, 1979, *The Dinner Party: A Source of Our Heritage*, New York, Penguin.

Commission on Urban Faith and Life, 2006, *Faithful Cities*, www.culf.org.uk.

Commission on Urban Faith and Life, 2007, *Faith as Social Capital*, www.culf.org.uk.

Drane, John, 2000, *The McDonaldisation of the Church*, London, Darton, Longman & Todd.

Galloway, Kathy, 1995, *A Story to Live By*, London, SPCK.

Giles, Richard, 1999, *Re-pitching the Tent*, Norwich, Canterbury Press.

Heelas, Paul and Woodhead, Linda, 2005, *The Spiritual Revolution*, Oxford, Blackwell.

Maitland, Sara, 1995, *A Big-Enough God*, London, Mowbray.

McLaren, Brian, 2000, *The Church on the Other Side*, Grand Rapids, Zondervan.

Nathan, Max and Unwin, Chris, 2005, *City People*, London, Centreforcities.

Nouwen, Henri, 1975, *Reaching Out*, New York, Doubleday.

Putnam, Robert D., 2000, *Bowling Alone*, New York, Simon & Schuster.

Seth, George (ed.), 1931, *The Tradition of St George's West*, Edinburgh, Edinburgh Press.

West, Angela, 1995, *Deadly Innocence*, London, Mowbray.

www.stgeorgeswest.com.

www.creativespaceedinburgh.org.uk.

8

The 'Emerging Church' at the
Centre of the City

BEN EDSON

The 15th June 1996 was a day that changed Manchester city centre for ever. At 11:15am a massive explosion ripped through the heart of the city centre. The IRA's 3,300lb bomb (the biggest ever planted on the British mainland) brought devastation to the people, businesses and the built environment. Initial surveys showed that over 1,200 buildings had been damaged, over 1.2 million square metres. However, Manchester's entrepreneurial spirit was not to be beaten. After the initial shock and despair had calmed the opportunist Mancunian attitude emerged.

> This is a one-off opportunity to radically treat an area of the city that may have developed over time. There has never been . . . an opportunity to look at a big (central) chunk of a city and impose some real quality on it. It is normally a piecemeal process which is full of compromises because you've put up a certain building in certain places because it fits . . . It's given us a chance to overview . . . to really redesign the city centre as we think it should be. (Peck and Ward, 2002, p. 137)

The city centre was redesigned as a modern European regional centre. It was re-invented as a commercial, retail and cultural centre. However, perhaps most significantly, the city centre was to be repopulated. In 2002, central government's Urban Task Force cited Manchester as an example of city centre repopulation at its best (http://www.manchester. gov.uk/business /econfacts/property.htm, accessed 11 June 2005). The repopulation has been dramatic. Whereas in 1991 there were 966 residents in the city centre, the 2001 census recorded that the number had risen to 5,496, and in 2004 the Office of the Deputy Prime Minister had the number at over 15,000 (see Office of the Deputy Prime Minister, *Making It Happen*).

The demographic makeup of the residential community indicates that gentrification is taking place. Apparently it is the most expensive city centre outside London; penthouse apartments have been sold for £2 million; 40 per cent of people have at least a first degree; and, perhaps most significantly, 82 per cent are aged between 16 and 44 (see 2001 Census, National Statistic Office).

In the summer of 2001 the Anglican Diocese of Manchester responded to this dynamic situation by appointing a city centre missioner with a brief to explore alternative ways of being Church in Manchester city centre. Sanctus1 is what has emerged. The remainder of this chapter will tell this story, and some of the theological themes that have emerged will be identified.

However, before those themes are explored it is first helpful to set a broader ecclesiological context and differentiate between two terms that are often used in reference to Sanctus1: 'fresh expressions of Church' and 'emerging Church'. In 2004 the Church of England published the *Mission Shaped Church* report. The report coins a new term to describe some of the new forms of church that are emerging: 'fresh expressions of Church'.

A fresh expression is a form of church for our changing culture established primarily for the benefit of people who are not yet members of any church. It will come into being through principles of listening, service, incarnational mission and making disciples. It will have the potential to become a mature expression of church shaped by the gospel and the enduring marks of the church and for its cultural context (Croft, 2006).

Fresh Expressions is a national initiative established in 2004 by the Archbishops of Canterbury and York and the Methodist Conference to promote and encourage fresh expressions of Church.

The emerging Church is a more fluid, less tangible entity. It is a bottom-up movement of people re-imaging church and is hence harder to define and measure. Between the years 2000 and 2005 Ryan Bolger and Eddie Gibbs, missiologists from Fuller Seminary, California, conducted research into the emerging Church. They carried out detailed interviews and visited a number of emerging churches in the UK and USA; from that research they produced the following definition:

Emerging churches are communities of people that practice the way of Jesus within postmodern cultures. This definition encompasses the nine practices. Emerging churches (1) identify with the life of Jesus, (2) transform the secular realm, and (3) live highly communal lives. Because of these activities, they (4) welcome the stranger, (5) serve with generosity, (6) participate as producers, (7) create as created beings, (8) lead as a body, and (9) take part in spiritual activities. (Gibbs and Bolger, 2005, p. 45)

The emerging Church movement has a different relationship to culture from most other ecclesiological responses to the move, in our time, from modernity to postmodernity. The deep distinction between the emerging Church and the other ecclesiological responses lies in the model of contextual theology that it employs, which understands the need for theological understanding and practice to be rooted in contemporary social reality. Others, however, tend to retain a 'modernist' model, as summed up by Anglican mission priest Ian Mobsby:

It is arguable that many church planting and cell church projects in the late 1990s were examples of specifically conservative evangelical and theologically revivalist inherited churches, attuned more to a modernist culture, which did not attempt to engage with a postmodern social context . . . This form of theological engagement conforms to Niebuhr's 'Christ against culture', where culture is seen in a negative form, that it may distract people from encountering Christ. (Mobsby, 2006, p. 26).

Experiments such as the house church movement did, in fact, become more conservative and more removed from their secular social contexts. The model of contextual relevance that they employ is 'more akin to a "translation" model where the emphasis is on retaining a Christian identity (as handed down in the tradition) as more important than cultural identity' (Mobsby, 2006, p. 26). The emerging Church, however, is utilizing a synthetic or correlation model. This model listens to both the Christian tradition and the culture for basic patterns and structures. Through such listening a variety of themes for a local experimental theology emerge. A local experimental theology and ecclesiology can be constructed that recognize that an 'ongoing dialogue is taking place between text and context, a theology which, in the nature of the case, remains provisional' (Bosch, 1991, p. 427). This is to say, the aim is to construct a theology and an ecclesiology that are unique to the context and yet faithful to the historical tradition – an ancient–future theology.

Sanctus1 began as an ecclesiological conversation in a third-floor apartment in the city centre. The conversation was between myself as the newly appointed city centre missioner and a couple in their mid-twenties who had been living in the city centre for two years. During their time in the city centre the couple had visited all the local city centre churches and had not settled in any of them. This was for a number of reasons, but largely because the churches had very little to say about contemporary city centre living. The conversation evolved and the group agreed to meet weekly, to study the Bible, pray and share bread and wine. A name was decided, Sanctus1; a website was launched, www.sanctus1.co.uk; publicity was produced and Sanctus1 was born.

At this embryonic stage a strategic missiological decision needed to be taken regarding for whom Sanctus1 was seeking to be Church. Was it for the 15,000 city centre residents or was it for the 300,000 city centre users? Was Sanctus1 for the people who geographically lived in the hub of the city centre or the people who made up the city centre network? This was not a simple decision, particularly as Sanctus1 is part of the Church of England, a church organized geographically. In *The Information Age* Manuel Castells makes a very strong case that a new sociology has been formed and that the social structure that corresponds to this new sociology is the 'network society' (Castells, 1996).

In a network society the importance of place is secondary to the importance of flows. A network society does not replace neighbourhood but changes it. The current organization of the Church of England, with diocese and parishes, gives place greater importance than flows. This a problem for the Church in a society based on flows rather than on place. The parish church, previously the heart of the geographical community, loses its role as community becomes disconnected from the locality and 'to live in one place no longer means to live together, and living together no longer means living in the same place' (Beck, 2000, p. 74). The local is fragmenting, whereas the network is connecting. So belonging and identity increasingly relate to the networks to which one belongs, whether of work, interests, cultural preferences or even family, all of which may be dispersed. Community is therefore being formed around networks rather than localities, whereas the parish church is connected to the fragmented local rather than the connected network. However, there are a number of forms of church or Christian connecting emerging that embrace this move to a networked culture. These forms of churches try to form 'hubs' and 'nodes' within the network society. Hubs are defined by the network, but link it to specific places with specific social and cultural conditions, locations which those in the network recognize as meeting places. Nodes are the 'location[s] of strategically important functions that build a series of locality-based activities and organizations around the key functions of the network' (Castells, 1996, p. 413). The city centre is a hub for a number of networks. Therefore Sanctus1 sought to identify the network of which it was organically part. The network that became clear fairly quickly was the contemporary creative arts network. This was largely due to the influence of three of the founding members, who were an arts consultant, an architect and a gallery outreach worker.

In February 2002 Sanctus1 held their first publicized, open act of worship. It was in Manchester Cathedral, called Sanctum, and sought to create a sacred space at the heart of the city centre. It aimed to be a place to wonder at the vastness of God and mystery of God, using music, imagery, art and film from contemporary secular culture. For approximately two years this pattern continued: weekly midweek small group meetings for the core members and others, and monthly openly advertised, alternative worship services. The importance of these early few months cannot be overstated: during this time strong relationships were built that have sustained Sanctus1.

These two activities, the small midweek group and public worship, embody two of the foundational principles of Sanctus1. The small midweek group is fundamental to Sanctus1, and the first foundational principle, as it seeks to create community in the city centre of Manchester. One of the great paradoxes of contemporary society is that we live in closer proximity to more people than ever and yet many people are still lonely. The city centre reflects this paradox: there are more people who live in the city centre than at any time and yet 73 per cent (see 2001 Census, National Statistic Office) of these people live in single residency accommodation. It is often a solitary existence, and because of this solitude it has been suggested that society is crying out for community. 'Men and women look for groups to which they can belong, certainly and forever, in a world where all else is moving and shifting, in which nothing else is certain' (Hobsbawm and Kaye, 1995, p. 428). In the city centre Sanctus1 has sought to create community because, quite simply, this is where we believe people find meaning, identity and purpose. A key issue for the Church to wrestle with in contemporary society is the dominance of the individual rather than the community. One consequence of the increase in individual human freedom is that traditional human security provision has shrunk and anxiety has increased. Unemployment, uncertain old age prospects and the hazards of urban life are, among other things, the cause of this anxiety. As the individual becomes dominant in a liquefied society old securities fall away as the individual is freed. The shift in society towards the individual has created an imbalance and, as Bauman says, 'the communitarian gospel can count on a large audience-in-waiting' (Drane, 2000, p. 171; cf. Bauman, 2005).

Sanctus1 seeks to offer people meaning through the hermeneutic of community. Generally within culture we have observed that the hermeneutic of language – that is, the words we say and what we mean by them – is being challenged by the hermeneutic of the deed – that is, our actions and what implicit message our actions give. To build an incarnational Christian community was, therefore, not merely about language, but much more importantly about deed, and when deed is outworked in community a different hermeneutic emerges: a hermeneutic of community. A hermeneutic of community is an authentic community of people living with an alternative world-view. Within this context Christianity is providing the framework for the alternative world-view. This is an idea that was first articulated by Lesslie Newbigin who referred to the 'congregation as the hermeneutic of the Gospel':

> Jesus . . . did not write a book but formed a community. This community had at its heart the remembering and rehearsing of his words and deeds . . . it exists in him and for him. He is the centre of its life. Its character is given to it, when it is true to its nature, not by the character of its members but by his character. (1989, p. 222)

Sanctus1 has sought to offer a hermeneutic of community in the city centre of Manchester, a community within which people find meaning, identity and purpose. However, community is a notoriously slippery term so it is helpful to explore a number of different types of community. Imagined communities and ethical communities offer us useful insights.* However, it is arguable that in relation to emerging churches – and, for that matter, to established churches – at the heart of the city

---

* An imagined community, as defined by Benedict Anderson, is the sense of belonging to a wide socially constructed identity such as a nation (see Anderson, 1991). An ethical community is defined by its adherence to a particular set of norms, such as faith, or cultural identity (see Bauman, 2000).

centre there are two types of community that we see: cloakroom or carnival communities and alternative communities.

> Cloakroom communities need a spectacle which appeals to similar interests dormant in otherwise disparate individuals and so brings them all together for a stretch of time when other interests – those which divide them instead of uniting – are temporarily laid aside, put on a slow burner of silenced altogetherness. (Drane, 2000, p. 201)

Cloakroom or carnival communities, and both metaphors refer to intentional but casual gatherings, offer temporary respite from the struggles of everyday life as individuals withdraw into this temporary community. The theatre (with its cloakroom), football match or church can provide this temporary community, where a similar interest brings a disparate group of people together. There are a number of problems with such communities, and rather than creating social cohesion they, in fact, break it. Cloakroom communities scatter rather than condense the untapped energy of social impulses; they therefore contribute and perpetuate the solitude so often felt in contemporary society. Cloakroom communities are a symptom of the social disorder specific to contemporary society and this symptom can be manifest in faith communities. Referring to the widely known American experimental-style church, which encourages outsiders, 'seekers', to explore the possibility of faith in their own way, Drane suggests:

> The Willow Creek model of seeker services trades on individualism and privatisation of these people, by offering them a context in which they can explore Christian faith in the same way that they might seek out information on a business competitor, by attending trade promotions or presentations in an anonymous capacity, and then by retreating to the privacy of their own inner lives in order to deal with what they have learned. (2000, p. 81)

I suggest that this model of church has the potential to become the dominant model in a city centre context, as the majority of city centre users are individual consumers.

The second type of community, the alternative community, is identified by Walter Brueggemann. He suggests that the Old Testament alternative community of Moses is a way that the contemporary Church can engage critically with society. Brueggemann's central claim is that the

Church is called to be a prophetic critic of consumer society and that the task of the prophetic ministry within the Church is to ' nurture, nourish, and evoke a consciousness and perception alternative to the consciousness and perception of the dominant culture around us' (2001, p. 3).

The alternative community aims to dismantle the dominant social consciousness rather than conform to it. Brueggemann looks to the alternative community of Moses which had at its centre 'God's freedom as an alternative to the static imperial religion of order and triumph and a politics of justice and compassion as alternative to the imperial politics of oppression' (2001, p. 9). The community of Moses is not about freeing a small band of people from their oppressor, it is about establishing an alternative community that provides an alternative social order to that of oppression and exploitation. 'Yahweh makes possible and requires an alternative theology and an alternative sociology' (p. 9).

The alternative community is the antithesis of the cloakroom community: a community that is radically engaged with society, committed to justice and establishing an alternative consciousness. Sanctus1 seeks to offer such a hermeneutic of community through establishing an alternative community that seeks to challenge the dominant consciousness of consumerism that is manifest in the city centre.

The second foundational principle of Sanctus1 is worship that affirms that God is deeply embedded in contemporary culture; worship that aims to provide an encounter with the extraordinary through the ordinary. Church can easily become a place that increases the fragmentation felt by many people in contemporary society, a place out of touch with the real world, and a place that has nothing affirming to say to contemporary culture. The style of worship used by Sanctus1 – 'alternative worship' – is experiential worship that is authentically rooted in postmodern culture because central to it is an incarnational theology that roots Christ in the ordinary everyday. This incarnational theology of alternative worship can be contrasted with one of ecstasy. Ecstatic experiences in worship, and by that I mean on the whole charismatic worship, seek to transcend the physical domain through an encounter with the other. Roberts, however, writes that 'alternative worship relocates God back within the physical domain, so to experience God means to encounter him in and through the created things around – symbolically, iconically, sacramentally' (1999, p. 5).

With this incarnational approach, the use of popular culture in worship powerfully brings 'the real world' into the presence of God and enables God's presence to be discerned back in that 'real world'. Any notion of a split between sacred and secular is rejected. Groups are willing to use ideas, materials and forms from the secular world in worship. Implicit in this incarnational approach is a very positive theology of creation and its redemption. (Baker, 2000, p. 6)

After two years, during which the Sanctus1 community was faithfully meeting in their midweek group and worshipping together, numbers were gradually growing. Eventually it was felt that there were enough people to divide into two midweek groups rather than one. It was felt to be important to keep the midweek groups small to build relationships and community.

At this point we started to get involved in a number of missional activities in the city centre. An affirmation of the *missio Dei* – that centripetally God is present and active in the world drawing people to himself – has always been fundamental to Sanctus1. We started to promote and run a night called 'II' in one of the bars in the city centre. 'II' is a high quality night of electronica and creative media, where DJs and artists combine to produce a stunning display of contemporary music and electronic media. Artists, performers and DJs offer their time, skill and resources as a gift to the city centre community. There is no entrance fee and hospitality is extended to all. The combined strands of gift and hospitality fuse together to produce an environment within which people feel comfortable talking about their faith, their lack of faith and other related issues.

A key decision taken in the planning process was that there would be no evangelistic presentation. A traditional evangelistic event would have a presentation mid-way through the evening; but Sanctus1 members felt that this would alienate the people attending. The Christian content would instead be implicit, though there would be some Christian content in the visuals and Sanctus1 flyers would be scattered around the venue. This proved to be a good decision. On the first night of 'II' I spoke with a variety of people and observed a number of conversations, all of which confirmed to me that mission was taking place, not least simply through the *presence* of a caring Christian community. For a professional evangelist to give a presentation might not only alienate visitors but also threaten to draw attention away from Sanctus1 members as they shared their faith; they might merely be seen as giving support to the 'main speaker', thus disempowering their witness.

A second example is the stand that Sanctus1 has at Manchester's annual Mind Body Spirit fair. The Mind Body Spirit fair is a 'new age' gathering at which people explore spirituality. It is also both the place of spiritual consumerism and also a place of great hurt and searching, where people reach out to loved ones who have 'passed on' and where they come for a quick fix to life's problems. In this environment Sanctus1 offers gift and hospitality within a place of quiet meditative reflection. The space contains a number of spiritual installations to encourage people to explore spirituality from a Christian perspective. We offer foot massages to people who are exhausted after being on their feet all day and also offer prayer for healing. In a context of Reiki healers, psychic healers and a variety of other spiritual healers it seemed culturally appropriate to offer healing from a Christian perspective.

The stand does not sell anything, unlike many other stands. Everything is a gift. We are there to be servants to those around us, serving the Reiki healers who are tired out, helping those overwhelmed by the event, and being a listening ear to those in need. We are careful to ensure that by being at the event we are not selling out to consumeristic spirituality; rather, we explicitly seek to show that the God of grace is a free gift for all. The dual strand of gift and hospitality has been key in Sanctus1 missiology and this was further outworked in the development of a 'third place'.

The 'third place' was a phrase coined by the sociologist Ray Oldenburg. According to Oldenburg third places are the places where you go to develop friendships, to discuss issues and to interact with other people. They are the cafés, bars and coffee shops that are appearing all over the city centre. It is what Starbucks aspires to be. The first place is where we spend most of our time, home; the second place is where we spend the next amount of time, work; and then comes the third place, sometimes called the proximity place. Under Christendom the church was, perhaps, the third place for a majority of people. That is no longer the case and the church must seek either to discover the third places in its locality or to create one.

In partnership with the Methodists in the city centre we started a project called Nexus in October 2005. Nexus has a number of functions: one of the Sanctus1 groups meets there weekly; it is a night café, supported by City Centre Safe; a base for the city centre churches' street angels project; and it is also a venue for a number of art exhibitions. The Night Café opens between 12 midnight and 4am on Saturday, and provides a safe place for people after they have been to a pub or nightclub to wait for a taxi while enjoying a coffee. Bogus taxis and the crime associated with them are a major problem in the city centre so this is a way that we can practically serve the city centre community. The third place enables us to contribute to the good of the city and facilitates meaningful encounters with the people of the city centre.

The alternative worship and missional activity highlight the fact that Sanctus1 has a positive relationship with the city centre and contemporary culture. The Sanctus1 website says:

> We believe that God is already in the world and working in the world. We recognise God's indefinable presence in music, film, arts and other key areas of contemporary culture. We wish to affirm and enjoy the parts of our culture that give a voice to one of the many voices of God and challenge any areas that deafen the call of God and hence constrain human freedom.

The revised correlation method that has been identified by David Tracy and Don Browning provides the most accurate definition of the relationship that Sanctus1 has with contemporary culture. This method is influenced by Tillich's correlation method but develops it further in two ways (Tillich, 1959).

> Firstly, rather than seeing theology as a process of correlating questions raised by culture to answers raised by religious tradition, a revised correlation approach envisages a more complex conversation involving questions and answers from both culture and tradition . . .
>
> [And secondly] is the notion that contemporary culture can be a mediator of truth and goodness in its own right and that contemporary culture can generate insights that require us to challenge or revise ideas and practices that have been part of religious tradition. (Lynch, 2005, pp. 103–4)

This approach has been subconsciously adopted for some key reasons. First, there is a level of inclusivity within revised correlation theory. Manchester city centre manifests many characteristics of postmodernity, one such manifestation being a celebration of pluralism. Culture has been pluralistic for a long time; it is only now that we can celebrate that pluralism. Pluralism demands inclusivity: the Church is one place where Christ is revealed but Christ is also revealed, among other places, in contemporary urban culture. This inclusivity enables Sanctus1 to engage in hopeful dialogue with contemporary culture because we believe that Christ is revealed in it.

The second key reason is that a revised correlation theory recognizes the complexity of the relationship that the Church has with culture. Tillich's original correlation theory is a one-way street because for him culture poses the questions and religious traditions have the answers. A revised correlation theory recognizes that the process of both questioning and answering is more complex and that answers will be found in both the religious tradition and culture.

One example of the theory at work within Sanctus1 is the way we use contemporary film. Film is used to provide us with a fresh insight into our understanding of culture and faith. In a recent series we looked at the Old Testament prophetic book of Ecclesiastes and contemporary film. An evening would involve watching some film clips and reading sections from Ecclesiastes. This would be followed by a time of discussion that sought to find points of correlation between the two. Questions and answers were found in both the film and the text. As Christians, Sanctus1 affirms that the Bible has a great number of God's answers to life's questions within it, but we also say that some of God's answers are also revealed in contemporary culture. One does not exclude the other but enhances it.

Sanctus1 has recently (2007) celebrated its fifth birthday. Approximately 50 people now attend the three midweek groups and there are now two Sunday services. On the fourth Sunday of each month we have our alternative worship service; then, two years ago, we started Sanctus2nds. Sanctus2nds is an intergenerational service that aims to be accessible to people of all ages.

Sanctus1 has positive relationships with the wider Church and catholicity is of central importance. The Fresh Expressions initiative has increased the level of possible structural connectivity between Sanctus1 and the Anglican and Methodist churches and this structural connectivity is currently being explored. This is further enhanced by the fact that two members of the leadership team are Anglican and Methodist ministers. There is an Anglican/Methodist steering group that ensures that Sanctus1 remains firmly rooted within the two churches.

There have been some good times on the journey and there have been some difficult times. There are weeks when Sanctus1 feels very fragile, and weeks when we feel dynamic and groundbreaking. I am not sure what the future holds. We may continue in our current model; we may change. However, the place of the city centre will remain as a significant place for Sanctus1. It is the hub of our network; it is the place that unites an eclectic group of people.

Bibliography

Anderson, Benedict, 1991, *Imagined Communities*, London, Verso.

Baker, J., 2000, 'Alternative Worship and the Significance of Popular Culture', unpubl. paper.

Bauman, Zygmunt, 2000, *Liquid Modernity*, Cambridge, Polity Press.

Bauman, Zygmunt, 2005, *Liquid Life*, Cambridge, Polity Press.

Beck, U., 2000, *The Brave New World of Work*, Cambridge, Polity Press.

Bosch, David, 1991, *Transforming Mission: Paradigm Shifts in the Theology of Mission*, Maryknoll, Orbis.

Brewin, K., 2005, *The Complex Christ*, London, SPCK.

Brueggemann, Walter, 2001, *The Prophetic Imagination*, Minneapolis, Fortress Press.

Castells, M., 1996, *The Rise of the Network Society*, vol. 1, *The Information Age: Economy, Society and Culture*, Oxford, Blackwell.

Croft, S., 2006, 'Fresh Expressions of Church', unpubl. paper.

Drane, J., 2000, *The McDonaldisation of the Church*, London, Darton, Longman & Todd.

Gibbs, E. and Bolger, R., 2005, *Emerging Churches*, Grand Rapids, Baker.

Haslam, D., 1999, *Manchester England*, London, HarperCollins.

Hobsbawm, E. and Kaye, H., 1995, *The British Marxist Historian*, London, Palgrave.

Heelas, Paul and Woodhead, Linda, 2005, *The Spiritual Revolution*, Oxford, Blackwell.

Jamieson, A., 2002, *A Church-less Faith*, London, SPCK.

Johnston, R., 2004, *Useless Beauty*, Grand Rapids, Baker.

Lynch, G., 2005, *Understanding Theology and Popular Culture*, Oxford, Blackwell.

Lyon, D., 2002, *Jesus in Disneyland*, Cambridge, Polity Press.

Mission and Public Affairs Council, Church of England, 2004, *Mission Shaped Church*, London, Church House Publishing.

Mobsby, I., 2006, 'Emerging Churches and Fresh Expressions: Are They Authentically Anglican?', unpubl. paper.

Newbigin, L., 1989, *The Gospel in a Pluralist Society*, London, SPCK.

Office of the Deputy Prime Minister, n.d., *Making It Happen*, London, HMSO.

Partridge, C., 2004, *The Re-Enchantment of the West*, Edinburgh, T&T Clark.

Peck, J. and Ward, K., 2002, *City of Revolution*, Manchester, Manchester University Press.

Roberts, P., 1999, *Alternative Worship in the Church of England*, Cambridge, Grove.

Tillich, P., 1959, *Theology of Culture*, Oxford, Oxford University Press.

Ward, P., 2002, *Liquid Church*, Carlisle, Paternoster.

9

City Centre Culture and the Churches

BARBARA GLASSON AND JOHN BRADBURY

Not far from the beginning of the Scriptures it was imagined that God was involved with the city. These biblical accounts offer us a fascinating insight into the way cities are perceived, and the way cities and culture are inter-related. Within the canon of Scripture, the first time a city is mentioned is the city that Cain built after he had gone away from the Lord having committed the first murder (Gen. 4.16–17). The building of the first city, then, arises out of the context of heinous crime, and Cain's having been 'driven away from the soil'. Any reader of the *Liverpool Echo* will recognize immediately the kind of view of the culture of a city that the writer of this part of Genesis is offering. It is a view of the city as somehow 'fallen', a place of murder and crime. It offers a suggestion that the city is a place that stands in contrast to the rural idyll of life on 'the soil'.

Interestingly, however, that is not quite the whole story of the city that Cain built. For, tucked away in the list of the descendants of Cain (and presumably it is implied that they too lived in the city that he had built) comes Jubal, who 'was the ancestor of all those who play the lyre and pipe' (Gen. 4.21), and Tubal-cain, who 'made all kinds of bronze and iron tools'. Out of the context of the city built on crime emerges, too, the city of culture (or, perhaps we should say, high culture). The beginnings of music and architecture, building as an art form, are seen to emerge. So it is that, biblically speaking, from the outset of the canon, cities are double-edged places of being: murderous and artistic in equal measure.

Moving forward in Genesis somewhat, we see that the next city in the story has an equally troubled reputation; for it is the city of Babel. The story does not need much repeating: the people seek to build a great city with a tower to the heavens, but God intervenes. The story tells us that:

> The Lord came down to see the city and the tower, which mortals had built. And the Lord said, 'Look, they are one people, and they have all

one language; and this is only the beginning of what they will do; nothing that they propose to do will now be impossible for them. Come, let us go down, and confuse their language there, so that they will not understand one another's speech.' So the Lord scattered them abroad from there over the face of all the earth, and they left off building the city. (Gen. 11.5–8)

It is worthy of note that this story is often seen as a story of human sin, but we should be careful not to read into the story what is not there. God is certainly displeased, but there is no sense of 'rule-breaking' having gone on, or God punishing people for that. Rather, God does not like what God sees, and comes to a decision that it is not good that human beings should take so much power to themselves. What is revealed is a divine decision for diversity. God does not want human uniformity, rather a diversity of language with people spread out around the world. As language is one of the bed-rocks of culture, it becomes clear that monolithic cultures are not what God wills, but rather a cultural diversity.

If we turn briefly from these stories that appear so early to the other end of the canon, we see a somewhat different perception of a city again. This time, we see the vision of the 'holy city, the new Jerusalem, coming down out of heaven from God, prepared as a bride adorned for her husband' (Rev. 21.2). Here the city is no longer the place of human crime, or human attempts to take power to ourselves; rather, it is the city of God, a vision and a dream of God's intended future for humanity. The city is thus the place of redemption as much as the place of condemnation. Cities, then, become the focus for dreams and aspirations, they are concrete manifestations of what we believe to be good. No town-planner or architect sets out to create a hell-hole, but rather attempts to build something approaching the perfect environment for human thriving (however often this actually fails).

These passages are what will travel with us, as we explore Christian ministry in the city centre in twenty-first-century Britain. What they offer us is an insight into the multi-layered reality of the city. Cities actually contain many different cultures, and the Church ministers within such multiplicity. There is indeed the culture of the underside of city life, of crime and abuse and suffering. There is the high culture of musical and artistic life. There is the diversity of languages and cultures, competing for space with one another, or seeking to live with one another. There is the culture of human power and dominance that is embodied within city centres, as well as the images that cities attempt to create (or have forced upon them) which are indicators of aspirations, hopes and dreams.

We can, of course, only truly speak out of our own context, which is the city centre of Liverpool. Barbara is the Methodist superintendent here, appointed to be a minister to the city centre. Out of this ministry has emerged a church that gathers around the baking of bread. John has joined this journey in the last three years, a more wandering ministry not directly tied to any one community, but rather to the city centre as a whole. Holding a post that is an ecumenical appointment, John, as a United Reformed Church minister, might find himself presiding at a carol service in the parish church, or baking bread with the Methodists, or drinking beer in a pub with a group of philosophers! What is interesting is that both of these posts exist to offer ministry not primarily to a church community, but to a city. This is something that as ministers we revel in, but we also feel the tension that comes with this approach from those within the church establishment who find it impossible to conceive of ministry being outside of the confines of hymn books and green tea-cups. City centres and their culture, however, will not be so confined, so neither can the ministry we engage with here.

Liverpool is, as we write, preparing to be the European Capital of Culture in 2008. The banners proudly proclaiming this from the street-lamps will not let us forget, neither will the multitude of cranes and scaffolding that clutter the horizon. It is impossible for us to escape this 'culture' thing. What does it mean to be a church and exercise ministry in a culturally attentive way? How does culture relate to the gospel and the life of the church and ministry? What, particularly, are the issues that are live within the context of city centre ministry?

To a significant extent our brief examination of Scripture has set the agenda for us, and it is an agenda that resonates with our lived experience of ministry within Liverpool city centre. One can walk past the Philharmonic Hall where the Royal Liverpool Philharmonic Orchestra might be rehearsing under the baton of their new Russian chief conductor. One might chat with one of the *Big Issue* sellers, who might well tell you a joke that somehow only quite works in Liverpool. One can wander down the hill to the women's collective bookshop, filled with the wonderful, the weird and the wacky; the notices calling on people to resist the ever-increasing culture of surveillance and monitoring that pervades life in Britain. One might then go upstairs to the rooms the Methodist church rents from the women's collective, and bake bread with folk who have travelled in from the inner city or the suburbs, to be in 'their' city centre. There might be folk around the bread table who pop in from work in the financial district of 'their' city centre. There might be those for whom the streets of the city centre quite literally are 'their' home. Someone present might be going off to see a play at the Everyman that evening, 'their' theatre in 'their' city centre. Perhaps the police have organized a meeting in one of the church rooms as the establishment culture of Liverpool makes its presence felt. In all of this, one sees that there is no such thing as the 'culture of a city centre', and no such thing as a 'city centre person'. Rather, city centres are where cultures meet, collide and mingle. City centres belong to everyone and no one. City centre people are not any more or less those who live there, but rather all who are present there for whatever reason, including those who are there because the city centre offers anonymity.

How then, are we to make sense of this word, 'culture'? What does this have to do with either city centres, or the work of the church and ministry? In attempting to get to grips with what culture might mean in our city centres, Timothy Gorringe provides an engaging place to turn. He opens his work with the comment: 'Human beings, says Clifford Heertz in a famous image, are animals suspended in webs of significance they themselves have spun. "Culture" is the name for those webs.' (2004, p. 3). This image translates well to the complex set of cultural realities within which ministry takes place in a city centre. Of all of the aspects of the culture of a city centre that we have alluded to, it is perhaps in the interconnection of all of them that one begins to find the 'culture' of a place. Beyond this, however, Gorringe engages with the conceptions of 'high', 'popular' and 'folk' culture. These offer us a way into examining the experiences of Liverpool and its culture.

The Capital of Culture bid was won supposedly on the back of a wave of support from across the city. It was supposedly a grass-roots movement that brought it about. However, the reality does not feel so 'grass-roots', for two very particular reasons. The first is the massive building site that the city centre has become – which was in the stages of planning before the announcement was made of Liverpool's success in the bid to host 2008, and in truth does not rely at all on Capital of Culture money for its completion (even though 2008 rather sets a deadline now!). The other is the cultural programming that the culture company offers. Here the popular perception is that the emphasis is on what is termed 'high culture'. The Royal Liverpool Philharmonic Orchestra, the visits of Welsh National Opera, the exhibitions in the Walker Art Gallery, the

Tate Gallery and the various museums, and the productions at the various theatres are all things pointed to as the fruits of the Capital of Culture. Gorringe relates the view of Matthew Arnold as representative of the high culture tradition. He quotes Arnold as offering the definition that culture is 'a pursuit of our total perfection by means of getting to know, on all matters which most concern us, the best which has been thought and said in the world' (Gorringe, 2004, p. 49). There is a sense in which this correlates very strongly with the injunction in Matthew's Gospel: 'Be perfect, therefore, as your heavenly Father is perfect' (5.48). As such, high culture can be a mediator of God's desire for the best in all who are created in God's image.

Church culture too can be an expression of this high cultural pursuit. The worship in Liverpool's two cathedrals, or at Liverpool Parish Church at the Pier Head, might be expressly this, with the innate power and beauty of high church liturgy and superb music, being not only a theological reality of the worship of the church, but a bearer of high culture simultaneously. The work of university chaplains is equally the work of those participating in what would be considered the 'high art' culture of academic life. The distinctions, however, become undermined before one can take this line of thinking too far. For where is the dividing line between this high art culture and the popular or mass culture, the folk cultures that Gorringe also identifies?

One dramatic production that we saw recently at the Everyman was by a Liverpool writer. The play concerned the murder of a prostitute that had happened in Liverpool and the effect this had on the lives of many prostitutes and those surrounding them in the life of the city. The words of the play were all directly transcribed words of interviews with those involved. This is clearly 'high art' culture. We had paid what for many people would be a significant sum of money to see this production. It took place in the theatre where all the normal rituals and rules of social engagement apply. Within this, however, we were hearing the words and thoughts of real people in their struggles in daily life in Liverpool. The humour could not have come from anywhere else – this was a manifestation of what one might call 'folk culture', the localized expression of identity within a place. The barriers come tumbling down straight away. The 'web' is well identified in the story of one of our friends who took a party of young people from a support service to see this play. They had to be stopped from shouting out in the middle of the theatre, for their only previous experience of the theatre had been the pantomime! This kind of 'clash' of cultures, while not exclusively a reality of the city centre, is an everyday reality of city centre life and ministry. Any city centre practitioner, who truly knows and understands the context, will continue to be humorously and painfully attentive to such tensions.

Popular culture and mass culture equally carry a very specific place in the life of city centres. In Liverpool, anyone out on a Friday or Saturday night in the Mathew Street area will experience mass-produced culture in local packaging. Mathew Street is one of the main partying districts of the city centre, and the place where the Beatles phenomenon was born. The present day Cavern is a re-creation on a different site of the original that was demolished back in the 1970s. The pints of Stella flow, the music pumps, and a sight will greet you much the same as in any city in the western world: young people, wearing not very much, drinking, partying, having a great time, and participating in a cultural world created by global brand names of alcohol producers and record labels. Except, of course, you will find an attention placed on the music of the Beatles that suggests you are probably in Liverpool and nowhere else. Indeed, in the case of the Beatles, one finds that what might originally have been 'folk' music, originating in a localized expression of culture in Liverpool, becomes mass culture as it is exported and branded around the world, and becomes high culture as it is studied in university music departments and becomes the subject matter for museums and exhibitions.

Where is the Church in the midst of these cultural expressions of the life of the city? In reality, the answer is, mostly, 'not present'. It is true that the independent evangelical group that runs a café in Liverpool might well be out on the street handing out cups of coffee and tracts; the Rector of the parish church has been known to head out with the police on their rounds. Certainly members of churches (maybe from the city centre, maybe not), or perhaps even the ministers of churches, might well be in the midst of the crowd, pint-glass in hand, enjoying the atmosphere. The opportunities to be visibly present to the city, however, are immense.

The language of Liverpool is yet another way in which one cannot possibly box off different aspects of culture, neatly label them and attempt then to dictate the response that the Church might make. John Belcham notes concerning Liverpool's accent: 'As an accent (and much more), Scouse is a recently invented tradition, a cultural response to the city's decline' (2006, p. 33). Belcham notes the origin of 'Scouse' as an accent in the melting pot of immigrations which results in a 'mixture of

Welsh, Irish and catarrh' (p. 41), but also an origin that both reflects and manufactures the humour of Liverpool. Comedians helped cement the distinctive Scouse accent (p. 50), and Belcham describes well the distinctive use of language in Liverpool humour:

> By the end of the Second World War, humour was firmly established as Liverpool's response to its psychological, economic and structural problems. Verbal wit – a cultural form which, like football, seemingly extended across sectarian boundaries – spread beyond the bonding rituals of workplace and local pub to become the defining characteristic of the Scouse. Surreal word-play was highly prized, distinguishing Scouse humour from the slow-building, anecdotal, character-based northern monologue and the fast patter of cockney dialogue. (p. 51)

Beware the minister who has not quite caught the hang of this yet!

This particular form of the use of language, however, is a cultural expression that once again cannot simply be confined. It is the same love of language that inspires the now famous Mersey-Beat poets expressing their experiences of life in Liverpool 8. The language finds its way into a culture of poetry that infuses the life of the city. The Dead Good Poets society gathers for open mike sessions, where the poetry offers a sometimes biting critique of the social and economic realities of Liverpool life. Within the Methodist church, we have found that poetry and creative writing offer expression and development of the issues folk carry around with them and cultural outlet for the many questions of faith that are around. Again, is this the high art culture of poetry writing, or is it the expression of a folk culture of Liverpool's language? Does it, one wonders, matter?

What is beginning to emerge is a sense of the pattern of inter-related expressions of culture within a city centre, none of which can truly be fully separated from one another. We have not at all discussed yet the questions of differing national cultures as they emerge within the life of a city centre. Surprisingly, the city centre of Liverpool can feel rather exclusive. While Liverpool as a whole does not have a particularly large ethnic minority, one is very aware that in the city centre life seems almost exclusively white. One has to wonder whether there are forces at work within the city centre that make it an exclusive place to be. If so, what should the response of the churches actually be?

The direction we are moving in, with this brief account of the culture of one particular city, takes us inexorably in the direction of diversity,

God's decision for diversity that we noted in the account of the Tower of Babel. Being ministers in the city centre we encounter this wide range of diversity at every turn; but what does it mean for the churches to exist within such a context?

City centres offer a real challenge to all faith communities in terms of how they define themselves and how they shape themselves. Those traditions that have worked exclusively with a parochial model of the church struggle to understand the context of the city centre, as most of the people in a city centre at any one point in time actually reside in a parish somewhere else. The tendency seems to be within such traditions towards a practical expression of a much more gathered ecclesiology. The parish church in Liverpool is a prime example of a gathered Sunday congregation failing to fit the received parochial model. The challenge to the clergy in such a situation is to balance ministry to a gathered, and essentially suburban, congregation with the needs of life in the heart of a thriving business sector of the city centre. There will be an inevitable tension between the demands made upon clergy from Sunday worshippers, and the demands of the mission context which calls for a radically different presence within the life of the city during the week. Such tensions simply reflect the nature of being in a city centre, where there is the inevitable pull between being a regional hub and a place in its own right. Such tensions often get expressed in terms of who represents what. For instance, the church may need to ask itself whether it is for the regional church leader or the local church representative to represent the views of the Christians in the city centre. A church that is being effective will not worry unduly about such protocol, but it is a *realpolitik* of church life that city centre practitioners need to address.

Where churches operate with an explicitly gathered ecclesiology, there are other inherent problems that arise. In Liverpool city centre, the large Presbyterian church moved out to the suburbs in the 1930s, and the large Congregationalist preaching temple which used to gather its congregation from across the region closed in the 1950s. The Methodist Central Hall closed in the 1990s. The reality is, no one wanted to come to such places any more. The fact that such churches have closed confirms the perception that all too often working with a gathered ecclesiology tends to leave no space for a fundamental concern for the surrounding locality. Hence it was possible to move out without worrying too much. The people no longer gathered there – so what?! But this shrugging of shoulders and leaving of city centres has left a vacuum of Christian presence and concern.

Instead of working with the received understanding of the gathered church, our discussions of the culture of city centres suggests that such narrow ecclesiological definitions are destined to fail, because they are not attentive to the cultural reality and diversity of the context. We have noted the very complex set of inter-relationships that make up the culture of a city centre in all its multi-layered complexity. Only a church that is truly of that complexity and place stands any possibility of being relevant. All too often our visions of the church have been as the Tower of Babel – a human attempt to build a monolithic, mono-cultural edifice in the face of God's decision for diversity.

The history of the presence of the Church in Liverpool is telling, and possibly indicates a way forward. In the late 1970s the United Reformed Church became concerned that it was not present within the city centre. Its response was to gift a full-time minister to work in a roving kind of way and to engage with the life of the city centre in ways that the city demanded and the gifts of the individual called to that ministry allowed. Therefore, initially it was a post that was deeply involved in the social and political life of the city, offering ministry in the political sphere through the turbulent times of the Militant era in the 1980s. Subsequently, the post has moved in the direction of offering chaplaincy to those in the city centre through work in shops and stores – an attempt at the church being where people actually are. Throughout all of this, it was a post that was an ecumenical gift to those churches present within the city and to the City Centre Ecumenical Team, an organization that offered a genuine grass-roots defiance to the sectarianism Liverpool has suffered from for so long. The reality of twenty-first-century church life, however, is that the heavy ecumenical bureaucracies bequeathed to us cannot survive, and therefore there was some general rejoicing when the burdens of the Team were formally lifted from us recently, to allow a more personal, sleeker and more flexible form of ecumenical engagement. The chaplaincy work in stores now continues under the auspices of Mission in the Economy, formerly the Industrial Mission, who now operate a small team of lay chaplains in stores. The URC post continues, although whether in these days of aims, objectives and targets it will be able to be as flexible and responsive to the needs of the city unfortunately seems in doubt.

The Methodist story is, in its way, similar. After the closure of the Methodist Central Hall for a period of time the city centre circuit existed only in name, although a Methodist lay chaplain did work unpaid in the stores, under the auspices of the City Centre Ecumenical Team. In time, however, the vision was for the continuation of Methodist work in the city centre. A minister was appointed simply to be sent to the city centre to work out whether or not there was any real scope for a Methodist presence there. Barbara's conclusion was that there was indeed. The work began by Barbara simply spending a year walking around the city centre, getting to know people, getting to know the place. That process is vital – without it, anything that does happen will descend upon a place, not in reality emerge from it. Over time, in a gradual and fragile way, a community has emerged that gathers around the baking of bread (see Glasson, 2006b, pp. 35ff.). This activity, which began accidentally, has become a parable of life together. It draws in very diverse people, as anyone can join in, around a common and unhurried task, where conversations lead to deepening relations. The product is something that can be given as a gift, not least to those in need; but which is also eucharistic, taking us to the heart of the gospel as bread is shared around the table. What is so interesting is that what has emerged is not so much a single community as a series of interconnected and inter-related communities. There are those who gather to make bread on a Tuesday or a Thursday, there are those who gather on a Tuesday evening to discuss in a no-holds-barred kind of way stuff to do with faith. There is a group of lesbian, gay, bi-sexual and trans-gendered Christians, related to the wider community, now tended on behalf of that community by John, the URC minister. Another piece of work that has formed another small community within the larger whole is a group that meets on a Friday night. Much to John's great surprise, this group that has emerged is essentially for young people to bake bread and explore the big issues of life. There is a women's group that meets for worship. There was a piece of work initiated to provide a worker with survivors of sexual abuse, which has now grown up, become regional and is managed ecumenically. Alongside all of this are other groups that use the space the church has that are to a lesser or greater degree part of the wider community: a bereavement society, the Stop the War coalition, and so it goes on. The community is like the city, in reality a series of communities, which overlap, and mix and merge and separate again. It is a church that has incultrated the gospel in the culture of the city of Liverpool as it is at the moment, rather than attempting to impose a gospel inculturated in another time and in another place into today's Liverpool.

So, we begin to discern some threads that help us make sense of being present in Liverpool during this exploration of culture, regeneration and church reshaping. These are interweaving strands that bring an understanding of God's decision for diversity. We find ourselves longing for a move towards 'city of cultures' rather than the monolithic assumptions that seem to be presented through 'City of Culture'. We have come to see diversity to be God's gift both to the city and to the churches, and long to find creative ways to give space for such diversity to be celebrated. And this longing is not simply that the city itself be a healthy and human place, nor that the message of the churches might bring a faith perspective to the built environment, but rather that there can be some conversation around 'life in all its fullness' for the people of Liverpool. Diversity and life we see to be part of the message of hope for our city's long-term sustainability and flourishing.

What does this mean in practice for us? We have highlighted four areas: a commitment to listening, persevering in the face of 'short-termism', a celebration of diversity, and an eye to environmental sustainability.

First, we seek a commitment to sustained listening and reflecting upon the issues that the city presents each day. Through the bread community we strive to be particularly attentive to the voices that are suppressed by dominant cultures, the lost, the battered or the fearful within the thrust of city centre life. It is our hope to continue to open up spaces for such voices to be heard and for the subversive narratives to be expressed and bring about realistic and long-term change. As theological practitioners, it is our role to sustain a community where the biblical narratives are held alongside such lived experience and to continue the struggle to critique and challenge structures that are oppressive or forgetful.

Part of our pastoral concern within all this is for people who have been rendered silent by systems or circumstances. The visionary town planner Leonie Sandercock refers to the need to make space for stories, to keep memory alive and to imagine different stories within the city context: 'An effective story telling practice is perhaps that which is able to conscript readers or residents to suspend their habits of being and come out in the open and engage in dialogue with strangers' (Sandercock, 2003, p. 227). She refers to aboriginal 'songlines' in which important human experiences are marked within an invisible labyrinth of story and song. Although, not writing from a Christian perspective, Sandercock points to what we understand as the inherent liturgies of the city, the stories told and remembered, confessions heard and absolutions given from the conversations over coffee and the attention of care workers and counsellors. This attention to 'songlines' we understand to be part of the call of the city centre church, which is perhaps uniquely

placed to open up 'safe spaces' for the most vulnerable and marginalized. Our work in the bread church is just one small example of how this
attention to story can be brought about in the simple attention to voices
often silenced within dominant narratives marketed as 'culture'. We are
learning this particularly with our work alongside survivors of physical,
emotional and sexual abuse whose experience of being silenced is
painfully acute. We have been challenged to think about what makes a
safe space and how the management of boundaries, personal and structural, can give space for people to be heard in safety.

With this in mind we have been pushed forward from the political
agenda of 'inclusion' within which the power still remains with the
includers ('I will include you'), and are endeavouring to broaden our
understanding of diversity ('We will be together'). For us, this has been
a much tougher journey, always questioning the structures of power,
which we often unwittingly embody ourselves, and endeavouring to
give space to contradictory and challenging stories that the people of the
city present. This is always leading us to challenge our own assumptions
and prejudices and to be changed. In tangible and practical ways we are
learning the cost of the divine decision for diversity!

Second, there is an intention to persevere among the challenges that
the city and the Church present. This is not always easy. After eight
years in Liverpool city centre Barbara is now the longest-serving
member of the ecumenical clergy. During the writing of this chapter we
have learned that John will be moving to take up a teaching job in
Cambridge. Persevering means nagging our churches to continue city
centre work even when there are no obvious increases in conventional
church attendance that result. This is particularly problematic when
inner city and suburban churches may be without ministers. We believe
that churches are called to be counter-signs to the 'short-termism' that
pervades and undermines city life and funding, but it is costly for
denominations that are struggling to find personnel and cash simply to
keep going.

This need to persevere is particularly pertinent in the context of City
of Culture. As we have watched the landmarks of the city centre up-
rooted it is becoming increasingly easy to lose our bearings. The 'songlines' that Sandercock refers to seem to have been disrupted to such an
extent that we sometimes hear only discord. Scousers are known for
speaking their minds but the good-natured banter that characterizes
most exchanges can soon turn to grievance, anger or naked aggression.
This is not peculiar to Liverpool. Even Cain and Abel found jealousy led

to violence. But we are aware that the language of surveillance, safety and cleanliness often disenfranchises those who don't fit the acceptable 'norms' of the redevelopment agenda, and this is particularly pertinent within a city that has often felt excluded in national, political and regional agendas.

Writing as a lecturer in criminology from Liverpool University, Roy Coleman challenges the agenda of surveillance and social control that we witness as City of Culture plans unfold:

> The mushroom growth of partnerships aimed towards governing a range of local problems has highlighted the issue of locating the 'powerful' within often dense and informal alliances that are relatively closed off from public access and scrutiny. The democratic deficit within urban rule generally, and with CCTV in particular, is high, where millions are spent on glossy marketing and legitimation strategies that appeal to inclusive ideals of 'the city' or 'the people', united by circumscribed notions of 'civic pride' and 'civic duty'. (Coleman, 2004, p. 239)

This scrutiny of the powerful to which Coleman refers cannot be achieved by clergy who have not shown themselves attentive to the many cultures within city life. Faithfulness to the city is a theological imperative that needs visible and embodied commitment. Being committed to the city means 'hanging on in there' and being prepared to speak with an authentic voice that can both celebrate and critique the trends that the redevelopment agenda brings. This may be particularly pertinent in the area of funding.

It is easy enough to talk about 'God's choice for diversity' in a chapter of a book but not so easy on the pages of a funding form! Funders seek outcomes and these are usually measured by quantitative, measurable results that fit into the agenda of inclusion. Yet people are nuanced, muddled, contradictory, multi-faceted and different. And people are a long-term project. Sometimes seeking funding resembles a kind of professional begging in which the needs of the intended recipient are pleaded and brokered by those with enough wit or blag to fill out funding applications. We often feel close to the language of the 'deserving and the undeserving poor'. With six degrees between us it has to be admitted that we often struggle with and fail in the process! On the occasions when we have achieved a successful funding bid the paperwork in managing the proceeds has at times seemed to outweigh the benefit of the grant. In a recent award from a government scheme to build the capacity of faith communities much was achieved, but only for a duration of the grant, which was for one year only. Such struggles with short-term funding, insecurity and uncertainty are unhelpful in a city context that needs stability and with chaotic communities that are familiar with being abandoned.

Churches need practitioners who have earned their credentials and speak with the powerful having listened to the stories of the dispossessed. Cities are a long-term project and require a clear signal that the Church is here to stay.

Third, in our discovery of the many cultures of Liverpool we are committed to celebrating diversity. That is, we believe diversity is a biblical imperative and in saying so we acknowledge that it is in this forum that we are often most challenged. To engage with the dilemmas of difference is not a woolly-minded 'anything goes' kind of approach to faith and culture but, on the contrary, is a call to enter the hard places of disagreement, anger, fundamentalisms and political oppressions this presents. In all this we are provoked to face the face of 'the other' and find opportunities for honest dialogue.

This maybe, is one place where the city 'speaks back' to the Church. Working within a community that represents a diverse range of sexualities, ethnicities, educational abilities and ages it is often a struggle for us to return to our conventional church structures. We find churches riddled with angst about who they are going to bless and in doing so missing the blessings of diversity that we perceive in the city. This has put us both in wonderful and yet lonely places. We often feel more at home with the city communities who embrace us than with the sending churches that can view us as at best enigmas and at worst threats. We sense that sometimes we have no path of 'return' to conventional congregations and yet we long for them to experience the breaking in of the Kingdom as we do among the bread makers and struggling people of the city. There are occasions when we are destitute in finding the vocabulary to describe the experience of being church in the city centre and we can often locate ourselves on the margins with relation to our churches.

Fourth, we believe this celebration of diversity brings us to a challenge of the sustainability of the earth. A return, if you like to ecumenism – the flourishing of the whole inhabited world – freed from the angst of church unity.

It is particularly pertinent for John and Barbara to be together, not just as colleagues and friends but representing different ecclesiological perspectives on the city. And, of course, this is particularly important in a city such as Liverpool which has emerged, like Belfast and Glasgow, out of a context of sectarianism. Despite the stalwart work of Bishops Sheppard and Warlock we are still aware that the longstanding, inculturated misunderstandings and suspicions between Roman Catholic and Protestant communities lie just below the surface. It is not uncommon for John to be told 'I'm not a Christian, I'm a Catholic' or for Barbara to be addressed as 'Father'! We still endure the marches of the Orange Lodge, who continue to finish their display of patriotism by urinating at the steps of the former St Mary's Highfield Street – the only thing is, it is now a film studio. And many faith conversations are prone to begin, 'I was baptized a Catholic . . .' Fifty per cent of patients booking in at the hospital will describe themselves as RC, although fewer and fewer attend mass regularly and there is only one Roman Catholic church in the city centre, the Blessed Sacrament Shrine.

So, it is true to say, we struggle with ecumenism, even at its most basic. The URC and Methodist churches that we represent have minority status and the Church of England fights for second position. We have two enormous cathedrals that face each other at the ends of Hope Street which sometimes feel as if they cast an ecclesiological shadow over the rest of the city. We can sometimes feel as though we are struggling to be noticed, let alone heard, and we continue to believe that ecumenism is so much more than this. It is about the unity and diversity of the earth, and the people of the earth and the factions and fighting within and between denominations can distract from this core agenda.

Alberto Magnaghi, Professor of Land Use Planning at the University of Florence, explores the issue of 'territorialization' (2000) and uses it to bring the city back to the agenda of sustainability. This is such an apt discourse for Liverpool, where we see the territory of the city centre eroded by the pressures of globalization and capitalism. Our only green city centre space, Chevasse Park, has just been bulldozed to make way for the relocated John Lewis – albeit with the promise of a lawn on its roof!

It is significant that the rift between Cain and Abel was centred on the use of the land. Written at a time of establishment of rural nomadic communities in urban settlements it represents much of the sense of alienation between rural and urban contexts that we experience today. The debate concerning sustainable environments is not only pertinent to the current political agenda relating to climate change but also at the heart of a theological understanding of God's involvement with the whole earth. If we are to assert that there is a divine decision for diversity, then we need to see this in the context of *oikoumine* – the involvement of the creator with the whole earth, both urban and rural.

> The 'Metropolis form' – with its tendency to devour environmental, human and territorial resources in the processes of accelerating the urbanization it has induced – is one of the main culprits for the environmental degradation of the planet and the exponential growth of the 'new poverties' in the so-called 'periphery' of the world. (Magnaghi, 2000, p. 1)

It seems to be one of the sadnesses of Liverpool's redevelopment that it has not been possible to think ourselves into this agenda. Rather than attempting to 'catch up' with our already redeveloped rivals in Manchester and London, Liverpool seems to have lost an opportunity to claim its unique position on the coast of the north-west and to be different. God's option for diversity is manifest not only in the multifaced aspects of humanity but within the whole created order in which our diversity is also our hope for survival. Cities are different and need to be different and also need to connect with their particular setting and context. An urban environmental policy that connected with the fragility of the coastal region north of the city, with the forthcoming threat of rises in sea level, of the endangered species that we protect – red squirrels and natterjack toads – and of the environmental cost of long-haul traffic, could have given a sign to other cities that the urban and rural environments can no longer afford to be estranged brothers. As Magnaghi writes:

> There are signs of renaissance, however: new ways of regenerating the territory, or rather new fertile relationships between human settlements and the environment. In these 'reterritorializing' activities lie the seeds of authentic and lasting sustainable development which here I call 'local self-sustainable development'. They involve exploring how to re-establish 'virtuous relationships'; new alliances between nature and culture, and between culture and history. (2000, p. 1)

We long for such 'signs of renaissance' for Liverpool and the alliances that lead to virtuous relationships and the link between culture, nature and history. We believe that God would call this 'resurrection'.

In her book *Sacred Longings*, Mary Grey argues for us to reconnect with the earth as a satisfying, healing and joyful process.

Reconnecting with the earth means at the same time reconciliation with the earth, a journey of turning toward the earth in humility and repentance. In the process faith communities – at the moment mostly confined to individualistic notions of repentance – become true to their original vision and calling to live justly with creation. They begin to speak and live out truth from the heart. Through a sense of the preciousness of creation's giftedness, they receive the transformative possibilities of living more simply. Compassion for the entire eco-logical community becomes mobilised . . . Reconciliation is both a symbol of healed creation, a vision that enables and inspires action for a future state of being, and something that one already tastes and lives from now. (Grey, 2003, p. 209)

Mary Grey talks much of the loss of heart of our present culture, a thought we can resonate with easily in the context of Liverpool where we have, literally, had the heart bulldozed out of our city. Yet she also brings a sense of yearning and hope that there can be a process of recon-ciliation and reconstruction. God's choice for diversity goes forward to speak to us within this context. We continue to believe, as did the vision-ary author of Revelation, that within the city there is the possibility of realizing God's intended vision and dream for the future of humanity, even though such a vision is often dimmed by the forces of destruction and greed. And we hear the natural image spoken even into a utopian vision of this idealized city, where 'the leaves of the tree are for the healing of the nations' (Rev. 22.2).

And we also hear the author of Revelation speak of the river, with the tree of life bringing abundance to the city, and how there will no longer be 'a curse'. In these words do we hear the end of the exile of Cain and the re-integration of the urban and the rural? Maybe this is too much to dream. But we do note that in the final vision of the Bible there is a tree of life and we believe that faith gives the option for life – life for every-one. We intend to enjoy city life, with all its struggles and confusions. We want to imagine God present with us and continue to live the imagining, even if the river bank we inhabit at present is that of the Mersey rather than Zion.

Bibliography

Belcham, John, 2006, *Merseyside: Essays in Liverpool Exceptionalism*, Liverpool, Liverpool University Press.

Coleman, Roy, 2004, *Reclaiming the Streets: Surveillance, Social Control and the City*, Uffculme, Willan Publishing.

Glasson, Barbara, 2006a, *I Am Somewhere Else: Gospel Reflections from an Emerging Church*, London, Darton, Longman & Todd.

Glasson, Barbara, 2006b, *Mixed-up Blessing: A New Encounter with Being Church*, Peterborough, Inspire.

Gorringe, T. J., 2004, *Furthering Humanity, a Theology of Culture*, Aldershot, Ashgate.

Grey, Mary, 2003, *Sacred Longings*, London, SCM.

Magnaghi, Alberto, 2000, *The Urban Village*, Turin, Bollati Boringhieri.

Sandercock, Leonie, 2003, *Cosmopolis II: Mongrel Cities*, London, Continuum.

Sheppard, David and Warlock, Derek, 1989, *Better Together: Christian Partnership in a Hurt City*, Harmondsworth, Penguin.

10

Working in the City

CATE ADAMS

Introduction: Working in context

This chapter will focus on the experiences of the City Centre Chaplain in Scotland's third largest city. Aberdeen has a population of roughly 207,000 people, speaking 60 languages and professing 14 faiths (Aberdeen City Council, 2004, p. 6). In 2003 a new post was created with the help of all the major denominations in Aberdeen and was financed by the Episcopal, the United Reformed, the Church of Scotland, the Roman Catholic, and the Methodist Churches. This ensures that the chaplain works in an environment that is completely ecumenical. In the first instance it was set up primarily to look after the needs of the retail sector in the city, in particular one of the city's major shopping complexes. Over a relatively short period the chaplain's brief has been extended to cover two centres, which have themselves expanded to take in many of the adjacent premises and, more recently, the local city council offices. The chaplain, as with many of her colleagues in Industrial Mission, works on the premise of being available for people of all faiths and none.

While it is acknowledged that large sectors of the city's working community are not covered directly by this chaplaincy, many interests, like tourism and leisure, the police and judiciary, health care and the voluntary sector, work in close co-operation under the auspices of Aberdeen Futures, thereby contributing to the city's policy and decision-making process. The chaplain has contact with some of these processes through being involved with the City Centre Association, the Scottish Council for Development and Industry, etc. However, this chapter will mainly focus on the needs of individuals working primarily within the retail sector with some input from the public sector.

It is necessary to understand some of the prevalent economic and social issues in order to appreciate the difficulties that may be faced by those who work within the city centre.

Because of the oil and gas industry Aberdeen continues to be a city of buoyancy and economic growth. However, while the level of deprivation is clearly much lower, notably, than that of Glasgow and some parts of the Strathclyde area, 27 of the Scottish Index of Multiple Deprivation (2004) most deprived data zones are found in the city. This accounts for just over 2 per cent of such data zones in Scotland, and Aberdeen is thirteenth highest among Scotland's council areas. This affects some 20,000 people, around 10 per cent of the population of the city (Aberdeen City Council, 2005b, pp. 1, 2, 11) .

As with many cities, Aberdeen is going through immense change. There are currently around 56,000 square metres of retail space within the city. New development within the city, costing approximately £200 million, is expected to bring around the equivalent of 500 new full-time jobs in retail and 300 construction jobs. This will mean an increase in the retail space of another 18,000 square metres, as well as new homes and the encouragement of more visitors to the city. Steps are thus being taken to cut down on money leaking to Dundee and Inverness, which compete in the north of Scotland's economy, and to attempt to entice those who have changed their shopping habits to the virtual kind to return to the streets (Aberdeen City Council, 2005a, pp. 3, 7).

The needs of the people

While the needs of all individuals working in large organizations with complex organizational systems may be similar, there are some needs that are specific to retail, and where this is so this will be made clear. It is proposed to break this section into three categories: the physical, the emotional, and the spiritual, but this is in no way an exhaustive list and many issues will be relevant to more than one of these domains.

Physical needs

There are many physical aspects of working, particularly in the city centre, that affect the individuals who work there. First are the practicalities of getting in and out of work. Parking for the day within the city is extremely expensive, with daily parking charges around the centre ranging from £8 to £12. Bearing in mind that many workers are still on the minimum wage, this is a huge chunk out of their living expenses. Many employers in retail have changed part-time workers' contracts so they are working, perhaps, five four-hour shifts. This means, of course, that they do not have to be paid for breaks. A daily bus ticket is around £3. Thus a week's journeys are almost one day's shift.

Contracts in retail in general are a huge cause for concern. Zero or low-hour contracts are good for the company. They mean that if the shop is not busy then the staff can be sent home, but they can also be called in, and expected to come in, when it is busy. For the individual this means never knowing if or when you are going to be working and how much money you will have at the end of the week. Taking on more than one job to compensate for this has huge difficulties and often results in conflict if the person is required to go in to both jobs at the same time, perhaps resulting in the taking of 'sick time'. The cost of housing in the north east of Scotland means individuals need to have a regular wage coming in and it needs to be relatively high. Thus even shop managers are often struggling with more than one job in order to survive financially.

This leads to the next difficulty, which is around debt, as many struggle to maintain a lifestyle that they think they should have but not one they can necessarily afford. A buoyant nightlife in the city means many individuals work to party, often forgetting the bills at the end of the month. Also, for many in retail or the hospitality industry this is their first job ever, or is coupled with studying at university and being away from home for the first time. The stresses are immense. On more than one occasion the chaplain has taken in basic food shopping for someone who has run out of their grant cheque early. Around half of the employees who are over the age of 25 are working in the hospitality industry or the wholesale and retail sector and earn less than £6.50 per hour. Within these sectors two thirds of the workforce are women. More than a quarter of all the employees over the age of 25 who earn less than £6.50 per hour are public sector workers. Similarly, half of all part-time workers earn less than £6.50 per hour (Palmer, MacInnes and Kenway, 2006, p. 67). It is no wonder that problems of debt are high on the agenda of the chaplain's conversations.

There are other dimensions of this problem that should be noted. First, these issues of poverty require the relationships between the chaplain and those who are in the position to make a difference, such as management, to be solid and respected. This is essential if the chaplain is in any way to be able to communicate between different levels of organizations and businesses. For this to happen respect has to be earned. It also, second, makes the chaplain's link with the churches even more important, to highlight these conditions that affect the majority of the city's workforce.

There are ethical dilemmas faced in retail, too. For example, workers are encouraged to entice the public into taking out store cards, though many of the workers know the customer can't afford them. Yet staff performance is based on how many they sign up.

Lack of physical space in shops means many do not have anywhere for making tea or coffee, and toilet facilities often double as a stock room. As trading gets busier toward the Christmas and New Year festive season, staff are forced to work longer and longer hours with fewer or no breaks, so that their well-being appears to be neglected. Added to this, of course, is the strain of standing for up to eight hours a day, lifting heavy boxes, and being responsible for stock when there are some dubious customers around, especially when there is only one person to staff the shop floor.

Increased commercialism means staff being expected to work longer and longer hours. With staff shortages there is little room for time back. Often head offices request store changes at a day's notice and, with staff never knowing when checks from regional managers might take place, these are always met with panic. The culture within retail never appears to be very positive, with few staff hearing the words 'well done' from those in charge. Instead staff are often left demoralized and upset as their best never seems to be good enough. The chaplain, therefore, is often the morale booster in these situations, always looking for the positives.

There is an increased pressure on sales staff to sell even if the economic trend is of reduction in growth. There are also the effects of continuing changes in the ways in which we shop, such as shifting to e-shopping, downloading music, or using the large supermarkets as one-stop shops for clothing, books, music, electrical goods and newspapers as well as food. These pressures look only set to increase (www.statistics.gov.uk, 2006).

Perhaps the most disturbing concern for those who relate directly with the public, whether in retail, the public sector or the judiciary and so forth, is the amount of abuse they have to accept from those whom they are trying to serve. Many are receiving the minimum wage and struggling to survive, yet day in, day out they are subjected to verbal and, in some instances, physical abuse.

Another issue, especially in larger organizations, is the climate of constant change. Change often means a different job title, a different area to work in, being separated from one's colleagues and perhaps being unclear of one's job remit or chain of command. When this also means possible changes in the contract of employment, for whatever global reason, there is a real sense of uncertainty and disquiet. Motivation can be affected.

Emotional needs

One of the greatest areas of stress for the people working within the city centre is that of their relationships. For many the stress of trying to continue in a steady personal relationship is too much, with the devastation of infidelity by one or both partners being a common thread in conversations. If this is a spouse it often results in marriage difficulties or even divorce. This can lead to one or both parties having feelings of low self-worth and being at a total loss as to how to cope with the day-to-day business of their lives.

Relationships between managers and their workforce are also a major concern. There seems to be a huge culture of mistrust in our society and the commonplace assumption appears to be that it is weak to ask for help or assistance. Thus folk who are unable to manage staff or workloads are put into positions where they feel they have to cope. Malfunctioning coping practices often mean that reactions to those below them are curt at best.

For many of the young staff the anxieties concerning relationships are much more basic, with personal safety, sexual health and morality being more commonplace. A lot of the issues that arise are around bereavement and coming to terms with loss, especially when this has been the result of a sudden death, as from road traffic accidents, suicide, substance abuse and so forth. When a colleague in one of the shops died suddenly one of the staff remarked that 'when someone dies at home you come in to work and have the support of your colleagues but in some ways you come in to work to forget. When a work colleague dies, every day you are reminded that they are missing.' As many of us spend more of our waking hours at work than we do at home the loss is that much greater.

Many individuals are trying to cope not only with the stresses of holding down more than one job, which adds up to more than a full-time working week of 39 hours, but also with home life, often with children and/or dependent relatives. It is no wonder that when a child or relative becomes ill the cracks begin to show. The chaplain often visits the relatives of those who are unable to get time off work so as to put the worker's mind at ease, knowing that all is well at home and that there is someone there to offer support.

As within all walks of life it is no surprise that those who work in our city centre carry the scars of abuse around with them. Abuse can take the disguise of many forms – emotional, sexual, physical – but can be much more subtle and can simply be the constant undermining of an individual's value and worth.

When the stress of work becomes too great or there is a predisposition to mental ill health, often it is the chaplain who has a relationship with the individual that is strong enough to help the person assess the situation dispassionately and to encourage him or her to seek professional help. The support needed by the worker in these situations often continues for many months which, at times, can be as draining for the chaplain, who therefore also needs a good support network. Trying to work with individuals and businesses to develop and sustain a healthy work/life balance does much to alleviate some of these situations before they arise.

Spiritual needs

Many of the spiritual needs are practical, with the chaplain being asked to take on many of the roles of a parish priest or minister: for example, funerals, wedding blessing services, or the renewal of marriage vows. The problem is compounded because many folk have already approached their statutory church authorities and have been either put off or turned down because of one reason or another.

Another of the many reasons the chaplain is asked to help is that an individual has been put off by the ritual and apparent inflexibility of the church. For example, at one point, a couple wished to renew their wedding vows but with a difference; they wanted to do so in medieval costume, and with their family from across Scotland, whom they had not seen since the wife had been through treatment for cancer. They approached four churches and the common response was that they were not members. Originally I was asked to find someone who would take the service, which I did. However, because I had been helpful, they asked me to do the service and of course I obliged. Such services are an opportunity of ministry and mission, and perhaps the churches turn these opportunities away at their peril.

The chaplain works not just at a pastoral level but at a prophetic one too. The Scottish Retail Chaplaincy Group has lobbied Parliament about issues relating to a Christmas trading bill, which has since been passed. Discussions have also taken place around the churches' response to Hallowe'en, and how to allow staff to have time off on Good Friday which, although a Christian festival, in Scotland is not observed as a public holiday.

The chaplain's visit often provides a good place to start when someone is soul searching or trying to answer those questions that no one seems to have answers to. One example was the discussion that took place over a counter about whether aliens go to heaven. There was no debate on whether aliens existed. That was taken for granted! Issues are raised like, why do we need so many churches if we all worship the same God? – a question I am still trying to answer myself. Often the only view of religion the workforce has has been gleaned from the latest soap. The thought that Christianity turns a person into a living, breathing version of Dot Cotton from *EastEnders* or Harold from *Neighbours* is fairly rapidly put to rest on meeting this chaplain for the first time. The huge difference between being a person of faith and being religious is not one often found portrayed by our media. We need these interactions, however basic. Why? Because of the situation represented by the young woman met last December in retail who, when asked 'why we bothered with Christmas', replied that 'it was a special day' (at which point I got excited), 'a day given to us by the government as a day to spend with our family'. Where has the Church gone wrong over the last two millennia?

On occasion some of the employees have asked to set up Bible study/discussion groups, which has been very rewarding. This is, however, often met with a certain amount of cynicism by some members of the management teams. It also sets up a tension between being involved in such one-faith groups and sustaining the open multi-faith remit of the Chaplaincy, which, as stated earlier, is the primary stance of industrial and urban chaplaincy work. It must not lead, however good the activity, to appearing to be available only to certain kinds of people.

Services and joint faith witness events are held within the city centre, especially at Christmas and Easter, in collaboration with the civic events team and those who live and work in the city. Thus, without compromising their commitment to their work, many who are working long hours over the festive season are enabled to enter into its spiritual dimension.

Part of the chaplain's task is to act as a link between the sacred and the secular. This can take many forms. Chaplains may find themselves suggesting church services that workers might wish to attend but be unaware of. In doing this, and acting as a facilitator in other ways, the chaplain is seen to be useful on a practical level, removing some of the misconceptions some of the workers may have about the Church. In the other direction, chaplains have the task of informing the churches of the current issues affecting people at work. Keeping this link is vital for the churches. The chaplain can often take away the fear of the unknown world of work and commerce, or some of the misconceptions of the different cultures found in the world of work, which can appear threatening to some. They can also advise on such practicalities as when would be a good time to have Christmas services that would enable shop workers to attend. Constant relationship building and networking with all the city centre denominations is vital, not least to ensure that the welcome a stranger receives who visits a church on the chaplain's recommendation is one of warmth and sincerity. So the chaplain is, as a recognized servant of the Church's witness, both an arm of the churches' mission and a prophetic challenge to the community of faith as it tries to renew its life in response to the challenges of the times.

The response – strategies and models

Chaplaincy in the retail section of business has blossomed and flourished in Scotland, as it has across the United Kingdom, over the last few years. Up and down the country chaplains can be found in big and small shopping malls, city centre shopping areas, local high streets and large supermarkets. It is estimated that the 15 people who work as retail chaplains in Scotland reach 15,000 staff members. There are also six chaplains working within local authorities throughout Scotland. Within public sector working there has been an increase of around 52,000 jobs created in Scotland since devolution, with a recent increase of 9,000 positions over a single year, accounting for over 23.5 per cent of the Scottish workforce. This in itself is a huge challenge (Scottish Executive, 2005; http://news.bbc.co.uk 2006).

It is a sign of the high regard given to chaplaincy that chaplains are welcomed and valued in business groups such as retail associations, merchants' meetings and business associations. There are also chaplains involved in city centre partnership groups and city centre management committees. People today are faced in their working life with not one pressure but many. The levels of responsibility now placed on them have substantially increased. Policies of competitive management undermine individuals and in some cases destroy the professional co-operation on which many of our public services rely. As trade union powers diminish many employees are worried that they can no longer freely express their concerns and that that they will not be heard (Rachel Jenkins in Rogerson, 1996, p. 141).

Mike West argues that the Church when looking at society uses linear models to 'do' theology, either using inductive theology, which explores the secular experience until, in that experience, there is uncovered the living presence of God, or using deductive theology, which draws on tradition and the ritual of previous generations to impose its ideas on today's society (West, 2003, p. 1). However, industrial and urban chaplaincy teams have built on the insights of liberation theologians and have found that it is more effective to use a circular model. So Ian Fraser's model (a version of the pastoral cycle) has been widely embraced by industrial chaplaincy, 'as a way to move from the secular experience, via political questions to a theological tradition and finally back to a secular situation' (West in Rogerson, 1996, p. 44). It is not enough just to 'do' chaplaincy. If chaplains are to be credible professionals then they have to be able to balance practice with theory. Indeed, Murray (in Norman, 2004, p. 213), in his essay on 'The school chaplain as professional', discusses this very point. Often professionalism is seen as some sort of status involving high monetary reward, but Murray goes on to outline a positive definition of professionalism from a theological perspective.

The pastoral cycle is a continual journey where those following it can enter and move around it at any stage. It flows from experience, to analysis, to reflection, to a theologically based response, and back to experience. At first glance it could be seen to be a little superficial and mechanical. But if one begins to reflect on experience in depth, as not just what one sees but using all one's senses, what is seen, heard, tasted, touched and smelt, and using every level of cognition, from the mind to the emotions, one begins to notice more and in greater depth (Fraser, 1980, pp. 59–60).

For example, in a shopping mall one could draw superficial conclusions when analysing this experience . . . they are people shopping, or going to work. However if one notices the expressions of people's faces one might begin to reflect that this person is happy, or sad, or lonely and the response to that person may therefore be different. If whilst analysing one takes in to account not only the market forces at play in that city, but also a recent factory closure, or a tragic train crash, then the reflective process, and thus one's response, change again. In other words the more one takes time and immerses oneself at the initial experience stage the more one can give a rounded response. One must, too, always remember to be 'rooted in Christ' (Monahan and Renehan, 1998, pp. 13, 22; Col. 2.7).

Brown and Morrison suggest that the theology of the Church today needs to be open to the activity and unique presence of God in the society in which one finds oneself. If the Church is parochially orientated it becomes distinctly limited, as it is only able to offer itself within the limitations of its parish. For the Church to be complete it is crucial that it lives, works and breathes in the secular society where God already is (Brown and Morrison, 1999, p. 28). It is primarily for this reason that industrial chaplains choose to 'loiter with intent' and immerse themselves in the society to which they are called (Monahan and Renehan, 1998, p. 106).

Sim suggests that the concept of servant leadership fulfils the desire for a calling which is so much bigger than the need for a job. He suggests that jobs are for the most part too small for our spirits and therefore do not make us complete. Every job needs some kind of sense of relating to another in service as well as support. He further suggests that servant leadership is a work that is large enough to liberate and provide growth for the soul and that it fulfils Jesus' teachings that to be happy one must first be the servant of all (Sim, 1997, p. 117). The role of City Centre Chaplain has indeed become a post that encompasses both servanthood and leadership in a spirit of serving.

In *The Rise and Fall of Marks and Spencer*, Bevan suggests that 'however well the company performs it will be a considerable time before its past reputation of excellence is achieved and as a company it will once again be regarded as a retailing standards benchmark' (Bevan, 2002, p. 262). It is in this environment of uncertainty and continual decline in morale that the chaplain functions daily. Many of the stories that are heard during the course of the day are deeply sad and they cause one to question, 'How does one share a loving God when this person has all this going on in their life?' The response is to offer to help in any way, which can often be very practical. It can vary from listening or bringing humour to the situation, to, if appropriate, praying, or buying coffee or lunch in order to give someone space to think and a safe environment in which to do so; or, again, visiting relatives in hospital or accompanying people to hospital for appointments, or referring folk on to other agencies, in each case asking God to help in giving the right response.

While it is important to share the gospel, it has to be in a low-key way. It is hoped that, through one's care for them, those one meets will see Jesus. The idea is to try to be, as much as is humanly possible, what he would be, without losing one's own particular identity. In much the same way Thackery (2000, p. 97) suggests using the 'shepherding movement', by which he means a long period of simply rubbing shoulders with someone. This can bring change because of what people have discovered by being alongside a companion or pastor who has travelled with them.

Serving yet leading also comes into play when one is faced with ethical dilemmas within the working environment. The chaplain attends many meetings and sits on many committees within both the church and industry. Part of the job in Aberdeen involves working as Chaplain to the Third World Centre. Aberdeen became a Fair Trade city in 2003 and there are many issues that arise from continuing to promote this ideal in the city. Again, for example, ethical issues are often raised which can cause unease within the Aberdeen City Centre Partnership, an association where the leaders of many of the industries meet. But being part of such groups has also given an insight into how the global economy affects daily working practices and has highlighted the need to be more globally aware when examining one's praxis theologically. For example, there has developed a separation between real wealth production and cash. Credit, technology and globalization have made money become a commodity in its own right (Doctrine Commission, 2003, p. 61).

Yet the heart of liberation theology and indeed the gospel message is to remember the dispossessed when another block of flats is built, or to remember the impact on small businesses another retail park will have, and, for those working on a day-to-day basis, just what the effect of being asked to work an extra shift might be on the work/life balance of these individuals (Dyce, 2001, p. 92).

It is only by being in the unique position of freedom that the chaplain is privileged to have that one is able and free to speak out. The chaplain needs to be not only with the people but also at the heart of the political agenda. As C. R. Whittaker argues when talking of the relationship of religion to politics and society, 'it is not so much that the former reflects the social order as that it shapes it too' (Clarke, 2000, p. 49). Without a willingness to engage in the political struggle the religious can become irrelevant.

Much of Fraser's model is about the process of being immersed in the society in which one lives and re-examining it with 'new' eyes at regular intervals and then reflecting on why it is like it is. One of the difficulties is that it is difficult to look at that which is familiar with open eyes. It is therefore very useful to bring visitors to the area of work and to watch as they engage with the environment for the first time. This is something that is becoming more common in Aberdeen as the post becomes more established.

The idea of servant leadership always brings us back to basic priorities; that of being a servant of Christ in the workplace and reflecting him in all interactions that take place. After all, he goes before, and is already there.

Theological interpretation is a major part of the pastoral cycle. Many situations facing society today were prevalent in our Lord's time (poverty, homelessness, corruption, high interest rates, etc.), and reflecting on his response is both encouraging and enlightening. However, this takes time and discipline, though the rewards are immeasurable. It is often assumed by the chaplain that one is judged on the time one is visibly present within the chaplaincy setting rather than on the quality of chaplaincy work that could come from reflective time away.

Reflection on one's own practice is always good, especially when seen through another's eyes. Feedback from those who work in retail and the public sector at ground level as well as regular talks with management teams is crucial to the constant re-evaluation of the post and one's own work.

Obviously the problems and challenges faced in particular urban settings will have their own perspectives and specialized responses, but the points covered here should give an overview of the type of issues that may need to be addressed and the responses and models that may be a useful starting point for practitioners and academics alike.

Bibliography

Aberdeen City Council, 2004, *Green Spaces – New Places*, Aberdeen, ACC City Development Services.

Aberdeen City Council, 2005a, *The Bon-Accord Quarter Master Plan*, Aberdeen, ACC City Development Services.

Aberdeen City Council, 2005b, *Scottish Index of Multiple Deprivation 2004: Analysis of Aberdeen Data*, Aberdeen, ACC Office of Chief Executive.

BBC News Scotland, 2006, 'Increase in public sector workers', accessed at http://news.bbc.co.uk/1/low/scotland/4609110.stm.

Bevan, J., 2002, *The Rise and Fall of Marks and Spencer*, London, Profile Books.

Brown, Malcolm and Morrison, R., 1999, *Church, Change and the Economy*, Manchester, William Temple Foundation.

Brown, Malcolm and Ballard, Paul, 2005, *The Church and the Economy: A Documentary Study, 1945 to the Present*, Peterborough, Epworth.

Clarke, A. D. (ed.), 2000, *Serve the Community of the Church*, Grand Rapids, Eerdmans.

Doctrine Commission of the General Synod of the Church of England, 2003, *Being Human: A Christian Understanding of Personhood Illustrated with Reference to Power, Money, Sex and Time*, London, Church House Publishing.

Dyce, J. W., 2001, *Breaking New Ground: The First Scottish Ecumenical Assembly*, Dunblane, ACTS.

Fraser, I., 1980, *Reinventing Theology as the People's Work*, London, USPG.

Monahan, L. and Renehan, C., 1998, *The Chaplain: A Faith Presence in the School Community*, Dublin, Columba Press.

National Statistics Online, 2006, *Retail Sales*, accessed at www.statistics.gov.uk/cci/nugget.asp?id=256.

Norman, J. (ed.), 2004, *At the Heart of Education: School Chaplaincy and Pastoral Care*, Dublin, Veritas.

Palmer, G., MacInnes, T. and Kenway, P., 2006, *Monitoring Poverty and Social Exclusion 2006*, York, Joseph Rowntree Foundation.

Rogerson, J. W. (ed.), 1996, *Industrial Mission in a Changing World*, Sheffield, Sheffield Academic Press.

Sim, B. J., 1997, *Servanthood: Leadership for the Third Millennium*, Boston, MA, Cowley.

Scottish Executive, 2005, *Public Sector Employment in Scotland*, accessed at http://www.scotland.gov.uk/Publications/2005/07/14174404/44045.

Scottish Index of Multiple Deprivation, 2004, www.scotland.gov.uk/library5/society/siomd-00.asp.

Thackery, C., 2000, *Epidemic of Life*, Milton Keynes, Word.

West, M., 2003, *Doing Theology, a Workbook: Using the Fraser Method*, Sheffield, Industrial Mission in South Yorkshire.

11

City Centre Living: A Twenty-First Century Icon

PETER WILLIS AND LEN SIMMONDS

Traditionally a magnet to the homeless and the addict, the city centre has been the place to find large numbers of marginalized and excluded people in the street and around the bus station, the worst examples of poverty concentrated in a small area. In the past, wealth has determined how far out from the city centre a family could go and how able they were to commute into work. The most attractive option for quality living has been suburbia and most middle-class people sought to move into leafy suburban housing estates and away from the city. However, in the last decade a sea change has taken place in people's attitudes and there has been a movement back into city centre living across Britain, a movement that has mirrored what has taken place in cities across the world (see Davey, chapter 1, and Baker, chapter 2 of this book).

Who lives in the city centres?

This recent movement into the city has largely been of those of the higher managerial and professional group. Cities are better at attracting and retaining the higher echelons of the workforce. The city centres' new populations are now made up of:

(1) Students. The expansion of higher education over the past 20 years has helped to boost many city centre markets as larger numbers of students find accommodation in the city.
(2) Recent graduates seeking their first career-level job. Retaining graduates has become a major policy objective for those city centres that are lagging behind in terms of economic growth and housing investment; but housing is only one factor: others are often more influential, such as accessibility to jobs or training.

(3) Migrants. Another factor affecting demand (which is poorly covered by the 2001 Census) is the impact of international in-migration, especially since 2004.

(4) Those living singly. A study of city centre living in Manchester, Liverpool and Dundee shows that it is the younger group that form the vast majority of residents in cities (Nathan and Urwin, 2006).

(5) The successful 'ager'. Old age is now seen as a productive, active, well-remunerated phase in life – these are people who have long-term housing equity. They are consumers of culture: theatre, concert hall, gallery and films.

(6) The 'counter culturist': those with alternative political views like the gay and lesbian community who take advantage of the city with its ethos of tolerance. These people tend to be high earners and form creative groups.

Thus the profile of new city centre dwellers suggests that they will tend to be single-person households living in the city temporarily and through choice because it is convenient, allows for longer working hours and gives immediate access to the 'buzz' of the city. While the rise of single-person households was previously dominated by older people living alone, the greatest rise in the number of single-person households today is among men between the ages of 25 and 44, a trend that is projected to continue.

Who is excluded?

It is important to ask also who does not live in the city centre. According to Lees (2003, p. 66), urban renaissance is intended to go beyond physical environmental objectives to include concerns for social inclusion, wealth creation, sustainable development, urban governance, health and welfare, crime prevention, educational opportunity and freedom of movement, as well as environmental quality and good design.

However, there are problems. For instance, planning rules usually require developers to include space for 'affordable housing' for key workers such as nurses and teachers. However, there is evidence that luxury developers build more than one project at a time so they can transfer their affordable housing requirements out of the way of their rich clients.

Again, for many city centre dwellers their city centre apartment is not their main home. While this can include people across a wide income range there is a particular concentration among those with household incomes of over £100,000.

Many in the lower income band are now priced out of the city centre and deeper into the less desirable and more threatening inner urban areas. One example of this was demonstrated in a recent BBC documentary that followed the sale and development of a waterfront council tower block in London, displacing council tenants by wealthy owner occupation. The poor do not choose to live in areas with higher crime rates and worse pollution; they simply cannot afford not to. The problem is poverty, not where poor people live. Inequalities of wealth in the UK are far more acute than can be explained simply by income alone. There is a strong political awareness of this social exclusion.

With the gentrification of city centres, too, there has developed a far more aggressive approach to the vulnerable and marginalized. It is no coincidence that alongside the city centre renaissance has come a raft of directives which changes the whole focus of care for these groups, moving away from 'day centre' provision to resettlement and prevention.

Why do people choose to live in the city centre?

The new wealthy professional class with ample disposable income and a new approach to work/life balance has given city centre living a new lease of life. Various factors have made suburban living less attractive, including the cost of travel, whether by rail or through congested roads entailing time lost in commuting and the new emphasis on a clean environment, which has led to transport restrictions and congestion charges. The new emphasis on entertainment and the '24/7' city scene has made city centre living more attractive, and all this has coincided with the attractive development of loft apartments.

For the childless households that make up the majority of the new incomers, moving into a city centre apartment is determined less by economic factors than by less easily defined 'lifestyle' reasons. They wish to be close to the 'buzz' that certain city centres provide, as well as to niche (and rapidly changing) 'leisure and pleasure' markets and services such as eating out, internet buying and communication, and access to private medicine. At the same time modern apartment developments deliver anonymity, a coveted privacy, selective exposure, co-operative exposure, and an individualistic personal identity. City centre living makes it easier to meet a selective group of people, do business, share information, clinch deals, and sell and buy goods.

Smaller cities like Norwich, Northampton and Portsmouth have gained from an inflow of higher managerial and professional people. Others, however, have seen a strong decentralization of this high-skill group, including Coventry, Middlesbrough, Stoke, Birmingham and Nottingham. Single elderly people, requiring housing within reach of main services, and empty nesters, spending regardless of any consideration of their legacy to their children, all also see the city centre as their new place to live.

What are the economic and social impacts of living in the city centre?

In the UK, proximity to city centres has in recent years been a positive factor in increasing property prices. However, the number of mortgage repossession orders made by county courts in England and Wales during the first three months of 2007 was nearly 22,000, a level not seen since 1993. The number of repossession claims made by landlords was over 25,000. To the extent that the buy-to-let market is driven by investor desire for profit, it becomes more difficult to predict future trends and tendencies. Large numbers of vacancies and a downturn in values is not a situation that investors, lenders or householders will want to admit to, due to fears of 'talking down' the market still further. One analyst has claimed that 17 per cent of the buy-to-let new-build stock has been vacant for more than 12 months (Hough, 2007).

The phenomenon of city centre living has clearly been an important element in the economic regeneration of cities like Manchester, Nottingham, Leeds and Cardiff. However, the extent to which city centre living may have positive regenerating impacts on deprived inner urban areas that satellite the city centre should not be overstated. At this stage, the growth of city centre living has had only a limited impact on neighbouring deprived inner urban areas (Allen and Blandy, 2004; Nathan and Urwin, 2006).

There is much evidence also that UK cities are characterized by mounting inequality. This raises some fundamental and challenging questions for planners and policy makers:

Who exactly are our cities for?
Who 'belongs' in contemporary cities?
How can we envisage the substantive nature of 'urban citizenship'?

Exclusive gated developments, built in the last ten years and often adjoining deprived estates, may have brought upper-class residents into the city centre, but they have completely failed to bring about the social integration politicians desire. Market-based systems of allocation and distribution tend to reflect, albeit imperfectly, underlying disparities in income and wealth. Subtle processes of social and economic sifting are taking place, leading to growing geographical concentration of poverty and affluence – in precisely the opposite direction from the government's aim of providing more mixed and sustainable communities.

City centre 'gated communities' are residential ghettos with restricted access. Public spaces are privatized, and typically advertised as a 'community' where residents own or control common areas, shared parking facilities, gym and swimming pool amenities while simultaneously having reciprocal rights and obligations enforced by a private governing body. Almost every country has examples though they have grown at a remarkable rate in the USA, Latin America, Asia and South Africa. For the very affluent there is a benefit; the suburban poor become harder to see.

Paul Cheshire (2007) offers a sceptical view about the possibility of securing any social mix in city living. He suggests that many of the poorest neighbourhoods have been among the most deprived since the end of the nineteenth century. The pecking order has changed little.

We must also remember that city centre regeneration is deeply affected by environmental issues. Unless cities consume a small fraction of today's energy and recycle virtually everything, they will never be sustainable.

Tackling exclusion?

Misery, despair and mental and physical health problems multiply among the socially excluded. Yet every city would benefit if all its children were able to reach their potential, if its workers were able to find jobs and all its citizens were able to avoid being isolated. However, housing inequalities are now much greater than they were 50 years ago and housing poverty is the most extreme form of social inequality in Britain.

Having different levels of choice is one of the greatest causes of inequality. The experience of 'choice-based lettings schemes' has shown that they can be effective in enabling applicants to be offered a home where they want to live. They have also been successful in enabling black and ethnic minority households to secure a fairer share of housing. However, there are policy choices that could dramatically reduce the scale of inequality, as well as creating more socially mixed and sustainable communities, making housing markets work more successfully and increasing housing choice. The gulf that divides the cultures of rich and poor isn't bridged by the marginalization of poverty. 'Just because you live near all of the things that go along with wealth doesn't mean you'll have access to those things' (Sugg).

Joseph Rowntree Foundation's CASPAR projects (City-centre Apartments for Single People at Affordable Rents) seek in some small way to tackle the problem of affordable city centre homes, with multi-million pound projects to be built in Leeds and Birmingham. 'We are trying to achieve three objectives simultaneously,' said Richard Best, Director of the Foundation. 'For many middle-income single men and women, and young childless couples, renting offers greater flexibility and freedom than owning. The resources of such people have much to contribute to reviving the social and economic life of city centres. With short journeys to work, the congestion and pollution of commuting is reduced and less housing development is needed on green-field sites.'

The emerging picture is of two segregated and separate life-worlds; the upper tier and the lower tier.

Those who live in the first of these life-worlds may be, like the others *in the place*; but they are not *of that place* – certainly not spiritually, but also quite often, whenever they wish, bodily.

The people of the 'upper tier' do not apparently belong to the place they inhabit. Their concerns lie (or rather float) elsewhere. Apart from being left alone, free to be engrossed in their own pastimes, and to be assured of the services needed for their comfort, they have no other vested interests in the city in which their residences are located.

For the upper tier the city is not, like it used to be for the factory owners and the merchants of consumables in days of yore, their grazing ground, source of their wealth or a ward in their custody, care and responsibility. The upper tier city centre dweller today is unconcerned with the affairs of 'their' city – it is just one locality among many, all of them small and insignificant from the vantage point of the cyberspace, their genuine, even if virtual, home.

The life-world of the other, 'lower' tier of city centre dwellers is the very opposite from the first. It is territorially limited and bounded by traditional geographical, mundane and practical necessities. It is defined mostly by being cut off from that world-wide network of communication with which the 'upper tier' is connected and to which their life is tuned. They are 'doomed to stay local' – and so one could and should expect their attention, complete with its discontents, dreams and hopes, to focus on 'local affairs'. For them, it is inside of the city they inhabit and where the battle for survival and a decent place in the world is launched, waged, won or lost (Bauman, 2000).

The city centre is the place where these two groups of people live, remain in each other's proximity, and yet remain, for the most part, strangers. City centre living is purposely faceless and anonymous; people choose to live in segregated communities, which does not eliminate loneliness but often accentuates it. In their search for 'meaning and identity', which they need and crave no less intensely than the next person, they may leave out of account the place where they live and work. Like other people, they are part of the cityscape, and their life pursuits are inscribed in it. Global operators may roam through cyberspace. But, as human agents, they move through and stay in the physical space, the environment pre-set and continually re-processed in the course of human meaning-and-identity struggles.

The troubles that afflict contemporary city centres cannot be resolved by reforming the city centre – however radical such a reform may be. There are no local solutions to globally generated problems. The kind of changes urban developers offer are impotent to relieve, let alone eradicate, the insecurity experienced in the fluidity of labour markets, the fragility of the value business places on their capabilities and behavioural skills, or the frailty and assumed transience of human bonds and partnerships. Reform of existential condition precedes reform of the city centre and conditions its success.

Future trends for city centre living

Living in the city centre involves a complex interaction of issues and ambitions that are shaped by the everyday choices of its residents as much as by their political leaders and their officials. The costs and obligations that come with the privileges of city centre life are a test of the limits of the power of persuasion, as opposed to compulsion. In the end, a genuine city can only be about persuasion and not compulsion.

First, city centre living is a lifestyle choice. City centre homes are less a place to live (for ever) and more a way of living (for now). People choose to live in city centres because it allows them to socialize easily and frequently and to take full advantage of the city centres' bars, cafes, pubs, clubs and restaurants. For many, especially those likely to move into new and recent developments, city centre living is attractive partly because it is affordable. If an economic downturn leaves people unable to live the lifestyle they bought into, city centre living itself may become less attractive for some.

Second, turnover is high in city centres. Each year a lot of people leave and a lot of people enter. Given that, it is always a buyers' market as apartments come up for sale. With signs of economic slowdown, the next wave of incomers will need to be happy with a different, less affluent city centre lifestyle. Property prices might need to fall further still before city centres became attractive again. Worse, the downturn in the national housing market has coincided with an emerging problem of oversupply in city centres. And the potential purchaser pool is unlikely to grow if people are getting nervous about the performance of city centre properties. Furthermore, investors may have failed to realize the extent to which city centre living has been led by students. As higher education growth rates slow, so will a key driver of demand.

It may also mean that residents are likely to be unable to move so readily. Lack of space both inside apartments and outside, plus the chaotic, dirty and noisy environment, mean that city centres are not thought to be suitable places to bring up children. These are deeply ingrained attitudes that are unlikely to change in the short term, but may have to.

People argue that city centre living is here to stay, that, in the long run, it is a market that will grow and thrive. Many of today's students envisage themselves as tomorrow's loft-living professionals. Furthermore, demographics indicate that the 20–30 age group will expand and, as trends for postponing families continue, the number of people at the stage of the life cycle when city centre living is most likely to appeal is increasing.

The residents of cities and their elected representatives have been confronted with a task they can by no stretch of imagination fulfil: the task of finding local solutions to global contradictions.

Contemporary cities are the battlegrounds on which global powers and stubbornly local meanings and identities meet, clash, struggle and seek a satisfactory, or just bearable, settlement – a mode of cohabitation that is hoped to bring a lasting peace but as a rule proves to be but an armistice, an interval to repair the broken defences and re-deploy the fighting units. It is that confrontation, and not any single factor, that sets in motion and guides the dynamics of the 'liquid modern' city (Bauman, 2000).

The Church and the city dweller?

Historically, the church has played an important role in helping to shape city life. However, today most city centre church members commute from suburbia. In many cases they have not only lost any connection with city centre issues but have no interest in the city centre apart from the building they inhabit. When Christians abdicate their role in the shaping of twenty-first-century city centres, developers, politicians and individual consumers will make those decisions by themselves. But the shape of the city centre should not be determined solely by politicians, sociologists and investors. The nature of city centre life, our responsibility to it, and the physical and social conditions necessary for human fulfilment are deeply theological issues.

A growing number of churches recognize that, for many people, the Church (like trade unions, working men's clubs and manufacturing industry) seems to inhabit a world that has disappeared. As a response to the new environment the Church finds itself, both in the city centre and elsewhere, experimenting with different ways of being church. Projects are mushrooming around the country. A community of 'Goths' meets informally in Soho, London. Youth congregations are emerging. Groups are being formed to explore spirituality, perhaps as a way into Christian belief. A skateboard park encourages young people to turn skateboarding into an act of worship. Café churches allow you to take latte with the Lord. Approaching 350 new and different forms of church have registered on the Fresh Expressions website and anecdotal evidence suggests there could be many more. However, amid all this change there is a sneaking suspicion that we are missing some vital clue to the future (see Edson, chapter 8 of this book).

Some years ago a challenge was laid down by a retired businessman, one of the wealthiest men in the city where we live, with the following words, 'It is the responsibility of people like you to tell people like me what God expects of us.'

He claimed that too many church leaders patronized 'people like him', fearful of offending and hopeful of gaining something, and, in the process, ultimately sealing the eternal doom of 'people like him'. Sobering words.

Some of the questions this prompts include:

What does it mean to be Church to those who live in the city centre?
Where should Christian influence reside and why?
What are the distinctive opportunities and responsibilities of the church? What is a good witness in the contemporary city centre?
What opportunities does the city centre offer?
What should the church contribute to city centre life?

Our problem is that the way we think about church in the city centre is still rooted largely in a framework that no longer applies. We don't yet understand enough about the shape of Church that the Spirit is now moulding and we can only guess at what might replace these older models. What doesn't help is that ecumenism has become, too often, a set of relationships in which unity predominates, limiting views of church primarily to meetings, buildings and programmes. Most of this is completely irrelevant to a modern city centre dweller who no longer utilizes a regular, weekly social gathering as his or her primary method of communication and community formation. Instead, the city centre dweller's culture relies on networks, communication processes based on 'infinity-based' gatherings and methods of communication/participation in the network. Postmodern culture, with its priority on pluralism, challenges the church to shape itself as a networking community.

The traditionalist will inevitably say: 'Stay firm. Keep doing the things we've been doing.' The city centre dweller will see what God is doing in the waters of culture and seek to engage it.

It is as though we began playing a game of football, but during half time the field had been rearranged for a game of rounders. Coming back out to play the second half of the game, we wonder how the bases we keep tripping over got there, but we go on trying to play football. Just below consciousness, there is a hint that something has changed; we ask, as we head toward the end of the field, why we can't find the goal where it is supposed to be. We have to stop thinking football and begin thinking rounders. If the traditional church order was about regulation, stability, singularity and fixity, the postmodern era is about chaos, uncertainty, otherness, openness, multiplicity and change. 'Post-modern surfaces are not landscapes but wavescapes, with the waters always changing and the surfaces never the same. The sea knows no bound-aries' (Sweet, 1999, p. 24).

Sometimes the things that are important are not the things we focus on but the things we only glimpse out of the corner of our eye. What is offered here are some eye-corner glimpses of what may shape the Church in its ministry to those who live in our city centres.

(1) Our task is that of finding the Christ who is beyond our Institutional Christianity, what has been called the 'Raw Fact of Christ'. The institutional Church with all its claims cannot lead us to the Christ; it can indeed detract our attention from Him; we have to continu-ally rediscover 'Christ, the Holy Spirit, the Kingdom of God' in the world today (Chenchiah, 1936, pp. 81–2).

(2) Christian mission is no longer about dogma or a mental assent to a list of beliefs learned, honed and presented. It is about our personal experience, authenticated by Scripture, tradition and reason and tested by lifestyle as we engage with others.

(3) The Church is challenged to go beyond the structure of membership or confirmation and build up a new partnership of Christians and non-Christians. We are called to live in the real world but out of the context of our Kingdom perspective.

(4) *Koinonia* (community) is that point of contact with the city centre dweller outside the institutional Church, the 'manifestation of the new reality of the Kingdom at work in the world of history' (Thomas, 1971, p. 60). This Christ-centred secular fellowship beyond the Church combines Christian self-identity and secular solidarity with everyone with whom we come into contact.

(5) 'Secular fellowship' does not mean making the gospel secular. What is intended is not for Christians to lose the religious or spiritual aspect of the gospel, nor for Christianity to be absorbed into other religions, but for the secularization of the Christian community in order to bridge the gap with the wider community and identify with the world. 'Secular' means the Christian community becoming 'truly "religious" without being "institutional"' (Thomas, 1972, p. 88).

(6) In this secular *koinonia*, place is important only if it simply means space. In the city centre the church is the last vestige of public space. Our buildings should offer space that authenticates and celebrates yesterday's experience and stimulates fresh encounter. It is not

about a special place or special presentation but simply creating space where the mystery may be encountered and, through Jesus, be recognized. Each new encounter takes us beyond the Jesus we know into new exploration and revelation of the Jesus we have not yet met.

(7) Mission is no longer about structures, policies, grand plans or great campaigns. It is about lifestyle and journey. If Christians are to have any effective credibility in a twenty-first-century city centre, the Church will need a strong network built on trust, using every resource, as wise stewards; a precision ministry that brooks no duplication, but capitalizes on co-operation. We must invest not in denominational preservation but in a mission focused on the Kingdom of God. It will mean moving resources to where the need is greatest. It will mean investing in people more than real estate. It will mean empowering the laity. It will demand of all denominations that they stop protecting vested interest and buy into a co-ordinated risk-taking ministry that gambles everything on a future only faith can see.

We need, as I like to put it, 'a Eureka theology for a peek-a-boo God'. God surprises us on the way to somewhere, or in a particular event; a theology of surprise and discovery.

For Moses it was an ordinary bush in the wilderness; he took his shoes off for it was holy ground (Exod. 3.5). For Jacob it was that night he slept, out in the open, under the stars; he said, 'Surely the LORD is in this place – and I did not know it!' (Gen. 28.16). For Isaiah it was just sitting quietly in the Temple. He cried, 'Woe is me! I am lost' (Isa. 6.5). It is what happens on the way to Emmaus (Luke 24.13–35); or going down the Gaza Road (Acts 8.26); or on that business trip to Damascus (Acts 9.2). It is seeing a shadowy figure standing on a sea shore, looking like a fisherman but you are not sure. He shouts to you, 'Have you caught anything?' Suddenly you recognize that it is the Lord, he cooks breakfast for everyone and it's a sacrament (John 21.4–14).

It is discovering the divine sacrifice in the film *The Matrix*. The God we met in the mass jumps out in a peek-a-boo moment through the Matrix and we shout Eureka! Our God is never safe. He embraces lepers (Mark 1.40); has tea with tax collectors (Luke 5.30); breaks the rules (Mark 2.24); talks to loose women and lets some prostitute pour scent over his feet and wipe them with her hair in public (Luke 7.38–39); lets an adulteress off the hook (John 8.1–11); and then has the gall to condemn the most important leaders in the city (Matt. 23). There is nothing safe or predictable about God as we meet him in Jesus! He is there in the father who will not give up on his wayward son (Luke 15.11–32). He hides himself in the man sowing seed (Mark 4.1–9) and the shepherd out on the hills looking for the one sheep that is lost (Luke 15.3–7). He hides in the everyday rough and tumble of life and jumps out to surprise us!

The twenty-first-century Christian is not called to take a packaged God to a needy world, as there are no certainties or absolutes. To think that we have all the answers and other people the questions is the worst form of arrogance. We need not defend God or his character as a system of belief. The Holy Spirit is his own defender. We merely carry with us a testimony of the God we have met, and as we engage with others we discover something new about him.

We are called to live in today's city centre not as faith's settlers but as faith's pilgrims. Yesterday's experience of God has shaped our lives so far. We take that experience, as others take their experience, into life's daily routine, where issues must be faced and decisions made, where people pursue questions of meaning and struggle for survival. We have to learn how to relax at parties and pray in pubs. We must begin to talk with our friends and workmates about our weaknesses and not just our strengths, our times of depression as well as our confidences. There is no 'them' and 'us'; only fellow pilgrims.

We have no need to hide anything, or to pretend to be any more or less than we are. A cup of coffee, a shared meal, or a night out with friends is every bit as sacramental as a consecrated chalice, for as we take with us the Christ we know it is there that he will jump out and surprise us; a peek-a-boo moment that will be for us and for them a moment of discovery, a revelation of him – and we will never be the same again.

Christ can still shake those in high office as we stand in their presence and still confound the academic with the wisdom of a fellow traveller. Business tycoons can still be stunned by the simplicity of a life lived for God. The greatest impact we can make today is simply to embody the Christ we know and go out to discover the Christ we have not yet met and do not yet know where people interact, love, grieve and search. More vital than this is to be emotionally and spiritually engaged, to laugh and cry, to be there in moments of desire when people reach out, or in that moment of despair when they cry out: in short, to walk alongside others. Only then can we share in the activity of the Spirit.

Mission is nothing but taking the God we know and in our engage-ment with those around us discovering through the unfolding revelation of Christ the God we have not yet encountered. It is to step out of the boat and stand on the water (Matt. 14.29), to place the precious seed in the ground and expect the harvest (Mark 4.26–29), to take up a cross and follow (Mark 8.34); knowing only that it will take us beyond the institutional church into uncharted territory.

We are unsure of what it will mean but those prepared to cross the boundary and explore the unknown will demonstrate the same risk-taking courage of the New Testament missioners, to go where people are, and discover God in new locations and through new experiences. Such exposure will challenge continually all we have learned, will over and again take us beyond our understanding, bring rejection, pain and crucifixion. Death and resurrection will be part of our daily landscape. We go assured only of one thing: God is still Emmanuel – with us!

Bibliography

Allen, C. and Blandy, S., 2004, *The Future of City Centre Living: Implications for Urban Policy*, Sheffield, Centre for Regional Economic and Social Research.

Bauman, Zygmunt, 2000, *Liquid Modernity*, Cambridge, Polity Press.

Chenchiah, Paudipaddi, 1936, 'The Church and the Indian Christian', in D. M. Devasahyam and C. N. Sunarisnam (eds) *Rethinking Christianity in India*, Madras, Madras Press, 81–2.

Cheshire, Paul, 2007, *Segregated Neighbourhoods and Mixed Communities: A Critical Analysis*, York, Joseph Rowntree Trust.

Hough, Jon, 2007, Vacancy Question?, www.insidehousing.co.uk.

Lees, L., 2003, 'Urban Renaissance', in R. Imrie and M. Roce (eds), *Urban Renaissance?*, Bristol, Policy, 61–82.

Nathan, M. and Urwin, C., 2006, *City People: City Centre Living in the U.K.*, London, Institute for Public Policy Research, Centre for Cities.

Sugg, John F., 'Movin' on down', on www.creativeloafing.com.

Sweet, Leonard, 1999, *Aqua Church*, Loveland, Group Publishing Inc.

Thomas, M. M., 1971, *Salvation and Humanisation*, Madras, Christian Literature Society.

Thomas, M. M., 1972, 'Baptism, the Church and *koinonia*', *Religion and Society* 19(1), (March).

12

Churches Together in and for a New City

MARY COTES

Introduction

Milton Keynes is one of the last 'new towns' to be built in the United Kingdom after the Second World War. The postwar recovery and renewal programme included a series of strategically placed new towns, built on the 'garden city' model that had inspired Welwyn Garden City and other towns before the war. These would provide centres for the new electronically based industries and make a major contribution to the problems of overcrowding and slums that bedevilled the older industrial cities. Milton Keynes was designated in 1967, situated halfway between London and Birmingham. It took its name from an ancient small village, but the area (21,900 acres) included a number of other larger settlements. The target was for a population of 250,000 but there is a further expansion programme planned for the next few years to help meet the current housing crisis (Baker, 2005, pp. 10ff.).

Milton Keynes is a buzzing, exciting place to live and in the next 25 years the population of the urban area is set to double. The first period of growth, which began in 2001, is set to last for ten years and will see the construction of some 21,000 homes. This development encompasses not only growth in the outlying areas of the current urban area but regeneration of some of the existing areas. The second period of growth, between 2011 and 2021, will include the construction of a further 26,000 homes both in outlying areas and along the central corridor of the existing city. Details for the third period of growth are less clear. All of this growth is being described as creating 'sustainable development', which is not only a reference to environmental sustainability, but a commitment to building safe communities with a 'greater sense of place', essential local amenities and community infrastructure.

While Milton Keynes is fast expanding, the traditional churches in the city can seem to be shrinking. Or at least, even though some of our many churches are showing considerable signs of growth, the rate of their growth is not the same as that of the city. We have a sense of shrinking, of growing proportionally smaller in relation to a population which is getting bigger, and which is increasingly unclear about the relevance of faith. This sense of our decreasing influence is compounded by the reality of shrinking resources, both in terms of finances and in terms of the personnel and deployment we are able as churches to sustain. Even in the four years in which I have been in post in Milton Keynes as Ecumenical Moderator, there have been noticeable reductions in the numbers of paid clergy, painful rises in the financial demands placed on churches, and a growing awareness that things are not likely to get any easier. The connections and contrasts we make between the outer and inner landscapes can often be painful ones.

In certain areas, the expansion has writ large the shifting position of the Church in relation to its community. As certain areas expand in one particular direction, for example, so church buildings which once found themselves pretty well in the middle of a housing estate or local area suddenly find themselves on the edge of it, or on the edge of the parish in which they were originally centrally located. This of course has practical implications, but more seriously than that reflects and echoes deeper questions about where the Church stands in the expansion itself and how 'central' a voice it might have in any consultation processes.

The churches are thus having to adjust to a new and complex environment and are being asked to find new ways of facing the challenges that are described by the facts on the ground. It is unknown territory which for us all demands a radical rethink of how the Church shapes itself, how it relates to the new communities, and how it engages with the civic bodies. In this chapter we shall describe how the churches have historically related to one another and to the civic bodies, as a background to a discussion of some of the issues that are currently facing us.

Presence and partnership: past

Forty years ago a church building Master Plan was created for Milton Keynes with church buildings at the heart of many of the new grid-square communities. There was often the intention that these buildings could also serve as a community centre, with the expectation that the church would be intrinsically involved at the heart of the community's life. (Strategic Working Party, 2007, para. 3.4)

The story of the ecumenical engagement of the traditional churches in Milton Keynes is an interesting one in its own right, and is well recounted in Robin Baker's *Milton Keynes Is Different*. Back in the 1960s and 1970s, when the new Milton Keynes was first conceived by planners, the churches of the Milton Keynes Churches Council – Anglican, Baptist, Methodist, URC and Roman Catholic – came together and, excited and encouraged by the national ecumenical scene at that time, took the decision to create ecumenical churches in the new areas of the city. These were heady days, remembered still with great excitement by church members who took part in the process, and engaged church members and church leaders at all levels – from grass-roots to regional and national. With vision and determination they brought to fruition in collaboration with the then Development Corporation a number of ecumenical church buildings, situated at the centre of many of the new communities in something of the style of a traditional village. These churches were then grouped into ecumenical parishes, in the north, south-east and west of the city. Older churches – sometimes centuries old – which already existed in the historic village centres that were incorporated into the urban area were encompassed by these parishes. These older churches also became ecumenical, belonging to the four traditional Anglican/Free Church denominations. At the centre of the new Milton Keynes a further parish was created and a central church, owned by Roman Catholics and Free Church and Anglicans, was opened in the 1980s.

The realization of this Master Plan articulated a particular story and a particular view of the church. With church buildings at the centre of newly built grid-square communities, an image was created of a church as intimately central to community life as it was central to the political processes and engagements that had allowed it to come into being. While for some of the denominations this was a situation to which they were accustomed, this was a new role for church members coming from other traditions. However, in terms of its representing a relationship between the powers and the churches *together*, it was a new and exciting venture for all of them.

Presence and partnership: present

Since those days, the Milton Keynes Churches Council, or the Mission Partnership as it is now called, has become a body to which are affiliated not only ecumenical parishes, but also three Churches Together groups to the north-west, north-east and south-west of the city, single-denominational churches in outlying villages which by choice or through membership of the URC district or Methodist circuit relate to the Partnership, as well as single-congregational Local Ecumenical Partnerships, one at least of which predates the establishment of the parishes. Further ecumenical, structural 'convergence', as it is referred to, has been achieved, allowing levels of ecumenical engagement at all levels. The partnership is overseen by a team of presidents, comprising the regional leaders of the five denominations in collaboration with one another.

As far as the churches' current engagement with the powers is concerned, the rather complicated and unusual history by which the Partnership has come into existence has meant a number of things. First, because the establishment of these ecumenical church buildings – and sometimes also community centres – demanded a close working relationship between the traditional churches and the Development Corporation, both sides – churches and civic bodies – have, to a degree, inherited a memory of collaboration and co-operation. Clearly, as the years have gone on and political and social realities on the ground have changed and developed, this relationship has evolved considerably. However, it is important for us all that the churches began with a sense of engagement with the powers and planners of the city, as it is undoubtedly this story that has influenced the subsequent strategy of the churches. The memory is held today, with pride and gratitude, both by church members old enough to have been involved in the negotiations in the past and who are still living in Milton Keynes, and by those who have moved into the city since those days, but who have nonetheless by virtue of their membership of the churches been incorporated into the story, who have inherited the memory and become holders of its values and energy.

With that memory comes a heightened awareness of the built environment and a sense of having an ongoing part to play in the construction of urban life. To an extent, the heightened awareness of the built environment is shared by all who live here. Anyone who lives in Milton Keynes is constantly aware of the changing and evolving landscape: of housing estates, shopping centres and schools suddenly appearing in places where last week or last month there was a field. The grid-road system means that for those who have a car there is quick and easy access to all areas of the city, enabling residents to travel widely and catch a much wider view of developments and the changing urban environment. But for the churches, their particular history undergirds this general awareness of the evolving surroundings. It also reaffirms the sense, within the churches, of the possibility and the expectation of being engaged in the process by which the city evolves, and of being able to contribute to its growth and evolution.

Furthermore, this history, and the way in which the traditional churches have continued to organize themselves, has enabled the authorities to recognize the traditional churches as working together within the city *as one body*. The traditional churches are to a relatively high degree perceived by the authorities to speak representatively and to be reached at one point of contact. This is a vital element in the whole process of engagement. The Mission Partnership now represents some 90 or so church congregations, from the five denominations, as well as a number of related Christian organizations. A number of chaplains are also encompassed by the organization. So, for example, if the authorities seek the participation of the churches, whether it be in the creation of a Holocaust memorial event, to invite representation at a colloquy or function, to update the churches on strategy and policy development or invite their consultation, there is one office to which they turn.

Equally, the ability of the churches to be organized in this way enables them to speak into the city's life with a stronger voice than if they had to speak on their own. Individual churches of course can and do relate to the authorities in their own way on issues that may particularly concern them, and there is no necessary obligation to speak through the organized body of the Mission Partnership. On many occasions, however, there is a great advantage to be gained by a church's concerns being shared and voiced by the whole Partnership community. So, for example, an individual parish's campaign to save a local school from being closed can be readily shared and adopted by the church community across the city; particular churches that find, thanks to the communication protocols in place, that they have particular issues in common are enabled to act together, pool expertise and resources; strategies can be formulated by one small group which then might be adopted by all the churches together. With a growing population drawing together people from a range of ethnicity and backgrounds, the churches are increasingly finding themselves aware of issues relating to asylum and racism, not to mention poverty and homelessness. Stories emerging from the different congregations can be held and voiced by the whole community. The ability of the Mission Partnership to draw together a number of chaplains from institutions across the city – the fire service, the prison, the hospital, the hospice, etc. – also adds to its capacity to know and react to ongoing issues across the city.

Relationships and representation

Thanks to a shared funding scheme the Mission Partnership has been able to sustain several separate posts which all, in their way, enable the Christian community to relate more effectively to the authorities. These posts may reflect the ecclesiology or traditional practices of one denomination rather than another, and the church tradition of the post-holder may affect the particular manner in which the job-descriptions are carried out. The point is, however, that these posts are accountable to the churches together. This is not at all to say that the processes of relating to the authorities are held entirely or exclusively by these posts; however, their creation has allowed resources to be directed into enabling the whole church community to be engaged with the issues of the city, and in channelling the voice of the Christian community in contexts where it can be more easily heard.

Our practical experience of ecumenism in Milton Keynes has demonstrated to us that both the church-related ecumenical processes and the ways in which we engage with the civic bodies are not only dependent on the structures that support them, but are fostered by good, solid and flexible working relationships, without which the structures cannot carry the weight of the work. This lesson has been learnt through the day-to-day living of the ecumenical experiment which is of a different quality from the formal ecumenical engagement that goes on at 'higher' levels. On the ground, the urgency for finding ways of relating that work and produce fruit is acutely felt and, in responding to it, the churches have built up a range of relational skills. This interpersonal dimension which is of such critical importance to all the ecumenical churches is reflected in the work of all the post-holders who each, in their own particular way, rely on the relationships that they create to enable and shape the representation they subsequently exercise.

Since the Mission Partnership was first created, the church scene in Milton Keynes has dramatically shifted, and whereas in past years the denominational churches may well have represented the greater number of churchgoers in the city, this is now much less the case. As churches and denominations have different ways of counting their constituent members, figures are hard to provide, but the situation is self-evident. New churches are appearing in Milton Keynes almost as fast as new housing estates, and the church landscape is changing as fast as the physical environment. It is a complex situation. The traditional denominations now find themselves in a city where independent churches abound and where relationships with black-led churches and other ethnic minority churches have become a priority.

While such churches very often guard their independence proudly and have no wish to subscribe fully to the kind of structural organization that the Mission Partnership represents, they are nonetheless often acutely aware that they do not share the traditional churches' history in Milton Keynes and the power that is assumed to go with it. Consequently there is often a strong desire on the part of many to create working relationships with the Partnership which may gain access to the kind of representation into the civic bodies which the traditional denominations have had in the past and which they are still perceived to have. On the other hand, very often the very breadth of position which the Mission Partnership needs to adopt in order to represent its wide constituency to the civic bodies is precisely what can discourage certain churches from engaging with the Partnership. There is consequently a complexity about these relationships which demands constant sensitivity.

The Ecumenical Moderator

A unique feature of the Mission Partnership in Milton Keynes is the position of the Ecumenical Moderator who acts as the executive co-ordinator. One of the key roles of the Moderator is to build and nurture the kinds of relationships that strengthen the body as a whole, overseeing the relationships and structures that draw the participating church communities together. As structures come to be seen as burdensome, and as business styles of working become to many less attractive, so the importance of this building of relationships becomes more crucial. Second, the Moderator represents the organization to outside bodies, be they civic bodies or church bodies at different levels, facilitating occasions where, for example, regional church leaders can respond to civic questions that relate specifically to Milton Keynes. Third, the Moderator is to be a catalyst in the process of reflection upon the life, mission and ministry of the Mission Partnership as a whole, enabling change and development to occur.

Increasingly the Moderator is involved in the building of relationships with other faith communities. In a city as diverse as Milton Keynes, this is an urgent task. Historically, a strong interfaith network has thrived, creating active relationships between people of different faith groups in a non-representational way. More recently, a representative Council of Faiths has been created to give a representational voice to the faith groups into the work of the council. This group is still embryonic and has struggled with questions of the nature of representation when the strength of the different faith groups is so varied. Such collaboration with other faith groups can have the knock-on effect of creating tensions in the Partnership in the relationships existing with some independent churches which may tend to hold a different, more exclusivist, theological stance. Relationships with the faith communities and with independent churches can thus pull the Partnership in opposing directions. As in many other areas in Britain, the traditional churches find themselves in a strong and unique bridging position. In the eyes of the authorities this can sometimes appear confusing, but more often it can serve to widen the representational function the Partnership is perceived to have.

The Chaplain

As residents of Milton Keynes we all find ourselves in a fast-changing, constantly developing environment, and not least the churches find themselves for hosts of reasons needing to relate to the new developments and the strategies that drive them. The Partnership has traditionally funded a city chaplain to Milton Keynes. Through the years the model of chaplaincy has varied according to particular circumstances, theological trends and individual gifting and interests. Currently, however, because of the pressing issues which the expansion of Milton Keynes raises for the whole community, the churches have designated the post as the Milton Keynes Development Chaplain. The Chaplain's specific role is to resource and encourage the local Church in its engagement with the local community, civic life, and the expansion of Milton Keynes. This is a key role in terms of maintaining the Church's engagement with the powers, especially at this moment in the city's story.

Again, relationships in a complex environment are vital. In the first place, the current chaplain's remit is to enable relationships and understanding to grow between churches across the city and local government officers, and to foster relationships with the voluntary sector and the various interfaith groups, thus creating opportunities for shared service and action, particularly in respect of disadvantaged groups. So, for example, alongside a huge range of networking activities, the chaplain might be involved in meetings of the Council of Faiths and engage with issues relating to land for faith groups in the expansion areas, and may well meet regularly with MPs and with council members, keeping them abreast of the churches' activities and concerns. These concerns may be formulated through the Partnership's own conciliar processes, or equally may be concerns relating specifically to one particular area of Milton Keynes and may have been conveyed to the chaplain through particular conversations with churches in that area.

In the second place, thanks to these relationships, the chaplain is better placed to enable the insights and concerns of the Milton Keynes Christian community to be channelled effectively and clearly heard and understood by those whose work impacts on the development and expansion of Milton Keynes. So, for example, the chaplain attends and engages in Local Strategic Partnership planning group meetings, attends policy consultations and offers a Christian voice in debates such as those relating to public transport or the establishment of eco-towns. The chaplain speaks for the whole of the Partnership in making responses to strategy consultations regarding matters such as regeneration or affordable housing.

Through all this the chaplain keeps abreast of the latest policy and strategy consultation and is better equipped to inform the churches on issues that concern them. The chaplain serves as a resource to churches within the Partnership and beyond that are able to access his expertise. Part of the chaplain's remit is therefore what might generally be described as training, enabling church groups to be informed and educated about community development and expansion issues. The educational part of the role is crucial in enabling churches to understand their own capacity to relate to civic bodies.

The remit of this current chaplain represents a development from previous chaplaincy posts to the city. Whereas in the past the chaplain has been offered by the churches as, in a sense, a lone voice speaking on their behalf, the current post has sought to place strong emphasis on the interface between churches and civic bodies, allowing the Church to have a voice to 'the powers that be' (Rom. 13.1), and allowing the 'powers' to address the churches. Equally, the remit of the current chaplain has been to stress the importance of the engagement of the local churches themselves in the process, raising their awareness of political issues and encouraging them to find their own voice in the process.

In the current climate, this remit represents a considerable challenge to the churches. As time goes on and as new residents stream into the city, and personnel in the council offices changes, so the memory of the Church's past engagement with the civic bodies is in danger of getting, if not forgotten, certainly diluted. Retelling the story of the past can be helpful, but it is not the solution. New and up-to-date stories of engagement need to be lived and experienced by a new generation. Furthermore, with increasing financial demands being placed on the local traditional churches by denominational bodies, and with increasing demands being made upon the churches to ensure their self-preservation and the increase of their numbers, church members can be engrossed with so many immediate concerns that urgent calls to relate to the civic processes can sometimes go unheeded. However, the Partnership as a whole remains committed to this model of engagement, recognizing that elements will need to evolve in response to change.

Presence and partnership: future

As the development of Milton Keynes continues, the churches find themselves faced with questions about the shape of their continuing presence in the city. While the Master Plan that was executed in the 1960s and 1970s was highly successful at that time, and while it has left a heritage that has been rich and important, many circumstances have changed and developed since those days, and questions now emerge about the appropriateness of simply rolling out more of the same some 40 years later.

Since those early days, the circumstances of the traditional churches have changed, not least in financial terms. Money is now tight, and is not easily found for new church buildings, even if land were readily being made available. Changes and developments have also taken place in the ecumenical movement at the national level, and this has a knock-on effect on the local scene. While, as this chapter tries to make clear, ecumenical work still flourishes in Milton Keynes and characterizes everything that the traditional churches are involved in, the national enthusiasm for experiments in structural ecumenism which fuelled the original Master Plan in Milton Keynes has waned, and questions are being asked at all levels about the direction ecumenical processes should take. This has an inevitable effect on the situation in Milton Keynes which has grown up as a highly successful experiment from that era, and which now finds itself asking what shape it needs to take on for the future, and how that will affect its relationships with the authorities.

Currently the Mission Partnership is in conversation with many of the black-led churches, and plans to create a new forum with a much wider constituency are well advanced. At the same time we are undergoing considerable internal changes to permit more varied and more flexible ways of creating collaboration and partnerships across the city, with both church and other faith communities and other agencies. This increasing flexibility may bring with it a greater sense of complexity, but we are convinced of the urgency of recognizing ourselves as part of a much wider ecumenical scene and of enabling a broader mechanism of representation. This will undoubtedly be a complicated road, trying to create sufficient structure to allow meaningful representation, while at the same time avoiding the dangers of heavy organization and control which are unacceptable to many possible constituent members.

We are convinced also that we need to understand our 'ecumenical' working not simply as the undertaking of churches in relation to other churches, but as an engagement in the great purposes of God who calls us to share in the ministry of reconciliation. The thrust of ecumenism must be not simply 'one church' but 'one world'. As the ecumenical movement in Milton Keynes has grown up, one of the 'key' biblical texts inspiring us has been, not surprisingly, the high priestly prayer of Jesus with its imperative summarized as: 'that they may be one . . . that the world may believe' (John 17.21). While this vision continues to inspire us we are anxious to widen and deepen our theological understanding of what the ecumenical process is, and to find creative ways to hold together both relationships with other churches and relationships with other bodies in an ecumenical vision of all things held together in Christ.

If the church landscape is changing, the nature of community life across the city has also changed. The original vision of the city planners, which was to create in each grid-square some kind of village centre, has been outgrown, if it was ever really there. The ease of movement around the city by car has meant that residents are less dependent upon their local centre for their community support, and can easily travel right across the city in some ten minutes in order to do their shopping or meet friends. Since the early days the exponential growth of virtual community, via the internet, has dramatically changed ways of relating. All of this points us to the view that local grid-square centres with church and community buildings at the heart of them no longer necessarily serve the purpose for which they were designed. Equally, postmodernity has brought with it a loss of commitment to and trust in the idea of the Master Plan, and the churches have needed to grapple with the shape that they will need to take if they are to speak relevantly to Milton Keynes in the twenty-first century. A recent report produced by the Partnership asserts:

> God has certainly blessed the Milton Keynes ecumenical projects these past forty years, but we cannot replicate this model in the new communities of the Post-Christendom twenty-first century: theologically, sociologically, financially, and numerically we are not in the same place. Rather we must discern afresh God's leading in new ways and with new shapes . . . We favour the establishing of a wide range of processes and the creation of environments where Christian presences can organically grow, responding to local initiatives, opportunities and resources within the context of widening and deepening relationships with those beyond our circle. (Strategy Working Party, 2007, paras 3.1 and 5.2)

Currently, this document is being discussed across all the churches in the Partnership in Milton Keynes, as well as by bodies outside. It invites those who engage with it to dream new possibilities of Christian presence in the new areas of Milton Keynes. We do not yet know what kind of response the document will elicit, what kind of new forms of Christian presence might be suggested, or which ones might come to fruition out of the discussion process. What we can be more certain about is that the new Christian presences will be less likely to mirror a picture of the Church at the centre of the city and at the centre of power, and more likely to depict a more flexible, less immediately visible presence, reflecting a more flexible and less immediately visible relationship with the authorities.

Bibliography

Baker, Robin, 2005, *Milton Keynes Is Different: The Story of the Ecumenical Movement in Milton Keynes, 1967–2005*, Milton Keynes, Mission Partnership.
Strategy Working Party, 2007, 'Christian Presence in the New Communities of Milton Keynes: A Report to the Presidents', unpubl., Milton Keynes, Mission Partnership.

13

Cathedral Ministry for City and Region

JONATHAN MEYRICK

These days you can avoid driving through the centre of Exeter. The summer holiday traffic now hurtles down the M5 and on to dual carriageways crossing Devon to Plymouth and Cornwall, leaving the city of Exeter on one side. But if you do turn aside and enter this small, ancient city you will pass under a huge sign which proudly proclaims that Exeter is the Regional Capital.

As an urban community, albeit rather a small one (population 125,000), it is not unique in seeking to affirm its regional role. Up and down the country cities and large towns will function in a magnetic way for a much wider area. Exeter was founded with that in mind. The Roman city in the first century AD was built to be a security and administration hub, and over the centuries, as its national importance waxed and waned, its regional role has continued. Like many of Britain's ports, it can claim – even if only for a few decades – a period of prime importance in national maritime trading. While there are two other larger urban communities in the old county of Devon (Plymouth has twice the population), the M5 and an increasingly busy airport combine with a strong sense of regeneration and a significant historical role to keep Exeter genuinely the hub of the region.

And, like many other such regional hubs, Exeter has at its own hub a large and eye-catching Church of England cathedral. The purpose of this chapter is to explore specifically how a cathedral is part of the 'regional hub' aspect of a city. I have been Dean of the cathedral in Exeter since May 2005 and before that served in cathedral ministry in Rochester, north Kent, for six years. In Rochester I had specific responsibility for the Education and Visits department and also held the reins as Acting Dean for two years. In both places, I have been closely involved in the 'regional hub' aspect of the cathedral's ministry and its interface with the city acting as a hub. Although I write primarily from my own experience, every English cathedral will have broadly similar stories to tell.

Shortly after my arrival in Exeter the Cathedral hosted an episcopal consecration for the new suffragan Bishop of Plymouth. It was a happy occasion, as such things are, and the service had gone well. When it was over and I was standing with Archbishop Rowan Williams at the west end, we started talking about the differences between Exeter and Rochester. He told me that each cathedral said something different to him. I asked him what he thought particularly distinctive about Exeter. 'Exeter smiles at me,' he replied.

That chimed with my own experience too. Exeter has two external towers which are all that remain of the early Norman cathedral. In between is a graceful fourteenth-century building, built entirely in the Decorated Gothic period. Thanks to the 'twin towers', there is no need for a central support and the beautiful nave ceiling flows seamlessly into the quire. When the sun shines through the clear glass of the clerestory windows and strikes the clotted-cream coloured stone with its delicate and varied tracery, the whole building radiates a warm and welcoming smile which, like all the best smiles, warms the heart of its beholder.

But, of course, if the cathedral is to be a worthwhile hub for its region, it needs to have a welcoming warmth other than just through its physical beauty. That will come through what its current community will allow, encourage, facilitate. Two occasions, one in each place, spring to mind.

Rochester Cathedral is set just behind the High Street with a ruined Norman castle 100 yards to the west – built by the same bishop who started the present cathedral (and indeed the Tower of London). To the north-west, across a wide road running down to the High Street, are a pair of pubs. They are owned by the same man. He came to see me one day and asked if we would allow him to have a memorial service in the Cathedral for one of his bar staff. This man had been serving behind the bar for many years and was highly respected and valued by many customers. Lots of them were asking for such a service, I was told.

The funeral had already happened, so we were able to design a memorial service from scratch with a wide variety of contributions and a fair amount of jazz. I enjoyed it, and as predicted a large number of people came. It did not seem to me that we were doing anything significantly out of the ordinary; however, it became clear that the publican (who became a good friend over the next few years) had expected me to say 'no' to his request. My (to him) surprising agreement transformed relations between the Cathedral and a significant part of the local community which had otherwise rather ignored us.

As a result, I and later on my colleagues found ourselves more warmly welcomed out in that wider community; and that wider community came into the Cathedral more frequently and much less hesitantly. For two years running, that same publican helped us to put on New Year's Day concerts with a number of local bands playing to a cathedral-full of locals.

More recently, Exeter Cathedral played host to a quite extraordinary funeral for a local street-cleaner. We were asked to host it because the family thought the parish church would be too small. When the parish church concerned told me it was quite happy for us to take the funeral, I agreed. A cathedral, particularly a so-called 'historic cathedral', by which is meant a cathedral built to be a cathedral, does not have large numbers of funerals, weddings and baptisms. That is principally because a historic cathedral does not have a geographical parish, though perceived self-importance can sometimes also be a factor. So while you might expect that a Lord Lieutenant might have a funeral in the Cathedral, a dustman surely not?

Even before the funeral, I was very glad I said 'yes'. On talking with the family I realized that the 54-year-old man in question had, up until his unexpected death, been one of the regular litter collectors around the Cathedral Green. Particularly in the summer, the amount of litter around the Cathedral in Exeter can be considerable. Recently the City Council has put a great deal of resources into assisting with that problem, and I had regularly encountered the deceased man grappling with it as I walked across to early services.

I also realized that we were talking about someone who combined a kind of 'likely lad' lifestyle with immense outgoing friendliness and genuine Christian saintliness, giving up his coat to a homeless man on one early, very cold, winter's morning as well as raising hell on his motorbike. They thought there might be several thousand people there. We had 650 chairs out and there were more people standing than sitting. The vergers estimated a total of 1,400. Outside the Cathedral were parked 325 motorbikes belonging to mourners. The same bikes had led the funeral procession through a city brought to a standstill, followed by a range of refuse lorries. It was a personal privilege to take such a funeral, but its importance for the Cathedral was to demonstrate how it could act as a very particular kind of hub for a series of interlocking communities coming together in an unusual way. Its importance for the Church as a whole was to show how the smile of the building could be echoed in the service it offers.

In his letter to the Romans, Paul writes that we can know the ground of Christian hope is no mockery because of the 'Love of God shed abroad in our hearts' – the Greek verb being the same that is used in Matthew and Luke for the shedding of Jesus' blood (Rom. 5.5 AV). I have always found in this phrase a motivation for my own ministry. A cathedral is in a very particular place to contribute to this aspect of God's mission.

The urban centres they inhabit vary considerably: Exeter is only the third largest conurbation in its diocese, Rochester is set in the middle of a handful of former separate but contiguous towns, now held together in the Unitary Authority of Medway with a total population of 250,000; cities like Manchester, Liverpool and Birmingham number their populations in millions; somewhere like Wells is minute in comparison; other cathedral centres – Chelmsford for instance – have a significant population but strictly speaking are not cities. In the same way cathedrals themselves vary: in size, in historic significance, in geographical relationship to their dioceses and, until very recently, in their governance.

Cathedrals that were founded as cathedrals were governed by a Dean and Chapter; cathedrals in more recently established dioceses were usually buildings that had been, and remained, significant parish churches. They retained Parochial Church Councils, though, following the Cathedrals Measure 1931, they had Cathedral Councils as well to ensure the fulfilling of the cathedral dimension.

I found a similar structure in most of the Episcopalian cathedrals in the United States. Not all their dioceses have cathedrals, but virtually all those that do established cathedrals in existing churches. The predominant pattern there was a continuing Vestry (their equivalent of a Parochial Church Council) presided over by the Dean and a Cathedral Council presided over by the Bishop. In several cases, I discovered that the latter hardly ever met and therefore it was the parish element of its mission that flourished, rather than the cathedral.

Michael Sadgrove's chapter in *Dreaming Spires*, entitled 'Cathedrals and urban life', makes clear that Sheffield Cathedral, originally a parish church, 'for the first 20 years of its life, like the other parish church cathedrals, remained wholly parochial' (Platten and Lewis, 2006, p. 88).

Dean and Chapter cathedrals were not all the same either. Broadly they fell into two categories: Old Foundations and New Foundations. The distinction is not to do with their age; Rochester, a 'New' cathedral, was founded in 604 while Exeter ('Old') was not founded until 1050.

The difference lies in the fact that Rochester had been administered by a monastic community from between the Norman Conquest and the Reformation. All cathedrals similarly cared for were given a re-foundation as secular institutions by Henry VIII. These cathedrals, regardless of their age, were then known as 'New'. I have discovered that 'New' and 'Old' feel quite different from each other. 'Old' cathedrals have more of a 'bishop's family' feel about them.

Since the latest Cathedrals Measure in 1999, which came out of the report of Lady Howe's Commission, entitled *Heritage and Renewal*, all English cathedrals now have a much more uniform governance structure. Michael Sadgrove again: 'Officially, "parish church cathedrals" do not exist, any more than "dean and chapter" cathedrals. There are only *cathedrals*, governed by chapters, presided over by deans, answerable to councils' (Platten and Lewis, 2006, p. 90).

In reality, for some time before the new Measure, all cathedrals were in the process of expanding a sense of their mission as 'hubs' for their wider communities in city, county and diocese. There are common threads in that expansion as well as more individual and distinctive contributions. Most cathedrals have been developing for some years internal education departments. These seek to encourage individual school visits, often at the top end of the primary school age and lower end of the secondary. Such visits will try to engender a direct experience of past cathedral life through simulating monastic-style days and medieval pilgrimage visits. They will focus on the buildings, on history and on current worshipping life. Rochester developed a trail, based on interpreting the stained glass, and gave visiting schoolchildren experiences in calligraphy and plainsong. Many cathedrals have also developed days when thousands of children have been brought together for a visit, usually in conjunction with diocesan Boards of Education and schools' officers. A recent set of three such days in Salisbury focused on Interfaith study – chosen as a subject that might be more difficult for individual schools to tackle. Rochester reckoned on seeing 17,000 to 20,000 schoolchildren a year on tailored school visits from schools across several south-eastern counties. Winchester attracts 25,000. Such schools would come back year after year, and comments from those who experienced the visits (both at the time and years later) indicate that they were both stimulating and memorable.

Cathedrals have not focused solely on the 10–12 age groups. A number have run successful sixth-form conferences, most have visits from much younger age ranges, and some are beginning now to develop links with adult learning. For some years now, Cathedrals as Partners in Adult Learning (CPAL) has, in conjunction with the Church's national Board of Education, been encouraging this development. Ely Cathedral has been at the forefront. St Paul's Institute seeks to be a forum for debate and education on faith, ethics and issues of relevance to the City of London.

A recent development has been in music outreach. A handful of cathedrals, including Truro, Salisbury and Exeter, have begun projects that involve cathedral musicians going out to local schools and then bringing children in to join with others (including the local cathedral choristers) in a concert in the cathedral. The intention is to assist in the raising of singing standards, to relate the 'professional' standards of chorister-singing to the development of singing more widely, and to work towards the establishment of county junior choirs. The initial signs have been very encouraging and the government is seeking ways of supporting this particular initiative.

A related project in Rochester which has been running for nearly a decade is a Christmas carol service for Local Education Authorities primary schools from the local area. Hundreds of children from a variety of schools rehearse through the morning together in the Cathedral and then do the service in the afternoon. The director is one of the county's music advisers who also worships in the Cathedral. His personal enthusiasm is so great that, whereas eight years ago one such service sufficed, there now need to be four each year.

There are two annual services in Exeter that seem to me to epitomize the way in which the Cathedral acts as a hub for the county. The first must be common to all 'county cathedrals' – the annual legal service, which is the High Sheriff's service for judges and magistrates. A colourful procession streams into the cathedral quire and the legal professions from across the county commend their work to God's guidance. In Exeter, that is followed by a reception in one of the city's halls and by lunch in the Cathedral's chapter house – a medieval building which can seat about 80 for a meal.

The Diocese of Exeter covers the whole of the large, predominantly rural, county of Devon. Agriculture is a key factor in its life and each year the Young Farmers' Clubs of the county gather in the Cathedral for a joint Harvest Festival service. Clubs compete in the decorating of the massive nave pillars and the Cathedral is full of young and old representing the farming life of the county. Again, such a service is likely to be held in those cathedrals with a strong county and rural connection.

Winchester is planning to introduce one and already has a Shipping Festival to affirm the role of merchant shipping. Winchester itself feels some distance from the sea, but Southampton is in the diocese. The fact that the service happens in the Cathedral rather than Southampton's parish church emphasizes the place that the Cathedral has at the hub of the county.

Structurally, cathedrals have been given an additional boost to their role as county or area hub through the 1999 Measure's establishment of Cathedral Councils for all cathedrals. The Bishop appoints to the council a wide variety of people representing the life of the county. He will seek to reflect both the geographical spread and a cross-section of the county's life and institutions.

Cathedrals, of course, are primarily hubs for their dioceses. Indeed, that is their essential purpose. They are cathedrals because they house the bishop's symbolic seat (his cathedra) and all cathedrals are required to express as their primary purpose that the cathedral 'is the seat of the bishop and a centre of worship and mission' (Howe, 1994, pp. 3–4). Exeter has recently sought to elaborate on the statement of its essential mission, adding 'teaching' to 'worship and mission' and making clear its missionary commitment to the city and county, to visitors, to working with other denominations and faiths, to the proclamation of the Christian story and gospel and to the maintenance of its worship and its various central communities. At the same time, our elaborated mission statement affirmed its commitment to the Bishop and to supporting the Diocese's vision of its mission.

We acknowledged the place that music and the arts generally have. The Cathedral in Exeter (as in many cities) is a premium concert venue; it houses periodically a variety of art exhibitions. Most of them will have a spiritual dimension, and many a specifically Christian focus. Day by day its own music echoes and evokes the glory of God.

Over the last few decades, cathedrals have recovered a greater sense of this central purpose. In every diocese of the Church of England, cathedral deans are full members of the Bishop's senior staff and expect to play their part as such. By contrast, in 2002, when I enquired of all the dioceses in the Episcopal Church of the United States and visited 20 of them, I discovered that fewer than 25 per cent of their bishops regarded cathedral deans or provosts as being part of their core diocesan team. Furthermore, most English cathedrals will now have on their chapters canons with some diocesan brief in their job description. Exeter has two executive Bishop's officers as Residentiary Canons; one is the Director of the Council for Mission and Unity and the other is the Director of the Council for Worship and Ministry. The Precentor (like many cathedral precentors) has been Chairman of the Diocesan Liturgical Committee, only resigning from that because he has been appointed to the General Synod's national Liturgical Committee. The Dean chairs the Diocesan Council for Mission and Unity.

Cathedral clergy preach around the diocese (I aim for an average of one Sunday a month) and the cathedral choir from Exeter sings Evensong in parish churches two or three times a term.

This increasingly close link is symbolized in big diocesan occasions throughout the year, as it is in every cathedral, with ordinations, the Maundy Thursday Blessing of the Oils and Renewal of Ministerial Commitment, the Diocesan Bishop's presence at Christmas and Easter and periodic consecrations and enthronements of new bishops. It is also symbolized in the College of Canons, affirmed as part of a cathedral's essential foundation in the 1999 Measure. Comprising the Chapter, the suffragan Bishops, the archdeacons and Honorary Canons (or Prebendaries as they are called in 'Old' cathedrals), the College has a key place in linking the diocese to the cathedral and vice versa.

There are always opportunities for a cathedral to be a hub for its city or local town. Indeed Michael Sadgrove quotes a dean of Chester in the 1920s writing, 'A cathedral will always be tempted to become too parochial in its city and its city will always love to have it so' (Bennett, 1925, p. 67). When I started in Rochester, the Unitary Authority was only a year old. The new Medway undoubtedly looked to the Cathedral as a key partner in establishing its identity. Links with the Mayor of Medway were extremely close throughout my six years there, as were links with the LEA and the Authority's Tourism department. Salisbury has close links with the Salisbury and Stonehenge Tourism Partnership (an independent body) as well as with its city. Such links are mutually beneficial of course.

There were, however, two disadvantages as well to Rochester's initial link with Medway. First, the major parish churches in the other towns (Chatham, Gillingham, Strood and Rainham) lost some of their previous civic status. Second, Kent County Council tended (at least in those early years) to treat Rochester as though it were now chiefly in relation with Medway. Kent also contains Canterbury, which was always more naturally the county's cathedral; the emergence of a separate Unitary Authority made it easier for Kent, but the cathedral in Rochester was of course still the cathedral for the diocese which covered most of West

Kent as well as two London boroughs. Its 'hub relationship' to this variety of authorities inevitably varied considerably.

One particularly clear example of the Cathedral acting as a hub for the city was the Holocaust Memorial observation. Facilitated by the Council and supported by the Medway Interfaith Group, though initially sparked off by a chance encounter with the leader of the local synagogue, Rochester Cathedral hosted the council's observation of the Holocaust in January 2004. While the main emphasis was on the Holocaust we remembered occasions when Jews, Christians and Muslims had all been victims of genocidal atrocities. At the end all the local faith leaders pledged themselves in a commitment to greater mutual understanding and a search for peace and a common hope for the future. The same group of people, including cathedral clergy, planned a similar event the following year too.

Cathedrals can also be places of Christian ecumenical co-operation. Again the structure of the Cathedral Council can ensure this: Rochester's Council had ecumenical nominations both from the Bishop and from the Chapter. The new constitution there also allowed for the appointment of up to three 'Ecumenical Canons of Honour'; they are not members of the College, but their presence is always invited on significant occasions. Cathedral clergy preachments elsewhere will often have an ecumenical dimension. Cathedrals will also be the natural host church for big ecumenical celebrations, for example diocesan affirmations of the Anglican Methodist covenant.

All of this indicates the significant extent to which Britain's cathedrals are genuinely supporting the regional hub aspect of their cities, and indeed operating as regional hubs in their own right. However, much of what has been described operates at the Bishop/High Sheriff/Lord Lieutenant county and city hierarchy level. And that is without having touched on the military connections many of our cathedrals will have. The last occasion on which Exeter's nave bulged before that extraordinary funeral was the afternoon that the Devon and Dorset Regiment handed over its Colours before it was absorbed into the new Rifles Regiment. The question remains: to what extent are cathedrals hubs for more ordinary citizens, or indeed the positively disadvantaged members of our society?

That was one aspect of ministry at which those American cathedrals I visited on my journey in 2002 excelled. Nearly all of them ran soup kitchens or the like. Seattle Cathedral was host to a 'city of tents' for the homeless; its lower car park was jammed full with a thriving community of people who would otherwise be on the streets. It is not there all the time, but moves every few months to another church site in the city. Perhaps it is more possible where the cathedral has less of a role in its diocese, but it was a very impressive witness.

It would not be true to say that such outreach ministry is entirely lacking in English or British cathedrals. In 1995, Michael Sadgrove arrived in Sheffield to find a Breakfast Project 'that provided a cooked meal five mornings a week to upwards of fifty or sixty needy and deprived people'. Together with a drop-in centre known as the Archer Project, which offers 'to the same constituency an array of social, educational, cultural and recreational facilities and comprehensive personal support', he finds these examples of the church relating to its local city 'a model of professionalism and excellence' (Platten and Lewis, 2006, pp. 90–1). There will be other examples of this kind of ministry, particularly in the more urban cathedrals, but it is nothing like as comprehensive as I found in the States.

Exeter is currently exploring the possibility of setting up a 'Night Church' such as its Canon Missioner, Mark Rylands, found in Copenhagen Cathedral. The cathedral there is open to the city's youth one night a week with a variety of spiritual and prayer-making experiences available. Many seem to make use of it. Exeter, through the appointment of a lay co-ordinator, is setting up a pioneer discipleship course and, with local ecumenical involvement, is researching how such an initiative might work there. The Cathedral Close draws a large number of young people to 'lime around', as the Barbadians called it when I was working over there in the 1980s. Mostly they are bored; occasionally they cause trouble and more frequently apprehension in others. By day Exeter's Close attracts huge numbers of people, as if it were a beach. On Saturdays in summer the Cathedral (again through the Missioner) supports an outreach we call '@Life on the Beach'. It is intended to be friendly and mildly evangelistic.

Part of the difficulty for all but a handful of English cathedrals is the lack of financial resources. They receive direct support from the Church Commissioners to the extent of three stipends (the Dean and two full-time Residentiary Canons) and a grant towards providing administrative support. This grant varies in size according to the individual cathedral's existing resources but is mostly a few tens of thousands. In order to maintain choral music to a high professional standard – and if they did not do so, the English choral tradition would soon wither – and in order for the cathedrals to be open and accessible, their financial outgoings are fairly considerable. They will also be responsible for looking after their own clergy housing (often in expensive ancient buildings); and all that is before the looking after of the cathedral building itself. They receive no direct financial support from their dioceses or from the government. Not many of them pay any direct contribution to their dioceses (though some do), but all of them will provide services to their dioceses considerably in excess of what participation in the diocesan 'parish share' scheme would cost them.

Major repairs to the cathedral building will attract support from English Heritage, though not to the extent that once they did. It is perhaps no wonder that so many cathedrals launch major fund-raising appeals from time to time. And, of course, if you are trying to find ways of using the space to raise a little more money from your refectory, tea rooms or cathedral shop, it is not easy to throw the institution enthusiastically into running a soup kitchen at the same time. Nonetheless, the challenge remains.

Combining a Christian welcome with seeking sources of income is not a new dilemma for cathedrals. Rochester had its own mini-martyr at the beginning of the thirteenth century. A Scottish baker was murdered there while making his pilgrimage; his name was William of Perth. A local madwoman who discovered his body was apparently cured by it, and the cathedral monks built him a shrine inside the cathedral. It is gone now, destroyed by Cromwell's zealous Puritans, but for the best part of 300 years it gave to Rochester its own pilgrimage – and therefore income-raising – draw. No doubt a large part of the later medieval improvements and new builds owed their financing to those pilgrimage visitors.

Cathedrals today also attract large numbers of visitors. All of us would recognize that welcoming them, enhancing their visits, reflecting some degree of hospitality in the way we treat them is part of the cathedral mission. It is also a significant part of our operation as a regional hub. More than regional, of course; particularly for the better-known historic cathedrals, this aspect of the mission makes us national and even international hubs. And, like Rochester's medieval forebears, cathedrals seek to find the right way of combining such hospitality with some element of income-raising.

For Exeter, as for many cathedrals, finding the balance between these two goals is an ever-present dilemma. Most cathedrals currently seek to do so with some kind of encouragement to visitors to donate voluntarily, though often with a suggested level of donation. A few, though an increasing number now, make a specific charge: St Paul's, Westminster Abbey, Ely, Canterbury, Christ Church Oxford and Lincoln, for example. In others like Salisbury and Wells it is difficult to tell, as the apparent charge is actually a requested donation. In Rochester I felt that imposing a charge would be self-defeating; the number of casual visitors there was not huge. Part of the reasoning in places like Westminster and Canterbury was specifically to reduce the numbers in order to enhance the quality of the visit.

In Exeter I am beginning to think that a clear charge might be more honest, more straightforward, easier to administer and easier, too, for the operation of a system of discounts and passes. How can you exempt a visitor if you are only asking for a donation in the first place? And yet it can seem to the hapless official behind the desk that some visitors get no less irate at being asked for a donation than they would if told they had to pay a charge. A more straightforward charging system would allow for a system of passes for locals, for diocesan parishioners or Cathedral Friends. To work properly, the right balance would require the providing of free and easy access to a chapel for private prayer and candle-lighting, to any shop or refectory, and ideally to an overview of what a visit to the cathedral could offer.

In Lincoln, for instance, where the balance seems to have been struck as closely as is possible, you can enter all the west end, absorb the general view down the Cathedral, reach a large chapel designated for prayer and the Cathedral shop; all before you have to decide whether to pay to see more of the Cathedral's particular delights.

Although I have focused on cathedrals in this chapter, it is by no means the case that they are the only churches to operate as hubs or to assist their cities operating as regional hubs. There are a large number of significant towns and cities with no cathedral; here a great deal of the 'hub' role is carried out by major city or town churches – not all of them Anglican of course. Plymouth has no Anglican cathedral, though it does have a Roman Catholic one. It also has a large central Anglican parish church which fulfils many of the functions of an Anglican cathedral. Both places have a 'hub' feel to aspects of their ministry.

For all of them, cathedral or parish church, Anglican or non-Anglican, the hub ministry is not sustained primarily by the building's size, history or beauty, though these may all be contributory factors. Where the hub ministry is most effective, it will be due to the extent to which others feel that the church and its communities have smiled at them in genuine welcome and Christian hospitality.

Bibliography

Bennett, F. S. M., 1925, *The Nature of a Cathedral*, London, A. R. Mowbray.

Howe, E., 1994, *Heritage and Renewal: The Report of the Archbishop's Commission on Cathedrals*, London, Church House Publishing.

MacKenzie, Iain M. (ed.), 1996, *Cathedrals Now: Their Use and Place in Society*, Norwich, Canterbury Press.

Platten, S. and Lewis, C. (eds), 2006, *Dreaming Spires? Cathedrals in a New Age*, London, SPCK.

14

London

LESLIE GRIFFITHS

People love London – or else they loathe it. One thing is sure, no one can ignore this extraordinary place which is at one and the same time a sprawling metropolis and a vibrant capital city. Those who live in the rest of Britain can very easily resent the monster that devours more and more of the national wealth while becoming a place that is wholly different from everywhere else. From the point of view of London itself, where 12.5 per cent (7.5 million) of Britain's population lives, it might be pointed out that the capital contributes a massive 19 per cent towards the national tax revenue. That means that roughly 12 billion pounds are paid out to the regions every year. So, love it or hate it, London forms an integral part of the country, its beating heart.

A city's centre is often defined as its Central Business District. This would seem a threadbare and minimalist description of the situation in London. From Tower Bridge to Chelsea Bridge, along the banks of the River Thames various instruments and institutions of power add up to make an impressive (if not intimidating) whole. The headlamp-like building of the Greater London Authority (GLA) keeps watch over the metropolis. The Mayor of London has particularly good views of the vast stretches of East London that are currently being updated in preparation for the 2012 Olympic Games. Efforts are being made to extend the Mayor's powers to give him greater executive control over planning and housing. The GLA, with its light-touch governing structures, has been a contributing factor to the new ethos currently observable in London. In comparison, the old and cumbersome Greater London Council (GLC), dissolved peremptorily by Margaret Thatcher in 1985, was wasteful of energy and talent, a bureaucratic juggernaut.

The Mayor can also see Canary Wharf and the Isle of Dogs, the subject of the last massive regeneration scheme during the 1980s, one of Margaret Thatcher's boldest initiatives. This extension to the historic City of London has attracted major financial enterprises to the United Kingdom and, after 20 years of existence, now seems a settled part of the total London scene. Well remembered are the demonstrations and representations made by churches and others to the then Docklands Development Agency lest the 'indigenous' (old white and new Bangladeshi) families should be shoe-horned out of an environment which, in any case, would be incompatible with them. Happily, some of the worst possible excesses were avoided and the Isle of Dogs is now a model of more or less well-functioning community life.

Moving up river from Tower Bridge, the City of London next comes into view. Any observer will at once be impressed by the number of cranes on display. One day, crossing Blackfriars Bridge, I counted over 20! Massive skyscrapers have been added to the City skyline and others will soon be joining them. Great care has been taken to preserve the iconic views of St Paul's Cathedral but nobody can doubt the sheer scale of the activity which, day by day, is transforming the historic City. Here, governance is being transformed and modernized, but no one seems certain of the outcomes of the present or proposed reforms. The traditional oversight of the affairs of the City has been arcane (if not Byzantine) for years. The Court of Common Council and the various Livery bodies (now numbering over 100) have produced Aldermen and Sheriffs and Lord Mayors since the days of Dick Whittington. Modernizers are now seeking to fast-track leaders from the business community into leadership in order to forge a more organic relationship between the commercial sector and City governance. Many are fearful that this will attract into political leadership those who have little understanding of the deep-seated needs and nature of the City. The sheer size of operations there is truly mind-boggling. Over 300,000 work in the financial services sector alone. In London 108,000 people earn over £100,000 a year, more than twice the national figure; 38,000 earn more than £200,000, over one third of the national total. Indeed, one observer has noted that 'if those working in the City of London were removed from the national earnings figures, Britain's income differentials would look far more like the more egalitarian continental European countries' (Parker, 2007, to whom I am indebted for much of the statistical information). Average annual earnings in London, at £37,323, compare with £24,301 for Britain as a whole. The generator of this wealth is the City of London.

As we continue upstream we will have noted the proliferation of arts-related institutions of the South Bank. From the Tate Modern gallery via the Festival Hall and Hayward Gallery, we reach the National Theatre. Who can doubt the pulling power of such a conglomeration of prestigious venues? Or their influence in shaping the output of artists of all kinds?

Across the river from them lie the Inns of Court and the High Courts of Justice. The Old Bailey is a mere stone's throw beyond them. To the common aphorism that everyone (without exception) can expect two things in life, namely death and taxes, many would want to add a third: there'll always be lawyers too! The mighty organs of the law straddle London's two cities. They relate to both the financial and commercial affairs of the ancient City of London and also the political and governmental life of the City of Westminster. Many rulings with significant ethical direction have been made here and no one should neglect or overlook this aspect of our national life.

Our brief *tour d'horizon* ends at the Palace of Westminster. Here our national laws are made and this is the place where our parliamentarians do their work and can be lobbied. Soon, the judges will move out of Parliament into their own Supreme Court which will be situated on the other side of Parliament Square in the existing (but extensively refurbished) Middlesex County Hall. Significant reform of the House of Lords now seems more distant than some had wanted. Many would avow that, even at a time when cynics scathingly dismiss the effectiveness of Parliament, a real relationship exists between the public and this national forum for public debate. Demonstrations have happened on a large variety of issues and Christians have often been in the fore. The nature and content of their representations need some investigation but the mere fact that they can register their presence and make their views known should not be overlooked.

This litany of institutions that shape and influence our metropolitan and national culture is surely unrivalled in the whole world. Global economic developments have undergirded London's position both in Britain and internationally. Since the 'Big Bang' which globalized financial markets from the mid 1980s, London has made significant advances. This, together with the relaxation of Britain's immigration rules, saw significant progress towards the flexible labour patterns that have distinguished Britain from some of its continental neighbours. There has been an annual net inflow of 100,000 foreigners to London since 1997 and this has saved Britain from suffering a fall in its population that would have amounted to 600,000 between 1993 and 2000. This 'churn' has produced a London population that is now 35 per cent foreign-born. This figure is expected to move towards 50 per cent.

All this makes London as diverse as New York and certainly far more diverse than any comparable city in Europe or Asia. The management consultants McKenzie have recently reported that Britain's relaxed approach to immigration and regulation is making London the best place for financial business in the world. London is an easy place to settle, with Britain's 'non-domiciled' tax rule encouraging rich people to avoid paying tax on income earned overseas. This has been a magnet for one million incomers at all income levels during the last decade.

But all this evidence of energy and vitality should not hide from view certain other facts. Housing is prohibitively expensive and in short supply. London has the highest unemployment rate in the country at over 7 per cent. Over half of London's children are living below the poverty line. Social inequality is producing problems of a political order. The tensions are highest in the increasingly Muslim East End – where the 2012 Olympic Games are due to take place, where the British National Party on the one hand and George Galloway's Respect group are vying to establish a power-base.

This is the London faced by faith communities. The sheer scale both of opportunity and challenge gives some urgency to the task. The Christian Church has a significant presence throughout the city centre and some truly magnificent work is happening on the ground. But too often it's pragmatic and local. There could be a greater sense of strategy.

Where is the Church in the city centre?

Threaded through the 'public square' described above is a string of churches whose very presence speaks both of another age and of another agenda. Dominated on all hands by a rapidly changing architectural scene, they speak the language of continuity and offer sacred space to the thronging multitudes who work and move around them. This visible Christian presence is, of course, dominated by the cathedrals – St Paul's and Southwark (Church of England) and Westminster (Catholic) – and Westminster Abbey. They bring together at frequent intervals the representatives of Church and State. The Queen's eightieth birthday, the funeral of Princess Diana, the fiftieth anniversary of VE Day are very public expressions of the contribution Christianity can make to a nation wanting to mark its moments of transition. But the cathedrals offer something else too. They respond to events. The bicentenary of the abolition of the British slave trade, the dreadful events of 11 September 2001, the ending of wars, the remembering of the Holocaust and the arrival of a new millennium, all gave rise to memorable liturgical experiences which allowed the nation to focus on some of the great themes and questions of our day. Many of these occasions were, of course, covered live on national television. This fosters the impression that we are all gathered as a nation to pay our respects, to nurture our memories or to gather our strength, according to circumstance. And it's very impressive these days to note how careful those compiling these great ceremonies are to include representatives of other faith groups in the action. No one should underestimate the contribution of these great moments in establishing the place of religion in the public arena and giving the whole nation a sense of social cohesion. In these cases, this is achieved largely by mere presence. Where else could such symbolic and highly charged experiences occur? Our sacred spaces are national treasures.

The cathedrals go well beyond this agenda. The creation of the St Paul's Cathedral Institute in 2002 added another dimension to the contribution of the Church in London's city centre. Its Mission Statement declares: 'St Paul's Institute runs programmes every autumn and winter on a major ethical issue of our time, in addition to working in partnership with other professional organisations on seminars, conferences and exhibitions.' The Institute has already mounted major educational programmes on the question of debt (Make Poverty History) and global warming. These are being followed by another called 'A good childhood? Growing up in the 21st century'. It's always very impressive to see the snaking queues of people wanting to attend the major speaker-meetings held on the floor of the Cathedral. Indeed, sometimes it's necessary to close the doors before everybody's accommodated. Those responsible are now contemplating overflow possibilities outside the Cathedral. Such meetings have been addressed by the likes of Professor Hans Küng, Secretary General Kofi Annan, Chancellor Gordon Brown and Archbishop Rowan Williams. Alongside these well-attended events are seminars, retreats and breakfast meetings which explore the various themes in greater depth and with more intimacy. These are usually attended by people working in the great financial or legal institutions that surround the Cathedral. Very often, one of these institutions will have contributed significantly towards sponsoring the programme (HSBC did this with the programme on global warming, for example).

Westminster Abbey contributes to the public discussion of major issues in a similar way, largely through the work of its Canon Theologian. Its

One People oration, the Charles Gore and other named lectures, and regular lunchtime teaching sessions offer a serious study of issues of the day. They draw in leading voices from various parts of the public square. And the same can be said of much of the work of the London Institute for Contemporary Christianity in Vere Street (an outreach organization of All Souls' Church, Langham Place) and also the lunchtime 'Conversations' that take place regularly at Wesley's Chapel, which lies just outside the City of London. These address the general theme 'Values in Public Life' and two may be worth a mention. The first looked at values in the City and featured the Lord Mayor, the Chairman of Lloyds, the Chairman of the Stock Exchange, the Governor of the Bank of England and the Bishop of London. The other, organized in conjunction with the British Association for the Advancement of Science saw a high-powered range of scientists (Professor Lewis Wolpert, Sir Martin Rees, Professor Helen Haste, Professor Susan Greenfield, Sir Walter Bodmer, Professor Stephen Rose, Professor Frank Close, Lord Sainsbury of Turville, Professor Peter Cochrane, Revd Dr Fraser Watts) engage in a serious discussion about the contribution of science to the values of our day.

The decision of the Anglican Diocese of London some years ago to use the historic Wren churches that cluster together within the City of London for imaginative purposes was a very significant one. Most of these have no Sunday congregation. The hundreds of thousands of people who work in the City spend their weekends in the suburbs or the home counties. They are commuters. Consequently, the City churches make great efforts to offer ministry to those who work in the City during the working week. Churches are open during the day and offer quiet space for prayer and reflection. There are widely advertised counselling opportunities. Music features strongly in the programmes on offer where many promising musicians, often students from the various academies and schools of music and drama, are given opportunities to exercise their skills and serve the needs of the working public. An intricate network of chaplaincies takes this one step further. Leading law firms, major theatres, high street shops and most of the institutes of higher education – all enjoy the quiet and regular work of chaplains. So too do the Livery Companies whose round of banqueting and arcane ceremonies is rarely far removed from significant philanthropy and public service.

The opening of the London Centre for Spirituality, based at St Edmund's Church in Lombard Street, in 2000 has shown another way of developing the life of one of our ancient churches in ways that resonate with needs of the twenty-first century. The Centre's stated aim is 'to offer a wide range of courses, meditation and discussion groups and resources, for all interested in spirituality, church-goers or not, both in the local and in the wider community'. It has already hosted several spiritual direction training programmes and has a richly resourced bookshop.

St Ethelburga's Church was one of the few pre-Wren churches to survive the Fire of London but fell foul of the attentions of the IRA when a bomb destroyed it in 1993. A coalition of interests within the City of London found the money to refurbish the church. A total of £3.6 million was raised by the Cloth Workers' Foundation, the Leather Sellers' Company, the City Corporation, Bridgehouse Estates Trust, J. P. Morgan the investment bank and others. It has been re-opened as a centre for peace and reconciliation and is now regularly used by Christians and people of other faiths. It has become another oasis where some of the intractable problems facing the world can be looked at by those with an interest in (or experience of) these problems. From its outset, St Ethelburga's became a meeting place for people of various faiths who wanted to look together at the social and political problems relating to the Middle East. Peace in Northern Ireland was also an early subject for discussion. It was significant that the venue was able to bring together important voices from across a wide range of opinion.

The West London Mission (WLM) of the Methodist Church has its headquarters in Hinde Street near Oxford Circus. The WLM represents the continuation of the extraordinary work of Donald Soper who oversaw the development of a number of agencies set up to address a variety of social problems in the capital. The St Luke's Centre for the treatment and rehabilitation of people who abuse alcohol and other substances, the Katherine Price Hughes bail hostel and the West London Day Centre for homeless people are examples of this work. Such responses are not unique to city centre churches, of course, but they undoubtedly allow such churches not only to address situations of human need but also to gather statistics and analyse trends in such a way that representation can then be made (with great immediacy and authority) to decision makers. This direct experience of social need can enable the service provider to explain the ability, or more usually the inability, of homeless people to access the Health Service, for example, or the interests of street homeless people during the implementation of the government's Rough Sleepers' Initiative.

The final example might be St Marylebone's Parish Church near

Regent's Park. This was re-opened after a major refurbishment in the 1980s to include a Centre for Healing and Counselling. Under its roof, various services are offered. Thus, counselling and psychotherapy, a mental health support group, spiritual direction, a variety of conferences for health professionals, professional development groups, meetings of the Guild of Health – all take place. It is an admirable piece of work. Once again, however, the importance, for the purposes of this piece, rests not only with the services offered but with the opportunity to make maximum use of the location of this facility. It is placed at the very heart of London's medical district with a plethora of hospitals and medical practices in the vicinity. The renowned Harley Street runs nearby. This allows St Marylebone's to address ethical issues arising from developments in the world of medicine with some authority. The Action–Reflection model can be operated with leading voices in the worlds of medicine, psychology and nursing. The work done is similar in kind to activities conducted in a range of projects across the land. But the location, in this instance, gives the church a strategic position from which to influence emerging trends and policy decisions.

So far, we have looked at the physical presence of the Church in the city centre. Its imposing set of properties, many of them attracting people for aesthetic and touristic reasons as well as spiritual ones, certainly ensures that the Christian message will continue to be proclaimed near the seats of secular power. Naturally, a great responsibility rests on these Christian (usually Anglican) churches to ensure that an adequate presentation of the concerns of other faith-groups is not overlooked. And this is being done with increasing sensitivity. But apart from these wonderful treasures, this range of historic and defiant churches, there are also the streets. Since biblical days, the message of faith has been proclaimed in the open air to great effect. This can be the case, of course, anywhere in the land. But when it happens in the centre of London, it does seem to acquire extra potency and urgency. The streets and squares of London can offer a platform from which to challenge public policy and even international events. Faith addresses Power to great effect when this is done properly.

In recent years, a public gathering on May Day in the open space in front of the Royal Exchange has allowed the Christian case for fair trade and debt relief to be heard by people working in the finance centre of London, the very engine of the British economy. Within hearing of people working in the Bank of England and the Stock Exchange, the case is made for the application of Christian principles to the economic and financial life of the nation. And, with poignant irony, this takes place under the plinth of the Royal Exchange (now used as a shopping arcade for top-of-the-range branded bric-à-brac) where the words of the opening verse of Psalm 24 add their own force to the case being voiced by the public speakers below: 'The earth is the Lord's and the fullness thereof' (AV).

The streets are also used for demonstrations. These are regularly mounted on a variety of issues. They often end up in Parliament Square (or else in Trafalgar Square) where the case continues to be made. Anti-apartheid rallies, protests against government legislation (on the incitement to religious hatred, for example), and a march into Battersea Park to call to mind the two hundredth anniversary of the abolition of slavery are all examples of this form of activity. In recent years rallies in favour of making 'Strangers into Citizens', events that bring the plight of asylum seekers into focus, have been held in Trafalgar Square after a mass in Westminster Cathedral. And then there's the Good Friday Procession of Witness through the streets of Westminster. The congregations of the Methodist Central Hall, the Abbey and Westminster Cathedral combine to remind the frequently startled members of the public in and around our seat of government of the meaning and potential of sacrificial love.

No one exploited the possibilities of the open air to greater effect than the late Donald Soper. His extraordinary ministry at Tower Hill and Speakers' Corner in Hyde Park over many decades became a feature of British life. In his own way, he was able to put the case for reasonable Christianity and apply Christian principles to the issues of the day. Others have used his methods, too, but usually with less effect. Soper nagged away at the agenda of peace and justice until the very end of his life.

Several reports on aspects of public theology have appeared in recent times. They often have a wider field of application than London or even the city centre. Yet their findings seem to have added force when applied to the capital's structures of power. *Doing God: A Future for Faith in the Public Square* by Nick Spencer (2006) makes a determined bid for an appropriate theological discourse for the discussion of public issues. It recognizes 'the inclination of both the government and main opposition party to partner with voluntary organisations, foremost among them religious ones, for the provision of public services'. To take advantage of this, argues Spencer, a carefully worked out strategy and appropriate ways of engaging with government will need to be developed. And there will always be the danger of selling one's soul if such partnership ends up by taking money from government. Yet the effort has to be made if the activities and values of faith-based communities are to continue to resonate in the public square. Nowhere is the need for such a developed discourse, born of deep theological understandings and honed in a way that engages properly with those who run our secular society, more to be hoped for than in Parliament, and perhaps even more particularly in the House of Lords. Here the presence of Bishops of the Church of England offers a very visible contribution to debate. In recent times, matters to do with religious discrimination and incitement to religious hatred, the discussion of 'assisted dying', the role of the churches in civil society and many other debates have given opportunities to people of faith to discuss the values and ethos of British society as well as legislative proposals before Parliament. Secular and sceptical voices are frequently heard condemning the contribution of religion to such discussions. It is certainly incumbent on all who contribute to such debates that the religious voice speaks within a register that communicates effectively. There is no place for sanctimonious utterance, and metaphysical truth claims will need to be made with great circumspection and in non-theological language. But theology can still be done in the public square. And Parliament is a brilliant place to do it. There are far more committed Christian people in both Houses of Parliament than one could ever imagine. Surely, here are the elements for shaping this new public discourse so clearly needed at this time.

Similarly, the recent report from the Commission on Urban Life and Faith, *Faithful Cities*, made a spirited case for our cities. The contents page points to the need to recognize the various factors affecting the modern city. It is a place that demonstrates both continuity and change, diversity and difference; it exhibits clear signs of wealth without necessarily engendering well-being; it offers anonymity to its residents but also establishes a need for places where real commitment can be offered. The Church, according to this report, offers 'faithful capital', a concept to stand alongside the more frequently encountered 'social capital'. The report is full of the language of regeneration and multi-culturalism. Once again, even a cursory application of this report's findings to the characteristics that are particular to London yields interesting results.

Theology, understood as 'a resource for transformation' and 'performative', seeks to address the real world of people's everyday life, and, therefore, it must address those institutions and systems that shape the conditions within which that life is lived out. It 'rejects any notion that religion is merely a private and personal matter'. 'Rather, it should give shape and substance to our engagement with ethical, social and political matters – since theology is concerned with a God who is present and active in the whole of creation and the entirety of human concerns.' Such theology, according to the report, 'provides the vocabulary of faithful action, it can never be simply the private language of a sectarian few, and should be prepared to engage critically and constructively with alternative points of view' (*Faithful Cities*, 2006, pp. 14f.).

The obvious and general application of these words needs no further explanation. But their particular appropriateness when applied to the ministries of those churches and gatherings of Christians in London's city centre should not be doubted either. There, it's not merely a matter of how things are on the ground, on the street, in the neighbourhood. Bringing insights from all such contexts, the voice of Christian theology can speak with authority to those who shape our laws, or frame our culture, or affect the economic climate within which we live and breathe, who hold responsibility for the policy and the ethos within which we all live. The 'public square' so often referred to these days would, in London, be bounded by Parliament, the Cathedral, our financial institutions and law courts. Similar conclusions could be drawn from a study of *Faith and Nation: Report of a Commission of Enquiry to the UK Evangelical Alliance* (2006) which went over the same ground and came to much the same conclusion. This report showed how the historic evangelical engagement with such issues as anti-slavery, educational reform, employment reform and workplace ministries and poverty relief has established a platform of good practice from which to continue to address such issues (or their equivalent) in our contemporary age. For this, we need an acceptable public discourse and a readiness to spring the ideas of Christian theology out of the community of faith and into the public arena. Once there, they can be shaped and honed and turned to account as they make the claims of justice and compassion heard both with insistence and authority in the places where power is wielded and decisions made.

Conclusions

No one should underestimate the simple fact of *presence*. Rapid and radical developments are in store for London's city centre. There is a call for more intensive development with an ever-increasing number of high-rise and skyline-dominating buildings. So the continuing existence, the defiant survival and the clear recognizability of church buildings in the very midst of all this activity gives a singular message of striking insistency. The presence of the Christian church, whether or not those who pass by avail themselves of its message or enter its portals, makes its own case in the market place of ideas and values. It affects the ethos of the city centre subliminally in this way.

For those who access the Church's programmes and join its worship, there is even more to recommend. The churches that cluster around London's city centre offer *sacred space* for all who work and live there. Here, artists can display their wares and struggling souls can say their prayers. The stillness and purity generated within these churches keep many busy people in touch with spirituality. It adds value to their lives. And, on the big occasions, it can and does foster a sense of national coherence.

The Church in the city centre offers Christians (and, increasingly, people of other faiths) a *platform* from which to launch their own agenda. In this way, prevailing economic, commercial, social and political proposals can be challenged. An alternative point of view can be established. Protest can be mounted and demonstrations organized. Naturally, it would be good to think that those speaking in the name of Christianity would get their facts right and know how to present them to greatest effect. But great opportunities abound.

Ten years ago, the Association of London Government organized a conference to begin what they called 'The London Study'. Anthony Giddens, Director of the London School of Economics, spoke on 'the future of urban society'. The Deputy Mayor of New York and the Mayor of Barcelona gave their perspectives. There were visitors from the worlds of broadcasting, the European Union and architecture (whose representative was none other than Richard Rogers). It was a great privilege to contribute to that discussion. I was asked to speak to the subject: 'The moral agenda for cities'. That occasion made me aware that the shaping of the city, the development of its culture and ethos, demands an interdisciplinary approach. And the voice of faith has its proper place in such an arena. Indeed, the doors of those in power are always open to a reasoned and reasonable presentation of the case for development as made by the community of faith. The city of London is constantly asking members of its community to contribute to various consultation processes. It actively seeks the views of those who live within its boundaries. It asks for contributions on issues such as accommodating future employment growth, achieving higher density development, providing better transportation and creating a more sustainable environment. The scope for creative dialogue is more than obvious.

The Church in London is well placed to affect the outcome of any discussion relating to the capital's development and also the national debate. It will have to earn the right to be heard, of course. But we should be confident that the insights and angles of view that are particular to people of faith can gain a hearing if they are appropriately engaged and expressed in the public square.

Bibliography

Commission on Urban Life and Faith, 2006, *Faithful Cities: A Call for Celebration, Vision and Justice*, London, Church House Publishing.

Parker, Simon, 2007, 'A City of Capital', *Prospect Magazine*, 13 April 2007.

Spencer, Nick, 2006, *Doing God: A Future for Faith in the Public Square*, London, Theos.

United Kingdom Evangelical Alliance, 2006, *Faith and Nation: Report of a Commission of Enquiry to the UK Evangelical Alliance*, London, Evangelical Alliance.

Index of Names and Places

Belcham, John 144f
Belfast 153
Bender, Thomas 40
Bennett, Fiona 123
Berlin 17
Best, Richard 175
Bevan, J. 166
'Big Bang' The 211
Big Issue, The 141
Birmingham 4, 173, 175, 184, 199
Black, James 115
Blackfriars Bridge, London 210
Blake, William 102
Blessed Sacrament Shrine, Liverpool 153
Blondy, S. 31
Bloomsbury Central Baptist Church, London 110
Blueco Ltd 35
Bluewater Centre 35f
Bolger, Ryan 127
Bosch, David 76f
Bowling Alone (2001) 99
Bradbury, John 111, 141, 148, 150, 152f
Bradford 49
Brannigans 38
Brazil 26
Bretherton, Luke 66, 72f
Bridgehouse Estates Trust, London 215
Bristol 4, 63
Britain; United Kingdom 2, 6, 7, 13, 19, 21, 30, 33, 37, 38, 43, 48, 52, 67, 96, 103, 105, 112, 122, 127, 141, 164, 172, 173, 174, 191, 196, 209, 211f, 217
British Association for the Advancement of Science 214

British Broadcasting Corporation (BBC) 172
British National Party 212
British Rail 37
Brompton Oratory, London 104
Brown, Gordon 213
Brown, Malcolm 166
Browning, Don 136
Brueggemann, Walter 103f, 132f
Buckingham Palace London 104
Buenos Aires 17

Cabela's Store, St Louis 34
Cain 61, 97, 139, 150, 153
Cambridge 150
Canal Street, Manchester 33
Canary Wharf, London 95, 209
Candlish, Robert 114
canons residentiary 202
Canterbury 203, 207
Canterbury, Archbishop of 127
Cardiff 1ff, 36, 47, 56, 57, 109, 111, 112, 173
Cardiff Bay 56
Cardiff Adult Christian Education Centre (CASEC) 111
Cardiff Churches' Centre 1, 4
Cardiff Conference, 2005 4
Cardiff University 1
Carphone Warehouse 35
Castells, Manuel 18, 129
Cathedral Councils 199
Cathedrals Measure, 1931 199
Cathedrals Measure, 1999 200, 202, 203
Cathedrals, Old and New Foundations 199f
Catholic Action for Overseas Development (CAFOD) 80

Index of Subjects

Index of Biblical References

239